MW00984711

DOCTOR NELLIE

Previously published under the title

A CHILD WENT FORTH

❧ ❧ ❧

There was a child went forth every day,
And the first object he look'd upon, that object he
    became,
And that object became part of him for the day or
    a certain part of the day,
Or for many years or stretching cycles of years.

WALT WHITMAN.

DOCTOR NELLIE

THE AUTOBIOGRAPHY OF
DR. HELEN MACKNIGHT DOYLE
WITH A FOREWORD BY
MARY AUSTIN

GENNY SMITH BOOKS
MAMMOTH LAKES, CALIFORNIA

This edition is a faithful and complete copy of the first edition (made by photographing the pages of a 1934 book) published in 1934 by Gotham House, New York. The illustrations by Merritt Cutler are from the edition published in 1935 with the Junior Literary Guild.

Cover: Below Mount Tom, Owens Valley
Original watercolor by Nina Kelley

Copyright © 1934, Gotham House
Assigned to Helen MacKnight Doyle and renewed 1961 by Morris M. Doyle.
New material copyright © 1983, Genny Smith Books
All rights reserved including the right of reproduction in any form.

Library of Congress Cataloging in Publication Data:

Doyle, Helen MacKnight, 1873-1957.
 Doctor Nellie.

 Reprint. Originally published: A child went forth. New York : Gotham House, 1934.
 1. Doyle, Helen MacKnight, 1873-1957. 2. Women physicians—California—Biography. I. Title.
 R154.D65A3 1983 610'.92'4 [B] 83-5720
 ISBN 0-931378-07-9
 ISBN 0-931378-06-0 (pbk.)

Manufactured in the United States of America

Distributed by William Kaufmann, Inc.
95 First Street, Los Altos, California 94022

ABOUT THIS EDITION

I remember that day so very well, about twenty-five years ago—the day I found Dr. Nellie's autobiography on the bookshelves at Tamarack Lodge. I was in the midst of gathering material for a book on the Mammoth region and my good friend Bill Putnam had urged me to search for a copy, though the book was then twenty years out of print. I wonder whether the worn copy I held in my hands that day might have been a gift to the lodge from the doctor herself, for I learned later that she had spent many summer vacations there on Twin Lakes.

I remember too the sharp thrill that afternoon, in my cabin on the cliff above the lakes, when I began to skim the pages. Vivid, first-hand accounts of days past grabbed my attention. The narrow-gauge Carson & Colorado Railroad; muleskinners, miners, sheepherders, buckaroos, ranchers, Paiute Indians; Laws, Bishop, Owens Valley, Long Valley, Mammoth City; people far from home, from the east, the south, from Mexico, Canada, Ireland, China; men and women, old and young, prosperous and poor—all part of an isolated, pioneer ranching community of the Old West.

I remember too the day I was wandering around the Mammoth Mine when I met Dr. Doyle's daughter Dorothy. From her I heard many more stories about life in Owens Valley and about vacations at Mammoth, when the Doyles drove a team and wagon from Bishop and put up a circus tent on a lake shore, to accomodate the friends and relatives who joined them.

My appreciation for A Child Went Forth has only grown with the years. By far the most descriptive book of Owens Valley's early days, it remains, as I wrote in 1959 in the first edition of Mammoth Lakes Sierra, "Must reading for those interested in the early days of Owens and Long Valleys." I have long felt that it deserved to be back in print, so it is with joy and some amazement that I find myself in a position to publish this new edition.

This edition brings back into print the work published in 1934 under the title A Child Went Forth. It received high praise from reviewers and was particularly popular in the San Francisco Bay area, where Dr. Nellie and her husband were well known in medical circles. The Commonwealth Club awarded Dr. Doyle its silver medal for nonfiction, and the San Francisco Chronicle listed it numerous times as a "Best Seller of the Week" among Bay Area booksellers. A Dakota schoolbook, Sod House Days, included the pages describing life on a Dakota homestead. A special illustrated edition for young people was published in 1935 with the Junior Literary Guild; it was made "special" by deleting twenty-one portions of the text considered not suitable for young eyes.

The only new material in this edition is the new title and cover, the photograph, and this publisher's foreword. Without the active encouragement of Morris Doyle and Dorothy Doyle Cook, this new edition would not be possible. Without the skills of Mike Hamilton, it would not be so handsome.

Mammoth Lakes, July 1983   Genny Smith

Courtesy of Dorothy Doyle Cook

DR. HELEN MACKNIGHT DOYLE

⚕ *1899* ⚕

CONTENTS

SEPARATIONS

AUNT SADE AND "AUNT" MARY

YOUNG DAYS IN THE OLD WEST

A STUDENT IN OLD SAN FRANCISCO

A DOCTOR IN THE "LAND OF LITTLE RAIN"

NOT TO BE EMBITTERED

FOREWORD

When I wrote, a short time ago, my own autobiography, I did not neglect to mention one of the few women who made of my long sojourn in the California desert a little less than desolation of my human contacts: Dr. Helen MacKnight. But no prescience warned me of being asked so shortly to write a foreword to the Doctor's own account of the courage and sprightliness with which she met the emergencies of a beginning medical practice in that remote, inhospitable land. And yet of all the women with whom I faced, hoped and prophesied about the early phases of the struggle for free expression among women in professions, there is none whose autobiography I could have felt more worthy to be written than that of Dr. Nellie, as she came affectionately to be called.

Pitchforked bodily into a profession for which editors of medical journals were pointedly stating their conviction of woman's physical unfitness, and serious journalists expounding that any avowed suffragist was a victim of psycho-sexual aberrancy, Dr. MacKnight has outlived the most strenuous years of woman's pioneering on her own. She has much to tell of an adventurous, heart-rending and amus-

ing character which in our modern acceptance of the woman physician as an accomplished institution we are disposed to forget. We are as far now from the incredible circumstance of a dean of a medical college recommending to the men students, on the advent among them of a young woman candidate for a degree, to "make it so uncomfortable that she cannot stay" as we are from the neglected and distressing condition of the "stiffs" on which her anatomical research was supposed to begin. Indeed, one gathers that medical practice in those days was frequently as messy as the state of mind of its practitioners toward the woman undertaking it. It is significant of the wholesome, free-hearted attitude with which she surmounted these difficulties that Dr. Nellie is able to look back upon them with humor tempering her philosophy. What patently saves her from the bitter and repressed reactions affecting too many women physicians of her day is her quick attention to pictorial incident and details of minor human interest in the narrative of her life story; the pointed note of personal characteristics of her instructors; the light but apt gossip of leading women of her era, Jane Stanford and Phoebe Hearst; the bustle that her graduating dress displayed; the items of women finding their legs through riding the bicycle, and going sea-bathing when it was the absolute mode that bathing skirts should reach the tops of shoes; and the warm, amused neighborli-

ness by means of which she oriented herself in her desert practice.

All these things are evident in the text. But one contributing factor neglected by her, I feel obliged to add to that one of her achieving graduation from the State Medical College while still too young to be legally entitled to be granted a license to practice, is that Dr. Nellie was an extremely personable young woman, of whom her rosy complexion, sparkling eyes and ready smile are salient memories. Perhaps these things had something to do with her achievement of a brilliantly successful marriage, but she was, taking that marriage into account, precisely the sort of mother who would—in spite of her amazement over it—grow up to find her daughter taking a foreign fellowship in Bacteriology. Her resistance to the narrow and unrelenting prejudices of her home environment, her attack upon the human elements in her professional practice, are wholly in the key in which she undertakes the recording of them. All of which tends to make of that record one of the most interesting as well as pleasantly informing pieces of modern autobiographical writing, equally free from introversions and from the disposition to pose herself as the central theme of her narrative.

Say what one may, it is difficult to separate Dr. Nellie's success in a difficult and exacting profession from her success as a woman. And in saying that, one has perhaps stated the final judgment of this whole vexed problem of women in professions. At any rate, one cannot read this forthright and explicit account of one woman's life and work without a satisfyingly real sense of the extent to which that life and work have supplemented and fulfilled each other.

Mary Austin

DOCTOR NELLIE

SEPARATIONS

❦ GOLD ❦ TEARS ❦ ↗A DOLL ❦
UNCLE SILAS

THE YEAR EIGHTEEN SEVENTY-EIGHT
seems a long time after the "days of old, days of gold,
days of forty-nine," in California; yet it took that many
years for the amazing stories of gold dust to sift through
to every corner and hamlet of the United States. The
narrative, sifting, drifting, lost nothing by the process;
rather it became more precious, until every grain of sand
grew to a nugget, every adventurer became a millionaire.

It was not until Christmas Day of that year that the
MacKnight family in the small town of Petrolia, in the
conservative state of Pennsylvania, felt the separating
power of the tales that seemed to filter between them like
particles of gold dust, growing and gritting until they
formed a wall—on one side, seclusion and intimate family happiness; on the other side, adventure, alluring tales
that led to a country of gold.

On that morning the pleasant home was filled with

bustle and anticipation. I, Nellie MacKnight—the only
child left of the three that had been born to my parents
—danced through the morning on eager tip-toes. I stood
at the window and watched the flurrying spits of snow
that nipped the faces of people hurrying by and dusted
the coats of horses drawing sleigh-loads of family parties
bound to the mid-day Christmas dinner.

Above my head Dick and Ned, the family canaries,
hopped from perch to swing, cheeping, trying to attract
my attention. I answered them, but did not take my
eyes off the window. Uncle Silas was coming to dinner.
Uncle Silas to my childish mind was a veritable Midas,
whose gifts were the outstanding events of my young
existence.

Soon, with the jingle of sleigh-bells, Uncle Silas appeared, looking like Santa Claus, himself, his snowy
beard flowing over the fur robe that tucked him, snugly,
in his cutter.

"Papa! Mama!" Breathless with excitement I ran
to call them from the kitchen, where my father was
filling the cook stove with coal and my mother was
basting the fowl, roasting in the oven.

"Merry Christmas!" I found myself hugged to Uncle
Silas's buffalo overcoat, and then put down in my own
rocking-chair, with a long package in my lap.

"Look what Santa Claus left at my house for you,"
Uncle Silas said, and while Papa and Mama watched,
I opened the package and found a doll, so life-like that I
gasped with joy and hugged it to my heart with a yearning so intense it was an ache.

Time passed like a fairy dream until I was summoned to put the chairs around the table and pour the

water, which I did, hugging my treasure with one arm. Not until the meal was served did I begin to realize that there was something unusual pending—something that made Papa look flushed and eager and somehow different, and seemed to take Mama's appetite, so that the much anticipated and deliciously realized roast goose (Papa always insisted on roast goose for Christmas) remained on her plate scarcely touched. Uncle Silas and Papa were talking so intently that they scarcely seemed to know what they were eating.

"You see," Papa was saying to Uncle Silas, "the trouble with this country is that it's all finished. I can always make a bare living here, but everything is surveyed and what chance has a surveyor in a country that is already laid out and finished? Think of the opportunities in California, not only in my own line of work but, through the work, being able to get in on the ground floor on good mining properties! Why, they're making millionaires out there overnight!"

"Gad, Smith, you're right." Uncle Silas had caught Papa's enthusiasm. "Tell you what I'll do. I'll stake you to the train fare out there. If I were a young man, I'd go with you. It's too good an oportunity for a young man to let pass."

Mama's hand shook, so that when she started to pour the coffee she spilled it on the tablecloth. She got up and went to the kitchen, as though in a hurry, and when she came back there were spots of red on her cheeks and her eyes looked as though she were going to cry.

"But, Smith," she said, breaking into the midst of their enthusiasm, "what about Nellie and me?" Even to my childish comprehension, Papa seemed suddenly different. I, who had always felt myself first in his affection, sensed a strange feeling of separation, a being set aside for awhile.

"I have thought it all out, Olive," Papa was saying to Mama; "we will sell the house and furniture, and you and Nellie can go and live with my folks until I send for you or come back."

Those were the days when the word of the husband was the Law-of-the-Medes-and-Persians, and although something went out of Mama's face that day that never came back, she only said:

"Oh, Smith, how can we leave our pretty home and be separated for an uncertainty?"

But if Papa heard, he did not answer. All that afternoon Papa and Uncle Silas talked and planned, with Mama a silent listener. I, who had always been the center of interest on such occasions, failed to focus attention as I had been accustomed to do. Cast out, as it were, from the circle of elders, I turned all my attention to my doll.

Conversation grew. Letters were read, tales were told. Letters from California. Tales of California, land of opportunity, of wealth, of gold, gold, gold. The house grew chilly. No one replenished the fires. Unnoticed, I took my doll, feeling that she must be cold, and drew up my rocking-chair in front of the base burner, where the glow from the coals shone through the mica windows of the big bellied stove, and held her up with her face close to the warmth. After a little, I laid her down in my arms to rock her to sleep. My heart stood still. Her eyes had left their sockets and were running down her cheeks!

At any other time, I would have cried out, have summoned every one to witness my grief. But a strange atmosphere in the house kept me silent. I rescued the eyes and pressed them back in their sockets, but my wax doll was ruined. Years later, when I saw a woman who was the victim of a beauty treatment that consisted of injections of paraffine that left her face in humps and hollows, I thought of how my doll had looked when I turned it from the fire.

Uncle Silas left, without knowing the tragedy of the doll, or realizing the greater tragedy that he had helped to bring about by making it possible for Smith Mac-Knight to leave his little family and go to California.

For the first time in my life, I knew what loneliness was. Papa kissed me as though he were thinking of something else. Mama hugged me too tightly and kissed me again and again, and then went hurriedly away when Papa called, "Olive," from the other room. I could not hear what they were saying, but I knew they were talking about "Out West, and Gold, and Opportunity"— and I knew that Papa was glad and Mama was sorry, and that I was to go with Mama to live with "his folks," and that, although Mama did not say anything, that made her very unhappy.

I thought of Papa, square-built, short and stocky, with a high forehead that bulged over his gray eyes,—Scotch, Papa was, and very proud of it, with a temper that was uncontrolled, sullen, devastating. Every one said that I was the "living image of Mac," my father. I supposed I should be pleased about that, since, my baby

brother having died, Papa said I must be the boy of
the family, but I would much rather have looked like
Mama—Mama, whose purple-black hair grew low and
soft on her forehead and was so heavy that there were
coils and coils of it in the braids on the top of her
head, and whose hands were small, with tapering fingers
that could make such pretty things. I did not know
that Mama's face was too angular for beauty, the cheek-
bones too high, the eyes already shadowed by unhappiness. Papa was often angry with her, and sometimes
he would not talk to her for days. But he was never
angry with me. Mama and Papa were own cousins,
first cousins; I afterwards learned what that meant,
when I had grown old enough to know about con-
sanguinity. My parents seemed very proud of the re-
lationship, never dreaming that the two babies who
had died in their infancy might have been sufferers from
this intermarriage.

The voices hummed on. Papa was doing most of the
talking. Once in a while Mama's voice would seem to
protest mildly, but it was promptly drowned out by
Papa's confident tones. I slept.

Next day Papa did not go to work. He began helping Mama take down curtains and take the tacks out
of carpets. I seemed to be in the way for the first time
in my life. I wanted Ned and Dick to be let out of their
cages and to see them fight as they did, standing one on
each side of the rocker of the big chair. But when
Mama started to let them out, Papa said no, they couldn't
be bothered; and, although I lay on the floor and kicked
and screamed, a proceeding that I had learned to follow
when everything else failed, no one heeded and my

display of temper only left me tired and cross and availed nothing.

Almost before I could believe it, Ned and Dick were sold, with all the things in the house, at auction. Papa was on his way "Out West." Mama and I, with boxed lunches to last throughout our trip, were on our way to "his folks," sitting night and day in the day-coach of the train. But that did not worry me, for I could sleep very comfortably on the seat and it was exciting to ride on the train.

Out of all these chaotic happenings there was one comforting thought. I had not had to tell Papa or Uncle Silas about the wax doll. Uncle Silas might never have found another gift from Santa Claus for me, and Papa might have been angry with Mama for not keeping better track of things. Mama knew but she did not scold—only said she was sorry and that Santa Claus would bring me another some day. But I never saw Uncle Silas again, and Santa Claus must have fallen upon lean years.

𝕏 GRANDMOTHER MacKNIGHT 𝕏
THERE WAS A WOMAN!

WHEN PEOPLE TALK OF THINGS THAT happened to them as children, it is difficult to differentiate between those things which they really remember and those occurrences which older people have so often recalled to their minds that they have accepted them as memories. There has been no one to recall them for

me, so that the impressions of my early years in New
York State are the experiences that were most vivid to a
child six or eight years old.

First, I remember Ogdensburg, where we changed
cars for our destination in northern New York. My
Lippincott tells me that Ogdensburg, now a popular
summer resort, is a city and port of entry of St. Lawrence County, New York, on the St. Lawrence River,
at the mouth of the Oswegatchie, opposite Prescott,
Ontario. The St. Lawrence is here more than a mile in
width. Trade is largely in grain, flour, lumber, and silk
and brass goods.

Such it is now, one of many cities, but when I first
saw it, to those who lived in the northernmost part of
the state, it was the hub of the universe. From there
came our weekly paper, the *St. Lawrence Republican,*
which formed our only contact with the outside world.
There may have been a Democratic paper, too, but to
my inexperience, any one who was not a Republican
and an Episcopalian was "beyond the pale." Any one
who traveled went first to Ogdensburg.

But it was not the city itself that really mattered. I
remember nothing of its buildings on that first visit,
but the river, frozen from bank to bank, broad, majestic,
captivated me. It was a picture of fairyland to a fat
little girl from a post-borough in Pennsylvania. I
watched breathlessly the beautiful swan-shaped cutters
that slid by on noiseless runners, the spirited horses that
drew them, arching their necks and raising their feet
high as though enjoying it all as much as the people
who rode behind them. Then the skaters—ladies in
polonaises over long skirts, bouffant over hips and bustle,

unbelievably small of waist, with question mark busts, and tiny hats set jauntily on their heads, ladies who glided with their bearded or side-whiskered escorts on fairy skates over the ice, green-blue as a diamond under the winter sun. Nor was all the scene given over to pleasure. There were men, in mackinaws and mufflers and fur caps, driving shining, wide-backed horses hitched to low, flat sleds heaped with hides and logs. There were others cutting huge blocks of ice for storage.

From Ogdensburg to Madrid, New York, it is eighteen miles. Mama's people lived in Madrid. Her name had been Olive Peck. We went to her father's home. I suppose we might have stayed there, but Grandfather had married again, and Mama always spoke of his wife as stepmother. I think Mama would have liked to stay, but there was a feeling that "his folks" should take care of Smith MacKnight's family if he wanted to go to California on a wild goose chase. About the only thing I remember of the visit was that step-grandmother smoked a pipe, which interested me very much. She seemed rather like a witch or goblin to me. Then, too, I remember the thin, silver spoons marked *SF,* which I was told stood for Mama's own mother's name, Sophronia Fish.

Uncle Alex, Papa's brother, came for us. He was of medium height, well muscled, pleasant-faced. He had a good cutter and shining horses that pawed the ground and kept the sleigh-bells jingling. Why should Mama look so sad when it was all such a great adventure? Over hard-packed roads, broken through the snow-drifts, Uncle Alex drove us to the farm, four miles from Madrid. We went in through the gate and along the driveway, which wound around the side of a long house, with gables and shutters loaded with snow.

Grandmother MacKnight—there was a woman! Through mists of fifty years I see her as plainly now as I did that day: stocky in build, rugged, rosy, with the most comfortable lap, the most cheerful smile, the softest skin. I used to love to stroke her face, pink and ivory white. Her only cosmetics were a dash of cold water at the kitchen sink in the morning and an occasional application of mutton tallow when her skin was chapped. Her hair was white and soft and smooth, parted in the middle and combed plainly back. Often, when she was tired or hot, she would dip her hands in cold water and smooth back her hair.

Just as Ogdensburg seemed to me to be the hub of the universe, Grandmother's kitchen was the heart and soul of the home. It was a large room, probably twenty by thirty feet. I don't remember the walls, but the floor was painted with yellow ochre, which was frequently renewed, so that the surface was always shining and seemed to lend a warmth and glow to everything. There were two large windows that looked into the front yard; double ones they were in the winter, the extra windows put on for protection from the cold and never opened until they were taken off in the spring.

Outside, the house was banked with manure, up to the sills, and this bank was drifted over with snow. Manure was supposed to have especial qualities of warmth. There was a large cook stove with mica windows in its front door, through which the fire glowed cheerily. There was a long table, covered with a checked cloth, and a wooden sink, and a pump which connected with a cistern underneath the house. This cistern was filled by the rain and snow water that collected on the roof and in the eaves, and the water was used for all domestic purposes except drinking. The tragedies that lay in those cisterns!

Off from the kitchen was the buttery, with a moulding board underneath a back window that looked into a frozen garden. There were shelves for dishes and food. Pans of milk stood here, the thick cream folding back in layers when Grandmother used the skimmer. There was everything in this buttery from saltpeter to drench the horses, and medicines concocted from rock candy and whiskey, to butter and homemade cheese, pumpkin pie and mince meat.

There was only one medicine that was kept in another place. In the grandfather's clock that stood between the kitchen windows, Grandmother kept a bottle of what was known as picry. This was especially for me. It was a dark brown, vile-looking and bitter-tasting medicine, and, oh, how I dreaded to see Grandmother go to the clock and take down the bottle and hunt a spoon. I should be very glad if I could find out what used to go into that mixture. That, with sulphur and molasses as a spring medicine, constituted the pharmacopœia of my childish rememberings.

Projecting from the end of the house was a lean-to. This, partitioned, formed the woodshed on one side, and an alcove, in which Grandmother's bed stood, on the other. There were curtains across the alcove, but they were nearly always opened, in the winter, showing a gay patchwork quilt and pillow, with hand tucks and knitted lace edges. In front of the bed stood the spinning wheel and a clock reel for taking the yarn off in skeins. There was a rocking-chair and a basket, filled with carded and rolled wool, soft and fluffy as sleeping kittens.

Two steps up from this kitchen was the "other room," with a great base-burner stove, windows that looked on the front stoop, and a bedroom where Mama and I slept. It was here that Grandmother came to change her dress in the afternoon, something which she never failed to do, and it was here, when neighbors came, that a fire was built and company sat. There were plants on a table by the window, and every winter night saw them swathed in newspapers, which were not always effective in keeping them from freezing. Here a calla lily struggled against great odds to produce one or two blossoms a year, and an oleander in a tub was the pride of Grandmother's heart. I now live in California, where there are hedges of soiled calla lilies, but never one so precious as those. In the Sacramento and San Joaquin valleys, oleanders flourish like a green bay tree. How I wish Grandmother had lived to see them!

Walls never seem to have impressed me, but I remember a Brussels carpet on the floor of the "other room," with a design of pink roses and green leaves. Beyond this room was the hall, which was the front entrance of the house, opening on the middle of the stoop. A stairway from the hall led to bedrooms, warmed only by the pipe that ran up from the base burner, and so cold in winter that you could see your breath. Beyond

the hall was the parlor, with three windows, the shades
of which were always closely drawn, except when house-
cleaning time came around. I remember the walls in
the parlor. On the outside wall hung an enormous
wax wreath in what we now call a shadow box frame of
mahogany, and on the inside wall a hair wreath similarly
finished. I don't know who made them, but they were
exquisite examples of that kind of work, and were
spoken of as rare and beautiful things. There was a
marble-topped, center table, on which lay the illustrated
family Bible. On rare occasions I was allowed to have
this taken into the "other room," where I could look at
the pictures and Grandmother would read the births
and deaths. Beside it rested an album, bound in green
leather with gold tracings and little white knobs that
made it stand up from the table. It held tintypes and
photographs about the size of an ordinary calling card.
It was a mystery to me how they were ever able to get
hoop skirts on such small cards. There were a black,
hair-cloth sofa and several slippery chairs. But most
fascinating of all was a kaleidoscope that stood on a
what-not in the corner. It was a source of unending
delight to turn the kaleidoscope in my hands, and watch
the ever-changing colors and designs.

From this room opened the spare bedroom with a
bed whose headboard was so high that it reached to the
ceiling—and the ceilings were high. On it was an
appliqué spread, with quilting so fine that it seemed
as though it had been done by fairy fingers. Why
those rooms had to be cleaned every spring, I never
could understand. There was no stove. There was a

stove hole, but the stove was never put up. The rooms were kept closed, as though waiting for a guest who never came.

In the "other room" the stove was taken down every spring and put up every fall, and great was the polishing of iron and shining of nickel and arguing with stove pipes that seemed either to shrink or expand over the summer so that they were always too large or too small at the stove end or the hole that went into the ceiling.

And so life on the farm began for Mama and me.

☙ WINTER AT GRANDMOTHER'S ☙ BUSY LEISURE

I HAVE SPOKEN OF UNCLE ALEX, THE ONE who came to meet us, but not of Uncle Gordon. He was a tall man, well proportioned, but his eyes held a great tragedy, for Uncle Gordon was deaf and dumb. He could communicate only by queer, animal sounds that no one but Grandmother understood. Was there anything about the sounds she did understand, or was it that she knew instinctively what his wishes were? How tender she was with him! How she would recall the fact (true or imagined), in his defense, that Gordon had been the brightest of her babies, first to walk, first to talk, when an attack of scarlet fever left him deaf and dumb, with only his eyes and hands to convey the emotions he wished to express. He had an ungovernable temper and broke into rages, when his eyes would burn like those of a wounded animal. How sorry Grandmother would be! How quick to shield him from the anger of others! Uncle Gordon knew no expression but hard, physical labor, and that he did with the strength of an ox and the intermittent application of a child—poor training for earning a livelihood.

Sometimes, on Sunday nights, a fire would be built in the "other room" and, dressed in our Sunday clothes, we would sit there. I am sure we all felt a little strange and not quite so comfortable as in the kitchen, but it gave a sense of having been on a visit, a change from routine. Those Sundays come to me as rather formal occasions. But the long winter evenings in the cheery kitchen remain a picture of peace and happiness and busy leisure that rests me whenever I think of it.

Busy leisure. A strange way to express what I want to say. After the chores were done and supper over, the reading lamp was lighted and set on the checkered cloth, Grandmother's spinning wheel began to hum, and straight, erect and sturdy, in her blue delaine afternoon dress, she would walk lightly, back and forth, whirling the big wheel with her right hand, and with her left running the fleecy rolls of wool back and forth to the spindle, every movement so deft and sure that the yarn was smooth and even, of uniform thickness and strength, with never a lump or bunch to mar its perfection.

Grandmother always seemed happiest when spinning. There was something very soothing in being busy at some task so perfectly synchronized that her mind could rove at will while accomplishing it. I am sure Sunday was a sore trial to her, for she never allowed herself or others to be occupied in any way on that day, except in tasks necessary for the preparation of meals and for the care of the animals, who really seemed part of the family. I can see her sitting, quite disconsolate, with her busy hands folded in her lap. Then, towards evening, the family Bible would be brought from the parlor and she would turn the leaves, showing me the fine steel engravings and reading the record of births, marriages and deaths. Monday was always welcome, and she plunged into the family washing with a zest. Soft water from the cistern, soft soap, made according to her excellent recipe, combined to make foaming suds. Then the clothes were hung on the clothes bars on the front stoop and were soon frozen stiff as pokers. I can remember watching them riding the bars like hobgoblins or ghosts.

While Grandmother spun, I sat in my little rocking-chair, as close as I could get without being in the way. She taught me to knit the wrists for the double mittens that Uncle Alex and Uncle Gordon wore whenever they went out in the winter. There was the block pattern and the zigzag and others, even more intricate, done in red, blue, white, or butternut—home-dyed wools. Grandmother did the rest of the mitten, carrying two strands of yarn, one white, one blue, alternating, so that the mittens were striped blue and white and double yarn in thickness.

When I hear the expression, "all wool and a yard wide," I think of those double mittens. I would knit with one eye on the spindle of the spinning wheel, for when the spindle was full of yarn, I was allowed to wind it off on the clock reel and help Grandmother tie it in skeins, an exciting diversion for me. Mama would be sewing, mending clothing for the men, darning, or making a pretty dress for me from one that had belonged to her or Grandmother. I had the prettiest clothes of any little girl I knew. Neighbors, and even Grandmother, spoke of Mama's sewing with great respect. "She can do tailoring," I heard them say—and that seemed to be something very expert.

When Mama was not sewing she was writing on the letter which she kept in a brown leather portfolio, etched in gold. There was always a letter in it for Papa. Once a week, when Uncle Alex went to Madrid, or a neighbor passed, she would send her letter to Smith in California and start another. There was never a time when there was not a letter to Papa on the way.

Uncle Alex would read the *St. Lawrence Republican,* or the *Home Veterinary,* or *Hostetters' Bitters Almanac.* I do not remember any other reading, never any magazines. Uncle Gordon would go to the cellar for St. Lawrence and strawberry apples—apples, red-cheeked, crisp and juicy, and to the attic for butternuts or popcorn. He would crack the nuts on a flat iron with the handle caught between his knees, and peel apples for each one. Perhaps all of us did not care to have them peeled, but he enjoyed doing it so much that no one ever denied him the pleasure. He always had the sharpest pocket knife, and he cut the red skin away from the white flesh of the apple in thin, delicate strips, round and round, unbroken from stem to blossom end.

There was never any liquor used except as a medicine. There was no tobacco, no beverage stronger than cider.

There was always a kitten, sometimes a whole family of them, to stretch and sleep on the rag rug before the fire, and to hold in my lap and snuggle to my neck one minute, boxing their ears and paws that threatened to tangle my yarn the next.

That is what I mean by busy leisure. I think of those evenings. One would not want to live them now, and yet . . .

Nine o'clock meant bed-time. Grandmother would go to the clock and change the weights, so that they were ready to start out again on their twenty-four-hour journey. The men went upstairs to bed. Mama and I undressed by the kitchen fire and scampered to our "other room" bed-room, each carrying a candle, and a hot brick wrapped in flannel to put between the hand-woven woollen sheets that Grandmother had made.

In the morning the men would start the kitchen fire and then go to the barn to do the chores. We would hear Uncle Gordon priming the pump to draw our supply of drinking water for the day. Mama and I would grab our clothes and make for the kitchen and the friendly blaze. No one who has not had the experience of jumping out of bed into a zero temperature and grabbing cold clothes to run and dress by the fire can possibly appreciate the luxury of a modern furnace-heated house.

Grandmother was always up and stirring before we were, getting breakfast started. My first thought was for the beautiful pictures that Jack Frost had painted on the windows overnight; parks and palaces, snow stars and fairies, finer than any picture books. They were the only picture books I had. The next thought, stimulated by the odor of warming potatoes and fried salt pork, was for breakfast. Of all the food I remember, fried salt pork and thick milk gravy seems to have been the backbone of every day's menu! Such good salt pork, sweet and nutty tasting, with milk gravy.

Mornings were always busy. Perhaps there was yeast to make from the "starter" that was never allowed to run out, or maybe it would be salt-rising bread made from emptyings started with meal and milk and sugar, kept warm and allowed to ferment and form a self-made yeast. Such wholesome, delicious bread, but giving off an odor during the making that was worse than over-ripe Camembert. Bread reminds me of butter and churning. In the winter this took practically all day. There was not so much cream as in the summer, so the tall stone crock, with the dasher, was used. The cream was brought from the buttery, icy cold, and poured into the churn. Then the churn was set in a tub of warm water to take the chill off, but not to get really warm—delicately tested with a finger for thermometer. Grandmother would give the dasher a few pumps and whisk it around to see if it was starting all right, and then it would be my turn to churn. It was a tiresome job, but stimulated in interest by Grandmother's occasionally lifting the cover, looking critically into the churn, and saying, "It's getting real thick. I think it's beginning to come," and I would churn merrily on again until finally a thick layer would form between the dasher and the hole in the cover, and then, just when it seemed that my short, fat arms couldn't raise that dasher another time, the cream would separate, leaving only a thin liquid and chunks of butter to cling to the dasher. The buttermilk was strained off and fed to the hogs, for the cream stood so long in the winter that the buttermilk was bitter.

Grandmother would put the butter in a shallow, wooden bowl, cover it with cold water, and work it with a wooden ladle until it was hard and smooth and free from buttermilk. In the winter it had to be colored with a few drops of Richardson's butter color. Then the butter was moulded into rolls the size and shape of a jelly roll.

In spring the whole process was very different. The cows "came in." There were little calves in the barn, and there was a quantity of milk. Then the big barrel churn, mounted on a standard, was used. The cream was poured into a bung-hole in the side of the barrel, and Uncle Gordon would turn the barrel by a big handle, much as he turned the grindstone to sharpen the scythe later in the season. Now the buttermilk was good to drink, nothing better, and no color was added to the butter, for it was a rich, golden yellow.

There were other exciting days when the snowflakes came down thick and fast, making the house seem even more snug and warm and secure. And, the day after, there was the fun of watching the men with teams and heavy sleds breaking the road. The men would beat their arms across their breasts to warm them, and icicles would hang from their moustaches and beards, and frost would form on their horses' mouths and nostrils.

Once, during the winter, an Indian came on snowshoes. He was dressed in buckskins, and he had things made from beaded leather to sell. Grandmother gave him something to eat, and bought me a pair of beaded moccasins.

When the sun had formed a hard crust on the snow, I could go out, bundled in coat, overshoes, mittens and muffler, and slide down the hill in the orchard on the sled which Uncle Gordon made for me. It took skill to steer between the rows of trees, but after many upsets, I became quite expert and would go the length of the hill and out onto the ice of Grass River, in breath-taking ecstasy. Then came the long pull back up the hill with my sled. How heavy those overshoes were then!

All that winter in Grandmother's home I never re-member having any child come to play with me, and yet I was never lonely. While all these interesting things were happening in the house, Uncle Alex and Uncle Gordon were busy out of doors, going to the woods across the frozen Grass River on their bob-sleds, getting out wood to last until the following winter, bringing the wood home, cording it, chopping enough into stove-wood lengths to fill the woodshed to bursting, stopping in their work to take off their mittens and cup their fingers in their hands and blow their warm breath on them to drive away the numbness; shelling corn in the corn crib for chickens and hogs, oiling and repairing harness, or making plow handles and axe handles from hickory wood, which was Uncle Gordon's specialty. It was a healthy, contented life, with good food and shelter for us all. There were warm barns for the cattle and horses, sheds for the hogs, chicken houses; a buggy house for the wagons and buggies, cutters and sleds; another shed for machinery; corn cribs, and tall, narrow smoke houses where the meat was cured.

🦋 SPRING 🦋 "SUGARING OFF" 🦋 A QUILTING PARTY

THEN CAME SPRING. I ALWAYS FEEL sorry for children who have had no experience of winter, with its snow and ice, followed by the thrill of spring. I never remember realizing beauty in nature until that first spring on Grandmother's farm, and then my heart fairly burst with the joy of discovery. From the gate in the picket fence along the drive that ran to the back of the house, Grandmother had beds of spring flowering bulbs, narcissus, daffodils, and tulips pushing their shoots valiantly up through the frozen ground.

In the front yard were large sugar-maple trees, four on each side of the path that ran to the front gate. It was fascinating to watch their buds swell and then burst into lace-like leaves. Beyond the driveway the orchard ran down a sunny slope to the river and apple and pear blossoms added their dainty loveliness to the spring festival. On either side of the front path Grandmother's peonies, in two round beds, uncurled their fern-like leaves to the sun, and in the back garden under the buttery window moss-roses began to leaf out.

There were little calves and colts coming at the barn and being turned out in the newly green pasture when the sun was warm. Baby chickens, like so many fluffy balls, were arriving, and I always had a chosen few in a little box, swathed in flannel behind the kitchen stove. There were little pigs to snuggle against their big, fat mother's teats in the hog pen.

Once, not many years ago, I was passing a little house and garden in Long Beach, California. The place looked so eastern, the garden so pretty, that I couldn't resist stopping and chatting with the elderly man who was pottering around among the flowers.

"Yes," he said, in reply to my questions, "we had a home back East, but we came out here one winter on a visit and the weather was so fine and everything grew so easily, we thought we wanted to live here. So Mother and I went back and sold our little farm and came out and bought this place. It's real pretty and things grow if you just stick them in the ground, but we get kind of tired of it. The old ocean out there just rolls and rolls and the flowers and garden stuff keep growing right along. No spring. No fall. We're plumb worn out with it, and we're going to sell out and go back where they have seasons. Where there is a real spring, with things coming up and surprising you all the time."

I could sympathize. I knew that homesickness. Mine was more for trees. Many times, among the forests of fir and pine and tamarack of the Sierras, or the palms and orange groves of Southern California, I would be suddenly overcome with a longing for the eastern woods, —maples and beeches and elms that rested in the winter and woke to leafy loveliness when winter was over.

When spring was running every place on tip-toe, came the rare treat of "sugaring off." Mama, Uncle Gordon and I, with a big basket of lunch, went in the buggy,

picking up a girl cousin of mine on the way. I was later
to learn that most of the people for miles around were
aunts, uncles, and cousins. Uncle Alex was to go in the
light wagon for his "girl" and some other young people.
When that arrangement was made, I saw the first
shadow on Grandmother's face. She was staying home
to superintend a hired man who came to do the chores.
But Grandmother's evident displeasure did not dampen
my zest for the lark on which we were setting forth.

We travelled the slushy road and over the bridge that
spanned the Grass River, where the ice was breaking up,
and then, in and out, among the trees of the sugar bush,
to the sugar house—a wooden, two-room shanty. The
trees had been tapped the day before and the buckets that
hung from spouts in their sides were full of sap. Uncle
Gordon collected the sap and poured it into the huge
kettle that stood on a stout iron stove. Then he started
a roaring fire and the sap began to boil. Mama, my
cousin and I roamed through the woods, finding May-
apple blossoms and violets—quiet, shy flowers that
clutched your throat with their beauty. When we came
back to the sugar house, a delicate odor of maple was in
the air. Uncle Alex came with his girl and the other
young people. I thought Uncle Alex's girl very pretty.
She was tall and slender and dressed more stylishly than
any one of my acquaintance. She made me think of
Ogdensburg.

We had such fun testing the syrup, and then, as it
grew thick, going to shady spots, where snow banks still
lingered, for milk pans full of glistening snow on which
the thick syrup was poured to make maple wax. If
there is any more delicious confection in the world, I

have not discovered it. The moon came up, couples wandered away with a milk pan to their bank of snow and lingered awhile, coming back with rosy cheeks and moon-touched eyes, to the group around the fire. Uncle Alex was so different that I hardly knew him,—so gay and tender to every one, especially to his girl. From that day on, Uncle Alex was a hero to me, for I knew that he was "in love."

For the first time, too, I realized how alone Uncle Gordon was in his world, shut away by the wall of silence, and Mama, too, was so alone with Papa gone. But these were only transient thoughts. Nothing could possibly spoil the "sugaring off" for a child greedy for life and pleasure. In the evening every one sang "Annie Laurie," "Coming Through the Rye," and "Seeing Nellie Home." And I blushed furiously when they all looked at me and laughed. But I went to sleep on the way home, and knew nothing more until morning.

As spring opened, letters began to come from Papa. The mails were so uncertain through the snowy winter that at first there were three or four at a time. The first letter was excitingly post-marked, Reno, Nevada.

"It has been a long, tiresome trip," he wrote. "Sometimes the train was stalled for hours, waiting for the snow plows to come and clear the tracks for us. This is a small town, only important because it is here that one changes from the main line to the Virginia and Truckee wood-burning train that runs to Virginia City and to Mound House, where I transfer for Bodie."

There was a later letter postmarked, "Bodie," California. "I came to Mound House on the Virginia and Truckee," it read, "through Carson City, the capitol of

Nevada. At Mound House I transferred to a queer, little narrow gauge train that runs to Hawthorne, and on through the desert to Owen's Lake. The good Lord only knows why it was built. As a man on the train said, 'This road was built three hundred miles too long, and three hundred years too soon.' I wish you and Nellie could see the coach that brought us to Bodie. It is a four-horse Concord stage. A shot-gun messenger, with a sawed-off shot-gun, sits up on the high seat in front with the driver. He has the Wells Fargo Express box between this feet. Going out, it is full of gold bullion; coming in, it is full of gold coin. The side rails of the stage turn up at each end like skates. The body of the coach swings between them on wide leather straps. They are very comfortable, and it was a beautiful drive over the foothills to the Mountain House, where we arrived at nine o'clock at night, had supper, and changed horses. All winter long the horses wear snow-shoes. They are about the size of dinner plates and clamp onto the horses' hoofs. At two o'clock in the morning we arrived in Bodie. The streets were all lighted, stores open, saloons and gambling houses filled with people. Big quartz mills were running at each end of town, men by hundreds coming off shift every eight hours. The hotel was so full I could not get a room, and was given a candle and taken to a cabin down the street."

The days lengthened and grew warmer and fragrant. The double windows were taken off and the banks of rotted manure were hauled to the fields and spread for fertilizer. The fresh grass was green under the maples in the front yard, and they were tapped and little buckets hung on the spouts to catch the sap. I would bring them when filled to the kitchen, where Grandmother boiled the sap and made flat cakes of maple sugar. Some of it went into my lunch when I started to school, but there was always one plain bread-and-butter sandwich, and on the way I would gather flat, juicy leaves of sorrel to put between the slices.

On the heels of sugaring off came house-cleaning. Every carpet and rag rug was taken out, hung on the line, and beaten. Feather beds were opened, emptied into sheets, aired and renovated; linens were washed and spread on the fresh grass in the sun to bleach. Grandmother waited until Saturday to clean the garret, so that I could help her. What a thrilling place it was! There were old trunks and boxes that had come over from Scotland and England with our ancestors; old dresses made with the full skirts that went over the hoops of Grandmother's girlhood, poke bonnets with wreaths of flowers, hand-knit lace mitts, collapsed hoop skirts, hung on nails on the wall.

In one trunk were Grandfather's clothes, and Grandmother told me about him—how handsome and tall and fine he was, how hard he worked to build up the farm, and how, while still a young man, he was paralyzed for two years before he died—in his chair out under the maple trees. I learned afterwards that he and Papa had quarreled violently and that the excitement had brought on the stroke from which he never recovered. Then I understood why Mama hated to go home to "his folks." But Grandmother's way with us was always free from censure or bitterness.

Up attic there were herbs hanging from the ceiling; catnip and camomile, and sweet anise and caraway, sacks and ears of dried corn and dried apples, a barrel, then nearly empty, of butternuts. All the herbs and corn and fruit were taken out to be replaced by fresh in the fall. The rafters and floor were dusted and swept. The spinning wheel and clock reel were brought upstairs and stored for the summer. Papa's Knight Templar hat with the beautiful feather plumes, which we had brought from Pennsylvania, was aired and put away with bags of spices and his Knight Templar sword. My fancy always clothed my father in romance, probably stimulated by the sight of the plumed hat and the sword that travelled with us wherever we went.

After the garret there was the cellar: apples to be sorted, potatoes to be sprouted, bins to be emptied, edibles to be put on the swinging shelf out of the reach of mice. I wonder how they did it all—just Mother and Grandmother, with Uncle Gordon to help. There was never any hired girl.

But, when it was all finished, what a feeling of rejuvenation! Everything spotless, fresh and clean. Spring brought into the house. And as the spring brought plowing and sowing outside, so the work inside the house changed. Patchwork was brought out and quilts started. Grandmother knitted lace instead of mittens. Worn-out woollen garments were cut into strips and sewn for hooking into rugs and weaving into carpets. There were no rummage sales in those days.

Neighbors visited and I became acquainted with my cousins and my aunts. There were quilting bees in the afternoons, with bread and butter and preserves and cookies. Here again Mama "shone"; she made the most intricate patterns, with tiny, even stitches, and was recognized as the best quilter in the neighborhood.

It was at one of the quilting parties that I first heard of "quick consumption." To die of "quick consumption" seemed quite as romantic a thing as to die of a broken heart, and it evidently happened much oftener. At this party some one, pointing to a particularly pretty piece of print in the quilt stretched on the frame (it was a design of red strawberries and green leaves, on a white background) remarked, "That's a piece of the dress Eunice wore the last time she quilted with us. She looked so pretty that day! Her cheeks were as red as the berries in her dress. That was a year ago come June and she was dead by fall."

It may not sound so in the repeating, but there was a flavor of romance in the way it was told. And it seemed to me it would be a rather lovely thing to have "quick consumption," and die prettily with it as Eunice had done. I learned that Mama's mother had died of it, and that was why Grandmother Peck was step-grandmother; also that various cousins and aunts had gone "that way" with "galloping consumption." No one seemed to wonder why. It was just the hand of God or Providence. There were no precautions against infection. The only wonder is that any one was spared, when I think of the double windows and the supposition that cold air was fresh air, and that, so long as your bedroom was cold, the sealed air was fresh even though the window was closed all winter.

In the midst of all these exciting happenings, I had to go to school. One smiles nowadays at tales of the little red schoolhouse and wonders if it really existed. It did. I know, for I attended one. The teacher "boarded 'round." She was young and pretty and had difficulty in handling the big boys, but when spring opened nature solved her problem for her, because most of them had to drop school and go to work on the farm.

I remember almost nothing of that spring term in school, but I can recall much of the road that I trudged every day to get there and home again. It was a mile and a half, and there was so much to see of birds and trees and spring violets that it never seemed far. Every morning Mama brushed my long curls over her finger, drew my hair back from my forehead to a bow on the crown of my head, and let the rest fall loose down my back. It was pretty to look at, but, oh, the tangle and the tears every day! There was always a fresh gingham apron, ruffled and tied in a bow at the back and starched, white panties, ruffled and tucked and trimmed with knitted lace.

I was a very fat little girl, and my most vivid recollection of school that first spring is walking home in the early afternoon when the sun was hot, with my fat legs rubbing against those starched panties until they were so chafed that I could scarcely endure the torture. I remember there was a sumac bush about halfway home, and I would stop and sit in its shade and wonder if I would ever get home, or if some one would come along and give me a ride. But I never took off my panties. Perish the thought! And although Mama was sorry and put on burned starch and mutton tallow, she never stopped starching those panties.

When school was out, there were long, summer days

full of wonder for me as things grew and bloomed and covered the farm with beauty. I had many tasks to do, but only one real "stint," that must be done every day but Sunday. Grandmother cut and basted blocks of cloth for me and every day I must sew one square made up of nine blocks before I was free to play.

I squirmed and my hands sweat, the needle stuck and squeaked, but Grandmother would get her little emery bag and scour the needle, and have me wash my hands in cool water, and keep at the task until it was finished.

After that, I was free to go and look at the heavy-headed pink peonies or smell the moss-roses and see if the wild Isabella grapes that grew over the buggy house were beginning to ripen, to eat the yellow June apples that had fallen to the ground, to chew sweet anise or lie in the red clover in the meadow and watch the bees and butterflies, or go to the pasture and play with the little calves and colts.

☙ *THE PRESIDENT IS SHOT* ☙
SUMMER DAYS
& TYPHOID

THE FOURTH OF JULY STANDS OUT BE-cause on that day Grandmother and Uncle Gordon, Mama and I started out early in the morning to drive to Waddington, six miles away. There we took a boat and crossed the St. Lawrence River to Morrisburg on the Canadian side. We walked around the town, bought

some silk ties, one for Papa and one for each of my
uncles, and a gorgeous hair ribbon for me. There was
great agitation about getting these things back to the
States, duty-free. Every one was gay and happy and
I thought we all looked so fine in our Sunday clothes.
It was a never-to-be-forgotten experience, that crossing
the St. Lawrence River for the first time.

Grandmother told me that day what a faithful river
the St. Lawrence was, how other rivers, like the Mississippi, broke their banks and flooded lands and destroyed homes, but that the St. Lawrence never changed
its course. It never rose or fell noticeably, but kept on
flowing from the Great Lakes to the ocean, sheltering
its Thousand Islands in beauty and calm. She told me,
too, of how the first mission for the Indians had been
established and called La Présentation, at the place
where Ogdensburg now stood. And how, during the
war of the Revolution a man named Jacob Brown had
worried the British by intercepting supplies on the St.
Lawrence.

And then she told me that the Fourth of July was
the day of the signing of the Declaration of Independence, which meant the war between England and the
United States; that England had owned all the country but we had broken away; that Canada still belonged
to England. Although there had been a great war,
everything was friendly now and the English were fine
people. But, of course, the United States was the greatest country of all. How she believed that; how she
watched every advance, each new growth, putting her
faith in God and the Republican party.

I shall never forget the day in July when Uncle Alex

came home with the news that President Garfield had been shot. Grandmother's grief was as real and intimate as though he had been one of her own sons. She would walk out to the road and ask for news of the passers by. She found reasons to send Uncle Alex to town more frequently. All summer long there was a feeling that some one very near and necessary to us was ill. Each night Grandmother, whose religion was more the practicing than the praying kind, would say a short prayer as she changed the weights in the clock. Long Branch, where Garfield lay ill, seemed very near and real to us and when he died in September his picture, with an American flag tied in black crape and banked with moss-roses, was placed on the marble top table under the wax wreath in the parlor until after the funeral was over, and on the day of the funeral a big flag was put out of the garret window to float all day in the summer breeze.

Next in importance to the President was Queen Victoria, a very real personage to me and, as far as I could learn, she and my grandmother were as like as two peas. To my mind they were equally great. Then, too, there was the Prince of Wales, a dashing figure, and Lily Langtry, the "Jersey Lily," most famous beauty of those days. I always had to have concrete examples to make people seem real, and so Uncle Alex became the Prince of Wales in my mind, and his girl the fascinating siren, Lily Langtry.

Every Sunday now Uncle Alex took his fine team of bays, hitched to a new top buggy, and went to see his girl, and because of his devotion to her a wall of restraint was growing between him and Grandmother. I never understood why, until one hot day, when Grandmother was ironing a stiff-bosomed "boiled" shirt for him, he came into the kitchen in a hurry and wanted it right away, for he was going out with his girl to some party.

"Are you going to marry her?" Grandmother asked, and I noticed that her usually firm hands trembled on the holder over the handle of the iron, pulling it awry and burning her fingers.

"I am if she will have me, Mother."

"Have you!" Grandmother said, scornfully; "don't give her the chance unless you want to tie a rock around your neck. O, Alex, son," she said with great tenderness, "don't marry her, I beg of you. She is no wife for a farmer. She will squander your money, your birthright that Father and I worked so hard to get for you and Gordon."

"She knows the value of money," Uncle Alex protested. "She has taught school to earn it," he said, proudly.

"Yes, to earn it to spend on her back, sending to Ogdensburg for her clothes. I hoped you would marry some thrifty farmer's daughter, who would be a helpmeet instead of a spendthrift."

I thought something must happen after that, but Uncle Alex went to see his girl just the same, and I never heard Grandmother speak of her again.

The odor of new-mown hay was in the air and I climbed to the tip-top of the fragrant loads as they were driven to the barn to be stowed in the haymow. Hens stole their nests, and it was an exciting game of hide-and-seek to find them and bring the eggs or maybe some downy chicks to Grandmother. The geese, that

were to furnish feathers for new feather-beds and grease
to rub on my chest when I had a croupy cough, ran
after me, stretching their necks and hissing. Grandmother and I took pails and went berrying, climbing
the rail fence beyond the pasture to a wood lot, where
wild raspberries and blackberries hung from a thorny
tangle ripening in the sun. Grapes that hung on the
buggy shed ripened, and delicious globes of tangy sweetness slipped from their loose skins. In the evenings
we would all sit on the front stoop and Grandmother
would hold me on her comfortable lap and rock while
she sang:

> *"The strawberries grow in the mowing, mill-may,*
> *And the bobolink sings in the tree,*
> *On the knolls the clover is blowing mill-may,*
> *Then come to the meadow with me."*

Letters came often from Papa, and Mama was happier.
Papa had a mine, the Nellie Mine, named for me.
There was plenty of surveying and map drawing, and
he was putting everything he could get into the mine.
He couldn't send any money. It was best for us to
stay where we were for the present, but he hoped it
wouldn't be long. Fortunes were being taken out from
the big glory hole. Stanford and Fair had struck it.
The Nellie Mine seemed to be on the same vein. It
only meant waiting awhile, and he knew we were
well provided for. Waiting awhile did not seem hard
when Grandmother was so kind and Uncle Alex and
Uncle Gordon made us welcome, but often in the night
I would waken to hear Mama crying quietly.

Grandmother got a piece of perforated card-board and

dyed some soft yarn in bright colors and taught me to do a motto in cross-stitch. The motto said, "God Is Love," and was to be used to mark the place where we were reading in the Bible. I found this much more to my taste than the patch-work and stuck to it diligently.

It was time to start school again. I began to be interested in reading, for I found it opened a storehouse of delights. The trees were turning gold and crimson, and the sumac bush was flowering red. Boys and girls planned parties to go beech-nutting and butter-nutting. Indian summer came, and the Adirondack mountains swam through a purple haze on the horizon.

One night plans were made for butchering the next day, and in the morning I went gladly off to school, relieved that I would be well away from the squealing and commotion that led up to the execution. I always had to shut my eyes and stop my ears when a chicken had its head cut off, or a pig was led to slaughter.

A never-to-be-forgotten picture was etched on my memory that night when I came from school. The sun was setting and all the world was crimson and gold. Grandmother in a clean print dress, her white hair shining in the sun's rays, was standing by the big, black kettle, filled with steaming water, above which hung a hog suspended from a crane. She was directing the scraping, and afterwards, when the hog was taken down, she selected the lard, separating the choice leaf fat from that which would be used as soap grease, and superintended the division of meat into spare-ribs and pork for salting, hams and bacon. It was the last task Grandmother ever performed on the farm, which had grown to security under her capable management.

That night her face was unusually flushed and I missed being rocked in her lap, for she was very tired and went to bed early. I had never heard Grandmother say she was tired before. She did not even wait to change the weights in the clock and it seemed strange to see Uncle Alex attending to it. Next morning she did not get up and I went to school, feeling that the mainspring of all our familiar, pleasant life had given out.

When I came home there was a strange horse and buggy in the yard. The doctor from Madrid was there. He said that Grandmother had typhoid fever, black typhoid they called it in those days, as though to add to its unspeakable horror. It came, he said, from using the cistern water.

"Stuff a cold and starve a fever" was the slogan in those days, and nourishment was withheld and the fever allowed to consume its victims. For a month Grandmother lay, her eyes burning, her mouth parched, her body shriveling day by day, taking uncomplainingly the nauseous mixtures the doctor prescribed on his daily visits, perishing for the nourishing liquids that should have kept up her strength.

Then Uncle Gordon was stricken, and Uncle Alex, and the struggle for life filled the house. Neighbors came to help, to sit up nights, to bring food for Mama and me and the watchers.

Grandmother asked that her spinning wheel be brought down from the garret and stood by her bed, and sometimes she would reach out a restless hand and start the wheel humming, then settle back with a smile on her face.

I sat by her sometimes, looking at the little reel with

tears running down my cheeks. When delirium came, I would try to swallow the choke in my throat and sing, "The strawberries grow in the mowing, mill-may," dreading what was ahead but not realizing that Grandmother was spinning her last skein.

Grandmother was dead. She lay in a black covered coffin, in the parlor, under the wax wreath. She was dressed in her Sunday dress and over that was a shroud. Uncle Gordon, too, the doctor said was dead and was laid out in the "other room." Uncle Alex was getting well. Mama had great circles under her eyes. Every one was too busy to notice me.

There were no flowers outside. The frost had taken them all; no flowers for Grandmother. But there was a bud on the calla lily. I stole into the "other room" carefully, so as not to disturb Uncle Gordon, and broke off the bud. Maybe it would blossom if I put it in Grandmother's hand. I curled the little motto that said "God is Love" around the stem, so that Grandmother would know who put it there.

A preacher came out from Madrid and talked about streets of gold and a house not made with hands, eternal in the heavens. I thought of Grandmother's busy hands and wondered if heaven would be like Sunday, and wished she might have a spinning wheel up there.

Uncle Gordon didn't stay dead. The doctor called it suspended animation and catalepsy, but the neighbors all thought he couldn't know his business not to know whether a man was really dead or not. So the other black coffin was carried away and Grandmother went down the front path to the gate alone. I had never seen her go down that path in life.

She was buried by Grandfather's side in the burying ground on the hill, and the choir sang, "We shall gather at the river," and I thought of the St. Lawrence River, and how Grandmother loved it, and knew she couldn't be very sad if she had gone to live by a beautiful river. The thought that we should all gather there was very comforting to me.

🏵 AUNT MARY 🏵 CHRISTMAS 🏵 JOCKEY CLUB PERFUME

I DIDN'T MIND VERY MUCH, AT FIRST, when Mama was taken sick, for the doctor said that she must be moved to Madrid to be near him, and so we went to Grandfather Peck's house in town. Everything seemed so strange and empty, since Grandmother had been carried out through the front gate, that I was glad to leave the farm. But Mama, who had been only "ailing," was really another typhoid case and there followed anxious days and weeks, with a nurse in the house, wearing stiffly starched white dresses, and Mama not knowing me but moaning and crying for Smith all the time. I began to realize that Papa was far, far away—farther away, even, than Grandmother, it seemed. Uncle Alex said it was no use sending for him, for it would be so

long before he could get home that Mama would be—
he hesitated—well. I drew a great sigh of relief. I
thought maybe he was going to say, *dead.*

Those were bad days for me. I seemed to be in the
way all the time. Grandfather was a fussy old man,
who hated being disturbed by sickness in the house, and
I overheard my step-grandmother say, the first day we
were there, that she "didn't see why Smith MacKnight
couldn't stay home and take care of his family instead of
leaving them dependent on their relations."

That night I cried myself to sleep. I didn't like the
nurse. She pulled my hair every time she combed it
and said she couldn't see why my mother didn't have
it cut off, it was such a nuisance. One day she asked
me why Mama didn't take her teeth out. I didn't know
what she meant and answered, "Why Mama never takes
them out. She can't."

"They can't be her own," she said, "I never saw such
perfect teeth except false ones."

I felt insulted that she should think Mama's beautiful
white teeth were false, felt as though any one who
thought that couldn't take very good care of Mama. But
I knew what she meant by false teeth when I found my
step-grandmother's teeth in a glass on the bureau.

Then I grew sick and feverish, and every one thought
I was going to have typhoid fever, and I hoped I would
and that I might die with it and "gather at the river"
with Grandmother and not have to stay with relations
any more. And I thought how badly Papa would feel
when Mama and I were both dead, and how sorry he
would be that he had gone away and left us.

But I was bundled up and taken away to Aunt Mary's.

Aunt Mary was not an aunt at all, but a very dear friend of Mama's. What a generous, comfortable, comforting soul she was. Instead of a relation, I was, all at once, a dear little girl whom every one loved once again. My curls were so pretty and Aunt Mary seemed to love to brush them over her finger, just as Mama did.

I sat wrapped up in a big chair, with Aunt Mary and Uncle John waiting on me and giving me cambric tea and soda-crackers to eat. Soda-crackers were a luxury those days. They tasted delicious to me.

I was soon well again. I suppose I had really fretted myself into a fever. Aunt Mary took me to see Mama, who was getting better, and when she was well she came to Aunt Mary's and they talked about our going to Bridgeport, Connecticut, to work in the corset factory.

"You see," Mama told her, "Alex is going to be married and I can't go on living there. Smith can't send me any money now." Mama seemed to accept that fact with no resentment. She never wavered in her allegiance and her faith that Smith was doing the best he could. I am sure she never wrote him one disturbing thing.

"I can borrow the money from Alex and pay it back as fast as I am able," she said.

Christmas was near. I realized that Mama looked years older than she had that last Christmas in Petrolia. Her black hair was clouded with gray, and there were always dark hollows under her eyes.

A letter came from Papa in California. Mama read me parts of it that told of the Nellie Mine and the prospects that looked so good. Papa was sending us a nugget, he said, white rock with wire gold running all the

way through it. They had struck a pocket, but it soon
ran out. It gave him some money to go on working
the mine. That was all Mama read to me. It sounded
fine, and I wondered what made Mama look so sad,
and why her eyes followed me as though she were wondering what to do.

I had gone back to Grandfather Peck's to be with her,
and later that day we went to see Aunt Mary. While I
was playing with some new kittens and they thought I
was not listening, Mama read Papa's letter to Aunt Mary,
and there were many things in it that I had not heard
before.

He was surprised to hear of Grandmother's death, but
of course she was pretty well along. Along what? I
wondered. He wondered about the property, supposed
he was disinherited, and that that upstart, Alex, would
get everything. Gordon would be lucky if he did not
have to hire out. It was the first time I had ever heard
the farm called property, and it was as though some cruel
instrument had scratched the beautiful, peaceful picture
that I treasured in my heart.

"I hope, Olive," the letter also said, "that you are
well by now, and I want you and Nellie to go right back
and live on the farm. You have as much right there as
anybody, and as long as I am not there to fight for it, I
want you to do it for me."

I had never before heard Mama rebel against anything
that Papa told her to do, and I could hardly believe my
ears when she said, "I can't do it, Mary. It is too much
for Smith to ask of me. I gave up our home and came
to live with his folks, but now that Mother MacKnight

is gone, I can't go back to live with Alex and his wife. Alex is kind, but he is putty in her hands, and she does not want me."

"Has she said so?" Aunt Mary asked.

"No, but Sade Carpenter does not have to say things to make you feel them. I'm sorry for Gordon, but it would only make it harder for him if I took Nellie back and tried to live there."

For the first time I comprehended that life is a complicated thing, that the farm that had seemed so safe a refuge was a refuge no longer, that its sheltering peace had been shattered when Grandmother went away. And all at once I knew that Mama was right—that we must not go back to stay; everything would be spoiled, and I wanted to keep my memories.

Christmas Eve I hung the pepper and salt stocking that Grandmother had knitted for me on the post at the foot of our bed. Santa Claus came, for in the morning there was a china doll head sticking out from the top of the stocking. No doll that has real hair and says Papa and Mama can possibly mean more than that doll did to me.

Her black hair was painted in ringlets on her head. Her unwinking eyes were bright blue, her painted cheeks and lips a vivid carmine against the china white of her face. Her head and china hands and feet were sewed to a body made of unbleached muslin, stuffed with saw-dust.

No doll ever had prettier clothes. Fairy fingers had fashioned a blue delaine dress that was just like the afternoon dress that Grandmother used to wear. There were lace-trimmed petticoats and panties, and doll stockings, knitted by hand with tiny heels and insteps, and toed off just as my own stockings were.

In the bottom of my Christmas stocking was a round, yellow orange, a rare treat. Really, Santa Claus is a wonderful person. When I see the demands made on him nowadays and how bored some children are on Christmas morning, I wonder if he remembers what joy a doll, a top, a jack-knife, and an orange, with perhaps a few "nigger-toes" could bring to children in those days.

Some relatives who lived miles up the Grass River had invited Uncle Alex and his girl and Uncle Gordon and Mama and me to come for Christmas dinner with other relations. They came for us in a two-seated sled, with long, curved runners. The sled was new and piled with buffalo robes. Uncle Alex had a new buffalo overcoat and cap and fur mittens and his girl a stylish browny-black fur jacket (Mama said it was sealskin), and such a pretty round fur cap to match.

She and Uncle Alex sat in the front seat and they were gay and happy and sang and laughed all the way. I sat between Mama and Uncle Gordon in the back seat and thought how wonderful it must be to be young and in love, and not sad as Mama and Uncle Gordon were. I wondered if Papa and Mama had ever been like Uncle Alex and his girl.

That day I knew what Mama meant when she told Aunt Mary, "Sade does not have to say anything to let you know how she feels." She hardly spoke to us on the long ride; she and Uncle Alex were so busy talking.

But the day was beautiful with the sun sparkling on the snow. The sleigh-bells played a merry tune as the horses trotted over the smooth ice of the river. There were people skating and doing figures of eight and all kinds of fancy things, then breaking away and racing us, shouting and laughing. Their bright colored toboggan caps and mufflers made them seem like carnival revelers.

When we arrived at our destination, Uncle Alex's girl was suddenly very nice to me. Mama was a favorite with all the relatives, and as soon as they welcomed her so warmly and said how glad they were that she was well again, Uncle Alex's girl patted Mama's arm and said, "Let me, too, extend my congratulations on your recovery." I thought that sounded very nice and lady-like.

And then she put her arms around me and said, "What a pretty dress you have, Nellie." But she did not really hug me like Mama and Grandmother and Aunt Mary did—just put her arm around me and held it there kind of stiff and I felt that she didn't really mean that my dress was pretty, nor what she had said to Mama, either.

But the hurts of childhood are very transient. There were other children to play with, dolls to pass around and admire. There were none so exquisitely dressed as mine, and I am sure she squirmed with embarrassment to have her skirts lifted and her underthings examined so critically, while my cousins and aunt exclaimed with wonder at the beautiful tucks and laces and the tiny, fairylike stitches.

Sixteen of us sat down around the table that day, ranging in age from a baby in a high-chair to a grand-mother who wore a lace cap and had little gray curls

down each side of her face. The table was covered with
a fine, white cloth. There was a silver caster in the
center, the pretty glass bottles held black pepper and
red pepper, vinegar, salt, and mustard. Clustered around
the caster were golden brown pumpkin pies, mince pies
with spicy juices oozing through the design of leaves
that perforated their top crust, fried dried apple pies,
turn-overs for the children and great cubes of yellow
home-made cheese. All the food was placed on the
table before we sat down, turkey, browned to a turn,
roast pork in a nest of whole preserved apples, mounds
of mashed potatoes, baked hubbard squash. At each
place were individual dishes of boiled, creamed onions,
and creamed dried corn. There were great bowls of
thick, brown gravy, mustard-pickles, sweet-pickles, pear
ginger, apple butter and soda-biscuit.

How strange it would seem, nowadays, to serve a
holiday meal without cocktail, soup or salad, celery,
cranberries, olives or salted nuts. I was a student in
medicine before I ever heard of a salad; yet I can as-
sure you there seemed to be nothing missing from those
dinners.

One was supposed to leave room for all the good
things to come and was torn between a desire for more
turkey and a longing for pies and steaming plum pud-
ding that was brought in when the turkey was finished.
I ate until, as Grandmother used to say, I was "only
mouth-hungry, not stomach-hungry any more." In days
that followed, when Mama and I had the most simple
and meagre fare, I would remember that holiday table
and the pies and puddings that were scarcely touched, and
sometimes I would dream that I was seated again at

the feast, eating until I could hold no more, against the time when the food would be taken away.

But whatever over-indulgence we committed that day was soon overcome by the games we played, Pussy-wants-a-corner, Drop-the-handkerchief; and when, late in the afternoon we were allowed to go into the kitchen and make taffy and put it in pans on the snow to cool and then pull it until it glistened and cracked we were as ready to eat it as if our dinner were already a thing of the past.

Once during the day I saw Uncle Alex and Mama talking together earnestly, and that night Mama told me that we were going to Bridgeport, Connecticut. She hugged me tight and told me what a comfort I was to her, and that it didn't matter much where we were, so long as we were well and together until Papa sent for us. Until Papa sent for us! How often I heard those words on her lips. With what supreme courage she packed our already shabby clothes with Papa's Knight Templar hat and sword and set out to go among strangers in a strange place to earn a living for herself and me!

Before we left for Bridgeport, Papa's Christmas package arrived. There was the nugget, and when Mama lifted the white quartz from the box, wires of pure gold hung from it and traced a pattern of gold in the white rock.

Then there was another box. I don't know what Mama expected would be in that. I remember I expected a miracle, something that would make life easier for Mama, maybe a nugget of pure gold that would mean money enough to go to Papa in California.

Mama's hand trembled, and she wouldn't cut the strings,
a thing that made it very trying for me, having to wait
so long. But finally she undid the last wrapping. There
were two bottles of perfume, White Rose, in a red velvet
box, for Mama; Jockey Club, in a blue velvet box for
me. Mama acted so queer. She cried and laughed at
the same time, and took me in her lap and hugged me
and said, "Wasn't it nice of Papa to send us perfume?"
and then she laughed again. But I looked at the stubbed-
out toes of my shoes and wished I might have had a new
pair instead.

I had learned to write, and at Mama's suggestion, and
with her help, I wrote to Papa and told him about my
doll and how much I liked the perfume. But of all
the things that were troubling Mama, and of how I hated
to go away from the farm and my cousins and school, I
said nothing. The perfume seemed to me to be very
foreign to our needs, but I had learned that Papa in
California must never be worried about anything.

🐝 *BRIDGEPORT AND CORSETS* 🐝
HANS ANDERSEN 🐝 *THE*
IMPORTANCE OF TWO
DOLLARS

LIVING IN BRIDGEPORT WAS A VERY
noisy, exciting experience after the peace and quiet of
the farm.

Mama clung instinctively to respectability. We might

have found more commodious living quarters in a
poorer neighborhood for less, but for the same amount
of money we could live on a better class street in the
garret. Mama chose the garret. I think Mama's idea
was that I would have better surroundings and companionship, but it was soon necessary for me to work
after school and holidays to help with our support and
the payment of the borrowed money to Uncle Alex.
Mama was proud, desperately proud. I must be properly dressed, and never must Smith know that we were
not self-sufficient and happy.

In school I was, apparently, a child of prosperous
parents, well dressed, neatly combed and brushed, and
from a good neighborhood. In reality, we lived up two
flights of stairs, the last flight opening on an unfinished
hall with low rafters. From this opened our only room,
our home, where we ate, lived, slept, and spent the few
hours left between sleeping and working in the factory.

Warner Brothers' Coraline Corsets. I can see them
now. Made of innumerable shaped pieces, back, side
back, under arm, side front, bust front. Each piece was
heavily corded with coraline, a material which did not
rust and would bend without breaking, so the adver-
tisements of the merits of Warner Brothers' Coraline
Corsets ran. Being unbreakable was an item in the
days of hour-glass waists when women tied their corset
strings to the bed post and pulled until flesh and bone
would yield no more.

No one counted calories. Hips and busts were proudly
exhibited by their fortunate owners. Beau catchers, they
were considered. The tremendous pressure consequently
exerted by both ends of the hour glass, caused the

corset to give way at the contracted waist line. Whale-
bones broke, wore through their covering and stuck into
the flesh of their victims. Coraline eventually wore
through and chafed and irritated. Such was the toll
exacted of those who would attain the fashionable figure.

It seemed to me that all the corsets in the world must
be made in Warner Brothers' Corset Factory. The buildings were so enormous, the rooms where Mama and I
worked seemed so immense in comparison with anything I had ever known. Great iron shafts ran along
the ceiling on which ran wheels which were connected
by belts with other wheels that turned the wheels of
the heavy sewing machines used by the stitchers. When
these machines were all running, the noise was deafening. They ran madly, for women were paid by the
number of finished articles turned in. The wheel that
ran the machine was controlled by a ratchet that switched
them on and off. The seams, in assembling the corsets,
were comparatively short, and so there was an incessant
broken rhythm as each worker sewed a seam, threw
the ratchet; while, perhaps, her neighbor threw the
ratchet, sewed a seam.

So Mama, who had loved to do hand sewing and had
been the finest quilter in all the country round, became
just another stitcher, sewing feverishly, backs to side-
backs, side-backs to under-arms, under-arms to front
sides, to busts, endlessly.

After school and Saturdays, I worked as a folder,
doing one of the simplest tasks in the intricate process
of assembling a corset. Two layers of stout material
with coraline corded between went to make up each
part of the garment. These, shaped, were given to the

folders. The folders turned in the rough edge of the outside of the piece, folded and creased the unfinished edge of the back over it, then turned this raw edge in so that it formed a pocket that the raw edge of the corresponding piece would fit into smoothly. The folders used a protector on the thumb much like a guitar thimble. If piecing blocks of a quilt had been tedious, this task, with sewing machines clattering all about and with the desire to finish and get out to play always pulling at one's apron strings, was torture.

How those raw edges would work themselves up out of the fold! With what venom the stitchers would expose an imperfectly folded piece that caused the seams to go awry! Mama would look so sorry when my work came back, but she never scolded me. I wished, sometimes, that she would, and then my conscience would not prick me so much. But I soon forgot about being sorry and did my work half-heartedly again. Mama's work never came back. It was perfect, but there was no joy in it for her.

I was happy. The world is so full of a number of things for a normal, healthy child. I longed for the good food that we had been accustomed to, but I throve and grew round as a tub on the well prepared, though economical, fare that Mama provided.

School became an absorbing and delightful place to be. I wonder how many teachers realize the importance of the contacts they make with those children who spend many hours of each day with them. There is a saying that Mama's eyes are baby's skies. I believe that holds good all through childhood. My Mama's eyes were sad and shadowed all the time now, and, although they rested on me with love and tenderness, yet I began to realize the heart-break that lay behind them.

Children turn to happiness as naturally as flowers to the sun. In school I found happiness, for there was smiling Miss House, Addie House. Among all the names that I have known and forgotten, that name is fresh in my memory. I thought she was beautiful. Her hair was brown, and she wore it in brushed-over-the-finger curls that fell to her waist, the front hair was caught up with a ribbon just as Mama combed mine, and she wore a fringe on her forehead. Her eyes were kind and brown and sunny, but best of all, she read to us every day from Hans Andersen's Fairy Tales.

The first story she selected was the Snow Queen, and I listened to it breathlessly, afraid to stir lest I should lose one word. When she finished the story, she told us that she was giving the book to the pupil in her grade who made the best marks in arithmetic.

I was nine years old, and I don't remember ever having wanted anything desperately up till that time. But right then a resolve formed itself in my brain that made my heart beat with high endeavor. Addition, subtraction, and multiplication tables became the end and aim of all existence. But there was a girl in the class who had a genius for figures. She really liked to add and subtract and do her tables. The class were on her side. I was not a favorite. I was too well washed and brushed and dressed to fit in with their democratic ideas; besides, they considered me teacher's pet.

The work in the factory suffered those days, but I did my sums heroically, always a lap behind the other girl but always hoping that a miracle might happen, and it did! A week before school closed in the spring, she came down with the measles and had to stay out of school. The prize came to me. In the precious volume Miss House wrote:

Reward of merit
Nellie Mattie MacKnight
Never give up the ship

Although Mama was too tired and busy at home on Sunday to go to church, she always helped me with my Sunday school lesson, dressed me prettily, and sent me happily on my way with the other children of the neighborhood.

Uncle Alex had given us the family Bible in which the span of Grandmother's life was now written. I always felt closer to Grandmother when I held it and read it and tried to understand the mysterious promises it held. Mama, too, read the Bible more than she had done before, and each night we would kneel and pray, Mama saying the Lord's Prayer, I, "Now I lay me," always finishing "Lord bless and keep Papa out in California and help him to send for us soon."

I felt disappointed when we prayed so earnestly, night after night, and nothing came of it, for Papa wrote that the Nellie Mine was not panning out as well as he had hoped, but that he thought they were on the edge of a paying vein. I redoubled my efforts and even said a silent prayer in Sunday School while the others were saying, "I believe in God, the Father," for it seemed to me that God must be listening then. But these intervals of devotion were often cut short by some little girl nudging me and winking at me through her fingers, or by the realization creeping in that all the other girls had new hats and dresses and wondering if Mama could manage to buy me some new clothes.

It never occurred to me that my well dressed appearance gave people a false impression of my background until one Sunday the Superintendent told the class that he wanted each one of us to ask our parents for a subscription for a new organ and bring the money with us the following Sunday. I was panic stricken. All the other children seemed to think it was quite a natural thing.

On the way home I tried to find out what they thought their parents would give. No one mentioned an amount less than two dollars. Two dollars! I folded in the factory all week after school for two dollars. I wanted a new hat. If Mama had to give two dollars for the organ, she would not think she could buy me a hat. I decided not to say anything about it.

When Sunday came, I said I didn't feel well and didn't want to go to Sunday School. I had a headache. One of the little girls called for me and Mama told her I had a headache and couldn't go. I recovered promptly and decided that unpleasant things were easy to avoid if one knew how. But that night, when it came time to say my prayers, my deceit crept out from the corners of the room and seemed to make the words strangle in my throat. I wanted to tell Mama, but I knew how sad she would be. After I went to bed, I spent a long time trying to explain to God that I didn't want to be bad but I didn't see how we could help to pay for the organ.

Your sins shall find you out. I had not long to wait

to learn the truth of that proverb. The Sunday School
teacher came to call. She climbed the two flights of stairs
and arrived at our garret room one night when we had
just finished supper and the dishes and scraps from our
meager meal stood on the table in the crowded room.

For the first time I saw Mama's courage break. Her
pride, which she had waved like a banner above all our
disaster, deserted her and to my amazement she tear-
fully told the pitiful story, still staunchly trying to show
that it was not Papa's fault. That he had a mine in
California. That things were not going so well right
now but that he planned he would soon be able to send
for us.

That Sunday School teacher was a righteous woman.
She seemed to feel that all the time I had been in her
class we were sailing under false colors. I remember
how tight her lips were when she said, "I came to see
you because the children said that Nellie was ill. I had
no idea, Mrs. MacKnight, of your circumstances. I supposed from Nellie's clothes and the address she gave
that she came from a prosperous home."

As she talked I thought of the snug, comfortable
homes all along the block where we lived, of the fathers
who went to business each day, of the mothers who
kept the house and did not go out to work. I understood
why I could never invite home the little girls who played
with me in their yards. All at once I was ashamed and
felt it was not quite honest to live in a garret on a nice
street.

The teacher told Mama about the organ. She said she
really felt that every child should have a part in paying
for it. She rolled her r's quite impressively. Of course,

she said we would not feel that we could give much, but since I was a member of the school I should be given the opportunity of doing my part, however small.

Mama asked her what was the least that anybody had given, and she said two dollars. Mama counted out two dollars from her shabby purse. The teacher patted me on the head and said I was a bright girl, and she was glad I was well again and she would expect to see me in Sunday School the next Sunday.

And so the two dollars was gone anyway. That night I cried out the whole story of my deception in Mama's arms. What a relief it was to be rid of it! But Mama seemed white and still the next day, as though she had lost something that she had prized.

✠ AN ACCIDENT ✠ A FIRE ✠ A FOURTH OF JULY EXCURSION

ONE DAY MAMA HURT HER FINGER. I was working with the folders after school when someone screamed, and all the ratchets were thrown off and the machines stopped. I ran with the others and saw Mama, all white and limp, slipped down in her chair. Someone was taking her finger out from under the big heavy foot of the sewing machine and others were saying, "She's fainted, bring some water!"

The woman at the machine beside her said, "She couldn't have been thinking what she was doing, and she got her finger caught and didn't think quick enough to throw the ratchet with her other hand. As soon as I seen what was happening I threw it."

Oh, I was frightened! I thought Mama was dead, and began to cry; but someone shook me and said, "Don't be a baby. She's just fainted. We gotta get her to the dressing room."

It seemed cruel that Mama's pretty hands should be hurt. The first finger on her right hand was all mashed and torn through with the needle. After it was dressed, Mama started to walk home, with me supporting her, but she was too weak and faint. She sat down on the curb and I went and found a man with a carriage to hire to take us home.

Mama had a bone felon from the bruising of her finger by the foot of the machine. She worked during the day at the factory, and at night she poulticed her finger, and I would go to sleep seeing her rocking back and forth holding her swollen hand clasped to her breast with the other one. It was then that I first heard her complain of a pain in the back of her head.

Months had come and gone and we were well into our second year in Bridgeport when this happened. In all that time the only diversion, outside of school and Sunday School that I remember, was going to see the animals from P. T. Barnum's Circus being loaded and unloaded from the trains when they were brought to their winter quarters in Bridgeport or taken away in the spring for their summer tour. We children who lived in Bridgeport felt that we owned the animals of Barnum's circus. When they were taken away we felt that they were only being loaned for a while so that other children might see them. Once when a baby elephant was born, we were as delighted as though a member had been added to our own family. I believe P. T. Barnum appreciated our feelings and the arrival or departure of the animals was always announced days before it happened. If we had not been there, I think he would have been as disappointed as we would have been to miss it.

But mixed with my delight in visiting the trains for these great events was a personal grievance that always gave me pain. I had grown so chubby that I was straight up and down with no suggestion of those waists that Mama and I and the other corset workers were striving so hard to maintain for the ladies of fashion. And so I was called "Baby elephant" or "Fatty" by all of my companions. This was the source of many heartaches to one who adored nothing so much as the slick, sinewy, snarling, striped tigers that scorned all proffers of friendliness.

Did you ever run away to a fire? Lose yourself in some spectacular calamity, so that you were not conscious of where you were nor what you were doing, caught up in the event? If you never have, you have been sadly cheated and I recommend attending a shipwreck or an earthquake at your earliest convenience.

I don't know how it happened. I was all at once in the midst of a surging crowd going to a fire. It was a summer evening and the tidings of the disaster were painted on the sky. I didn't feel alone for there were whole families with their children on their way to the big display. I was pushed and shoved, and sometimes almost smothered; but I fought and kicked when I had to, and sometimes a man would pick me up and carry me a ways, but no one stopped me. No one asked where or why I was going, a question which I could not possibly have answered.

I overheard snatches of the conversation of my comrades in the march. The Singer Sewing Machine Factory was a great manufacturing plant. Its destruction meant that many people who depended on it for their livelihood would be out of work. And I thought of the machines in the corset factory, and how big and heavy they were, and how one of them had mashed Mama's beautiful hand, and her finger would always be blunt and ugly; and I was sorry for the people who would be out of work, but I felt that I wouldn't mind seeing the machines burn up.

I was so eager that a policeman held me up to see, right by the ropes that had been stretched to hold the people back. My experience of fires had been the haze of the Northern Lights that formed a fanfare of color in the skies of northern New York, and the great blaze under the iron kettle in the yard at butchering time. But I had no conception until then of the glorious sight a fire can be. The great dogs of flame leaped and barked. Fire engines arrived with great clanging of gongs and valor of firemen. Horses responded to orders with human intelligence. When it was all over and a cloud of copper-colored smoke hung in the sky, the policeman asked me where I lived and when I told him, he took me home. On the way he told me about the horses and how they were trained so that when the fire bell rang they ran from their stalls and stood in their places under their collars that were lowered on to their necks from above, and were all ready to go before you could say Jack Robinson.

Mama was not there when we got home and my friend left me with the people down stairs, and when Mama came, she hugged me and cried and laughed and the people said I ought to be punished for running away. But Mama was so glad to have me home that she did not even scold; but I knew I must never run away again from her.

The great temperance lecturer, John B. Gough, came to Bridgeport. Mama and I went to the big tent with some of the other people from the factory to hear him speak. I had never fallen under the spell of an orator before, and I was touched deeply. I knew nothing, by personal experience, about the evils of drink, but I was convinced that something should be done about it. I went forward and signed the pledge, and was proud to repeat the slogan "lips that touch liquor shall never touch mine!"

When school closed, the days grew long and hot. The factory, with its clatter of machines and constantly revolving wheels, was like a cauldron filled with steaming, sweating people, and when night came our garret was breathless and offered no relief.

One day a letter came from Papa to me. He enclosed a post office order for five dollars, and said he wanted Mama to take me to New York for the Fourth of July. They were to have a great celebration in Bodie, Uncle Sam, and George and Martha Washington were to ride down the main street and there would be ropes of gold to keep back the crowds. Perhaps, the next Fourth of July, Mama and I would be there and see it all.

The excursion boat to New York was hot. The holiday crowd jostled one another. But everyone was happy, intent on making the day a real holiday. I know why people like to go to Coney Island. I know what it means to get away from a crowded tenement, even to a crowded excursion boat. It is the urge for pleasure, for something different, even if it is only another kind of misery. Mama and I forgot the factory and the garret. We had a blissfully happy time with the crowd on that excursion boat, and sight-seeing in New York.

Years afterwards I read the letter that Mama wrote to Papa about that day. She told him what a pleasant time we had had, and how much we enjoyed having the five dollars to spend just for pleasure. She quoted some startlingly bright things I had said about the trip and the Statue of Liberty. I don't know whether they were fabrications or not. I do remember that I had ice cream; it was the first time I had ever tasted it and it seemed to me the most delicious thing in the world.

🌊 *LAUDANUM* 🌊

AT LAST THE DAYS WERE COOLER. Mama's finger was well, but she still complained of the pain in her head. She thought it might be better when fall came, but it seemed to grow worse. I grew used to her gesture of putting her hand to the back of her neck as though something was pulling her. And when she did that she would look at me so strangely that I was almost afraid. I went with her to the doctor's. He said, "Mrs. MacKnight, you must stop work and worry. Something is worrying you." And Mama took the medicine and went on working and writing to Papa that everything was all right and that I was doing fine in school.

Fall came with the frost painting patterns of gold and crimson under the dust of the leaves on the trees in the city parks. How I longed for the maples in Grandmother's front yard and the tangy taste of the wild grapes that hung on the buggy house.

Mama had never recovered from the pain of the bone felon; she looked sick and white. She complained always of the pain in her head. Her work sometimes came back from the finishers and she was not earning as much for she could not work as rapidly as before. I was in another grade in school and I did not like the new teacher as well as Miss House.

My clothes were getting shabby, and the little girls on the street were not as cordial as they had been. Even the romantic story of Papa, who had a gold mine in California, could not offset the fact that we lived in a garret and Mama worked in a factory.

I went again with Mama to the doctor's. He said, "The medicine won't do you any good, Mrs. MacKnight, unless you can stop working so hard and, more important, you must stop worrying. I don't know what it is, but I am sure you are worrying about something. Can you tell me what it is?" And Mama said, "I am not worrying. There must be something that you can do for me with medicine." Never a word about Papa, Mama was waving her banner again.

Then a letter came from Papa. The Nellie Mine was closed. The vein had run out. Bodie was on the down grade. People were deserting it as though it was a sinking ship. They were walking out of their houses, leaving everything. They had no money to move their belongings. He was going to Sweetwater. He had heard of a good prospect there.

Mama did not cry or even say it was too bad. But she kept rubbing the back of her neck as though something was pulling her. I was grasped by a childish fury. All at once I resented everything, the way we lived, the going without the things that the other little girls had. I began to cry in angry self-pity. I didn't want to live this way. Why couldn't I have a Papa like the other little girls, a Papa who gave them nice homes to live in and pretty clothes to wear? And then, shamelessly, the immediate cause of my rebellion was revealed. I wanted a red plush poke bonnet like the little girls next door. The more I cried, the more my self-control was lost. I didn't care if I hurt Mama. I wanted to hurt somebody. And finally, in an ecstasy of revolt, I lay on my back on the floor and kicked my heels as I had done long ago in Petrolia.

Mama didn't even try to stop me. Just looked at me with dry, sorrowful eyes, and rubbed the back of her neck. But when I pounded the floor with my heels, she came and shook me and said, "Stop, Nellie, the people down stairs will hear and come up to see what is the trouble. Haven't you any pride?" And I remembered the Sunday School teacher, and knew that I must be quiet and not disturb the neighbors.

In my heart I was sorry and tried to help Mama very

nicely, and dried the dishes and put them away just as she liked to have them. But I wouldn't say that I was sorry. I said my prayers quickly and mumbled through the part about Papa in California. Mama must have been very tired. She did not comb her hair and braid it in two braids as she always did before she went to bed. She knelt and. prayed a much longer time than usual, so long that I fell asleep with her still kneeling there.

I woke sleepily. A light was still burning on the table. Mama was asleep beside me and she was making queer noises in her throat. All at once I was wide awake and frightened. I leaned over and shook her, but she was sleeping so soundly she did not wake, but moaned as though she did not want to be disturbed. I climbed over her and got out on the floor and stood by the bed and shook her hard, and still she only moaned as though she was very tired and did not open her eyes.

I thought it must be that she was uncomfortable because her hair was not in braids, and maybe the hair pins were sticking in her head. I raised her head from the pillow and took out the hair pins, one by one, letting her lovely heavy hair down all around her, but still she went on moaning with that queer choking sound, and her head was very heavy, so heavy I could hardly hold it up. I wondered if it was pulling the way it did some times, and I tried to rub the back of her neck as I had seen her do. But nothing seemed to make any difference to her.

I shivered with fright and cold. I had been so naughty to Mama, I began to cry and tell her I was sorry, and that I didn't care whether I had a new plush bonnet or not. But Mama seemed very far away and nothing I said or did made any difference. I took her by the shoulders and shook her and sobbed, "Mama, Mama, wake up! I'm sorry! I'll never be such a bad girl again." Her head only rolled from side to side, and she moaned in and out with every breath.

I was afraid to call anyone. Mama would not want them to come and see her with her hair all down and the bed all mussed. I waited a little, shivering in my bare feet, and then tried to rouse her all over again. And then, all at once I couldn't stand being alone with her any longer. I ran stumbling down the stairs, pounded on the door of the man and his wife who lived there. When they came I told them, between sobs, that Mama was sick, that she seemed to have a pain and I could not wake her.

The people down stairs had never been friendly. Perhaps they resented the way Mama had of minding her own business. It had not been easy to get acquainted with her. But the woman came upstairs with me, and when she saw Mama, she screamed to her husband to come. Almost before I knew what was happening, it seemed that the room was full of people. People in the neighborhood who had never even spoken to Mama.

They looked curiously around the room and patted me and told me not to be frightened. Somebody found a little bottle on the table at the head of the bed, and they said, "Yes, that must be it. She took an overdose. Probably took it on purpose. I've heard that her husband deserted her!" I knew Mama wouldn't want them to say that. I stopped crying and said, "It isn't true. Papa loves Mama. But he went to find a mine in Cali-

fornia and he's going to send for us." No one listened
to me. They were saying, "We'll wait till the doctor
comes, but the coroner's office will have to be notified."

I went around to the table, when no one was looking,
and saw the bottle and I spelled out the word on the
label, LAUDANUM. There was a head without any skin
over it on the label and some bones, like bones a dog
has gnawed, under it. I had never seen the bottle
before and wondered where Mama could have gotten
it, and if she had made a mistake.

The doctor came, and pretty soon another doctor.
They had a kind of pump, like a bicycle pump, and they
put the rubber tube in Mama's throat and pumped.
And then they shook their heads and said, "I'm afraid
it is too late," and I wished I hadn't waited to tell Mama
about the red plush bonnet, and had called the people
downstairs right away.

The woman from downstairs built a fire and made
strong coffee. I was glad to have a fire for I was so
cold. The doctors took Mama out of bed, and made the
people stand back and they held Mama between them
and tried to make her walk back and forth, back and
forth. The room was small and they had to keep turning and turning. Then they would stop and pour coffee
into Mama's mouth, and try to get her to swallow it;
and then walk, back and forth, back and forth. But
nothing made any difference to Mama. She just kept
on moaning, and her head fell back as though something
was pulling it from behind.

As I grew warm, I became sleepy. Surely, now that
the doctors were here and everyone was taking such
good care of Mama, she would soon be well. A neigh-

bor, who had a little girl about my age, said she would
take me home with her. They had put Mama back
into bed, and she lay sleeping very soundly. She was
not moaning any more. So I knew she must be better,
and I was glad she was going to have such a good sleep.

The lady took me home and put me to bed in a pretty
room. She left the light burning in the next room so
I would not be afraid and I snuggled down and did
not know anything until morning. The lady was very
kind and helped me dress. I was sorry I did not have
my prettiest panties and petticoat with the lace on then
as Mama would have wanted me to do if she had known
I was going to stay all night.

The little girl and her Papa and Mama and I had
such a nice breakfast, with oranges, and I tried to be
very polite and eat nicely as Mama would like to have
me. Then the lady took me on her lap and told me
that Mama did not wake up. That she had written a
letter that said I was to go and live with Aunt Mary till
Papa sent for me to go and be with him in California,
and that she told them to send for Uncle Alex and he
was coming to take Mama and me home with him.

Then she took me to see Mama. She was dressed in
her prettiest dress. I remembered there were some worn
places in it that Mama had mended, but they had fixed
it so they did not show. Her hair was all nicely combed
and she looked rested and happy with a sweet smile
on her face. I cried, not because I was sorry for Mama,
but only sorry that she was gone away from me.

Then the lady gave me a letter that Mama had written
to me. It said, "Be a brave girl, Nellie. Do not cry for
Mama." And I choked back my tears, and only tried to

think how glad I should be that Mama's head did not
hurt her any more.

What a blessing that children's sorrows are so transient.
How near they are to healthy animals! In spite of the
fact that Mama lay dead, I really had a very nice time
that day. I was suddenly the center of attention, all the
children wanted to play with me and were envious of
the little girl at whose home I was staying. My favor
was as eagerly sought as though I was some fairy queen.
Small wonder that my childish grief was submerged by
this excitement. That night we had beefsteak for dinner;
I remember how good it tasted, and I must have eaten
like a young savage.

When the little girl's Papa read in the paper that
night that Mrs. MacKnight, a stitcher in Warner
Brothers' Corset Factory had committed suicide, it
seemed strange that Mama, who had been so lonely and
unknown, should suddenly have become a person whom
the whole city was glad to read about. All her letters,
the one to Papa, the one about sending for Uncle Alex,
and that I was to go to live with Aunt Mary, were in
the paper. I felt a sense of importance in being connected with so remarkable a tragedy.

Uncle Alex came and Mama was put in a coffin and
carried down the two flights of stairs to the hearse with
black plumes waving and beautiful black horses to draw
it. Uncle Alex and the neighbors, who had been so
good to me, rode in a carriage behind it to the station.
All the children gathered round and waved good-bye as
we drove away. I was dressed in my new dress that
Mama had made for me. It was a black and white
shepherd's plaid, and I had new high buttoned shoes,

black with white tops. I remember looking in the mirror which faced the seat where I sat and feeling all confused and wondering if it was really I.

And then we were on the train and Mama was in the baggage car. We would have to change cars at Ogdensburg at night. Uncle Alex was very kind and tender with me and I was interested in the people in the train. As we traveled through the country, we flashed into woods so gay and riotous with color that one forgot to be sad.

In the pastures there were sheep puffed out with wool until it seemed as though their thin legs must bend with the weight. I thought of Grandmother and wondered if, now that I was going back home, I might learn to spin as well as she had done and if maybe some day I would have a little girl to take off the skeins on the clock reel. But I felt sorry that I would never be able to sew as nicely as Mama had, and wondered who would make pretty clothes for me now that she was gone.

At noon Uncle Alex and I ate the lunch that the nice lady with the little girl had put up for us. It tasted so good and I wished I might be like that other little girl with my Mama still here and a Papa to make a nice home for us.

When we got to Ogdensburg, it was dark. We had to get out of the warm train into the cold, blustery night with snow blowing in our faces. We went into the station and had some warm food. Then Uncle Alex said he would have to go and see about getting Mama put on the train that went to Madrid. There was a big stove in the waiting room, but the fire was almost out. The wind blew in around the windows; I felt cold and lonely and miserable. All the excitement had ebbed. I was all alone in the deserted waiting room with Mama in her coffin and Papa away out in California. I did not even know where he was. He seemed even farther away since I could no longer place him in Bodie.

I sat with my hands in my pockets and my elbows resting on the hard iron arms that separated the bench into seats. I would have liked to lie down but the railroads had no such comforts for people who had to wait in a station. It seemed as though no one cared any more, that I might just go on sitting there wretched and cold and forgotten. The tears rolled down my cheeks, quietly. Then all at once there was a presence in the room. I raised my eyes. Mama, in her pretty dress, was over near the wall with her arms stretched out to me. Her eyes were sorrowful. Her lips moved, and I heard her say, oh, so softly, "Be brave, Nellie, do not cry. It will make Mama very sad if you do. Be a good girl." That was all, but it was healing to my loneliness. Mama's presence was real to me. I did not question it. My cheeks were dry. Mama had wiped away the tears. From that night on I was conscious of her nearness.

We took Mama home to the farm and put her in the parlor where Grandmother had lain. But the parlor was so changed I could hardly believe my eyes. The hair wreath and the wax wreath were gone. There was an enlarged picture of Uncle Alex and his girl taken at Niagara Falls on their honeymoon. The hair-cloth sofa and chairs were gone and there were new cane seated chairs. There was a table with feet like a tiger and each foot had a round glass ball in it. There

were long pink curtains at the windows and a soft pink
carpet on the floor. I had thought that Mama would
be glad to come back to the nice parlor after living in
the garret. But it was all so strange and different that I
felt sure she would not feel at home.

The relatives were there to meet us. I slipped out to
the other room to see if I could find a calla lily bud for
Mama. But the calla lily and the oleander were frozen.
Their leaves hung limp and swollen looking. When I
went back to the parlor, Uncle Alex's girl was there.
She had a lovely fat baby in her arms. Somehow she
wasn't so pretty any more. She didn't look quite tidy.
She kissed me and let me kiss the baby, and she said
that I might hold the baby and that she was married to
Uncle Alex now and I must call her Aunt Sade.

Then she got up and went around talking to everybody, and left the baby with me. Pretty soon I felt
something warm in my lap, and putting my hand down
to see what it was, I found that the baby had wet a little
puddle. I was so embarrassed I did not know what to
do. I did not have any other dress to put on. Aunt
Sade was clear across the room talking to someone.
She seemed to have forgotten all about the baby. One
of the women sitting by me saw what had happened
and said she would take the baby that I might go and
dry my dress. When I came back into the room, Aunt
Sade met me. She looked angry and she whispered to
me as though she would like to slap me. "What did you
give the baby to someone else for? Why didn't you
bring him to me? Do you suppose I want him handed
around with his diapers all wet?"

I wondered why she didn't feel sorry for me with my

dress all wet and Mama dead in her coffin. Then Aunt
Mary and Uncle John came. Aunt Mary hugged me and
cried over me. I forgot all about the baby and was
glad Mama had said that I was to live with Aunt Mary
until Papa sent for me.

The casket was opened and the preacher did not
preach a sermon, but only said a prayer for those who
take themselves out of this world by violence before the
Lord sees fit to take them at their allotted time. Then
I knew that he thought Mama had been wicked in the
face of God to take LAUDANUM and never wake up. And
I wondered whether he would have thought that the
Lord would forgive her, if he had known about the bone
felon and how her head had pulled and hurt. But I
did not get a chance to say anything to him about it.

Mama was buried in the burying ground on the hill.
Her grave was by those of my brother and sister who
had died and been buried there before Papa and Mama
moved to Petrolia. The red and gold maple leaves fluttered softly down, making a patch-work quilt over her
grave. What the preacher had said did not trouble me.
I felt sure God understood how tired Mama had been
and that when she was rested He would let her walk
in the streets of gold. I felt glad that even though Papa
had not been able to find gold in California, Mama could
have it all around her now.

AUNT SADE
& "AUNT" MARY

✥ AUNT SADE ✥

UNCLE GORDON SEEMED GLAD TO SEE ME and he motioned with his hands to show how tall I had grown since I went away. His beard didn't look neat and nice as it used to when Grandmother trimmed it for him. His hair was shaggy and beginning to turn gray. I knew he felt very sad about Mama, for when the preacher prayed I saw the tears run down his cheeks into his beard. He wiped them away with a red handkerchief like the ones the men carried in their working clothes. Grandmother had always kept a nice white one in his best suit. The suit looked mussed as though he had not thought to hang it up properly and brush it. The bosom of his boiled shirt was dull, not white and shining the way Grandmother used to do it up.

One of the relatives stayed with the baby so that Aunt Sade could go to the funeral. When we came back, the chairs were all fixed in the parlor, and it was hard to believe that Mama had been in there at all. The woman had a fire in the other room, and hot tea and

little cakes all fixed on a table for us. I wondered why
we didn't eat in the kitchen, but thought this new way
seemed quite grand.

Aunt Mary and Uncle John came home with us. Aunt
Mary said how glad she would be to have me stay with
her until Papa sent for me. But Uncle Alex said that
wouldn't do at all. That he was willing to give me a
home until Papa came or sent for me. That he felt,
under the circumstances, it was his place to provide for
his brother's child. Aunt Sade said she needed someone
to help with the baby. I was old enough to learn to
make myself useful, and since Uncle Alex had been to
the expense of going to Bridgeport for us she couldn't
afford to hire anybody. Aunt Mary hugged me with
tears in her eyes and said that she was sorry, but I must
come to see her often.

After Aunt Mary and Uncle John were gone and
Uncle Gordon and Uncle Alex and Aunt Sade and I
were left all alone with the baby, Aunt Sade said that
she must nurse him and put him to bed. That Uncle
Gordon had better build a fire in the kitchen and I could
do up the dirty dishes before supper. Uncle Alex started
to say something, but Aunt Sade looked at him and he
changed his mind and kept still.

Aunt Sade went into the bedroom that had been
Mama's and mine. Uncle Alex talked to me and said
he was sorry about Mama. He hoped I would be happy
there with them, and I said I would because I knew I
would love the baby, and it would be nice to have him
to play with.

Then I went out into the kitchen. I couldn't believe
it was the same place as the one that I had held in my

memory as the heart of peace and contentment. The shiny yellow ochre floor was stained and tracked and spotted with grease. The stove was no longer black, but red and rusty looking, and the nickel trimmings were gray and sticky. There were crumbs on the table-cloth and the lamp chimney was streaked with soot. The spinning wheel and reel were gone and Grandmother's bed had some soiled quilts and playthings on it, and there were some diapers spread out to dry.

I was ten years old when Mama died, and I had never seen such a sink full of dirty dishes in my life, much less endeavored to get them bright and shining again. The water in the reservoir on the back of the stove was only lukewarm, but there was a tea-kettle of boiling water on top of the stove. I was anxious to please Aunt Sade by getting things in order before she came into the kitchen. So I cleared, as best I could, a space in the sink large enough to hold the dish pan and began. I dipped the luke-warm water from the reservoir into the pan, then added some hot water from the tea-kettle. The iron kettle was heavy and when I tried to tip it up, the spout swung around in my hand and the steam burned it. It hurt cruelly and tears came into my eyes, but I remembered to be brave. The dishwater was soon cold and grease had collected on the top. There was none of Grandmother's nice soft soap. The soap in a big, yellow bar did not seem to cut the grease.

Aunt Sade came out and made some sour cream and soda biscuits for supper. The moulding board in the buttery had to be scraped and cleaned before she could roll them out. I set the table and Uncle Alex took a paper and cleaned the lamp chimney. We had fried

eggs and tea and dried apple sauce. The biscuits were
yellow and smelled of soda.

But all of these things would not have mattered so
much if only Aunt Sade could have loved and directed
me a little bit. I was as helpless in many ways as a baby.
I had never combed my own hair, a real undertaking
the way Mama had always done it. I had never made
a bed nor swept a floor or kept my clothes in order. I
had been petted and spoiled and tenderly loved by Mama
and Grandmother. Now I was suddenly expected to
do all these things and the unaccustomed tasks that Aunt
Sade set for me, with no reward for doing them well,
and unkind, even insulting, words if I did not perform
them properly. I have never known anyone who could
put so much mockery and insult into words that sounded
perfectly decent when used as they were meant to be.

As I look back on those days and the miserable life I
led, I realize that Aunt Sade was a bitter, disappointed
woman. She had, undoubtedly, thought that the resources of the farm were inexhaustible. Their marriage
began with an expensive honeymoon to Niagara, returning by way of New York where the purchases that did
over the parlor were made, and Aunt Sade outfitted with
clothes such as the people of Madrid and the country
round had never seen before.

At first she had hired girls to do the work and every
few weeks she and Uncle Alex went to Ogdensburg to
skate or dance or ride on the excursion boats. The
rhythm of labor, so necessary to the successful working
of the farm, was neglected. Uncle Gordon was a fine

worker with someone to supervise and keep him company, but his interest soon flagged when he was left by
himself. When the baby came, Aunt Sade had been
obliged to stay at home more and, although she loved
the child with a strange fierce passion, she resented the
restraint his coming had placed upon her. I didn't know
all these things in a day or a week or a month. Even
after two years I was still puzzled. Only living and
experience have helped me to understand Aunt Sade.

Uncle Alex took me upstairs to my bedroom. It was
the one over the "other room" and the stove pipe that
ran through it was supposed to keep it warm. But the
fire had died down and it was so cold up there I could
see my breath as I undressed. My shepherd's plaid was
spotted with dish water, but I was too tired to care,
too tired even to say my prayers. One of Grandmother's
warm feather beds enveloped me. I felt that I should
get up and kneel by the bed, but it was too cold. I said
"Now I lay me" in bed, and added "God bless Aunt
Sade and help her to love me." Maybe if I prayed
properly she would see how hard I was trying and forgive me for not knowing better how to do things.

Letters finally came from Papa. He was heart-broken
to hear of Mama's death. He had loved her so! He
could not understand what made her want to die. Of
course, she must have been out of her head. It seemed
to me she was very much in her head when it pulled
and hurt her so all the time.

When the trunk came from Bridgeport, I had my

Bible and Hans Andersen's Fairy Tales. Uncle Alex
wrote in the record of Mama's death for me.

*Olive Peck, born, Madrid, St. Lawrence Co., New
York, 1843.*
Married Smith Peck MacKnight, Madrid, 1863.
Died, Bridgeport, Conn., 1882.

Grandmother had always been Grandmother to me.
I never remember hearing her called Eliza. But the
record of her life was of Eliza Smith MacKnight. Those
two names, Olive and Eliza, became enshrined in my
heart as the symbols of all that was kind and loving and
beautiful in life. Never, while she lived, had I tried
so hard to do as I knew Mama wanted me to do, as I
tried now that she was gone.

Life on the farm was no longer something to be
enjoyed, but a host of disagreeable things to be endured.
When I got up that first morning, the room was so cold
that I dressed as quickly as possible, smoothing back
my hair with my hands expecting that Aunt Sade would
comb it out and curl it for me. When she saw me,
without even saying "Good morning," her first words
were "What a snarl your hair is in! Don't you ever
comb it?"

I had come downstairs rested and looking forward to
Aunt Sade and the baby. But her greeting humiliated
me, something that she always contrived to do. I went
back to my room, and there, with my teeth chattering,
combed my hair as best I could, and braided it in two

braids. Then I went downstairs and started my first day in the house that was now Aunt Sade's.

For a long time I felt something akin to love for Aunt Sade. If there had been anything to nourish the feeling, my first liking would have grown into real affection. I was so lonely. I craved love and tenderness. I admired her face and her figure and her pretty clothes, and, especially, her air of worldliness. Her cleverness with words fascinated me. I do not know whether she was really ill or not, but much of the time she claimed to be feeling wretched, and more and more of the household tasks devolved on me. Try as I would, I could never gain a word of approval. When she did not scold I felt that I was gaining.

The baby was fretful and peevish, but I loved him. Aunt Sade soon took advantage of that fact and left to me more and more the task of caring for him, which was evidently irksome to her. She would put him on the quilt on the bed that had been Grandmother's, and I would wring my greasy hands out of the dishwater and dangle his playthings before him or change his wet diapers. If he fussed too much, Aunt Sade would come out of the other room to ask querulously, "Why can't you keep him quiet?" At other times she would sweep into the kitchen in a charming negligee and come over to the sink and shrug her shoulders and say, "Ugh, I don't see how you can endure washing dishes in such greasy water!"

I don't remember ever resenting it, only feeling sorry that I could not do things to please her, for she was such a discouraged housekeeper. I knew that the bread was sour; the potatoes often boiled dry before they were done; that the fried salt pork was too salty; and the milk gravy full of lumps. Uncle Alex looked tired and worried all the time.

Uncle Gordon had changed, too. His quick tempers that Grandmother had always known how to control developed into sulkiness, only relieved at times by violent outbursts against some inanimate thing—a wheel that stuck when he was trying to take it off to grease, or an axe handle that refused to fit into the axe. He was never cruel to animals. He loved the baby devotedly and would sit and play with him and rock him by the hour when the weather was stormy and he was kept indoors.

In the evenings Aunt Sade and Uncle Alex would sit in the other room and read; and Uncle Gordon and I were left alone in the kitchen. I found some yarn in the garret and tried to knit a pair of mittens to send to Papa, but when I dropped a stitch I could not pick it up before it raveled, as Grandmother had always done this for me; and I did not remember how to shape the thumb.

Sometimes Uncle Gordon would peel an apple for us, but he did not go to the garret for popcorn or butternuts any more. Before Christmas Aunt Sade found out that I still believed in Santa Claus; she laughed at my credulity and said I was old enough to forget such fool-ishness. But no child is to be really pitied who has a copy of Hans Andersen's Fairy Tales and can read them. The print was poor, the light miserable, but I lost myself as completely between the covers as though

I was in an enchanted forest. Although Jack Frost still painted the windows, and the snow glistened on the orchard slopes, I had no time or heart to enjoy them. But a story was something different. It took one far from present cares and troubles.

When spring came, Uncle Gordon quarreled with Uncle Alex and hired out to a man who lived a long way down the Grass River. Aunt Sade had been planning to go to Ogdensburg and leave the baby with us. She was furious when she found that they could not go. She insisted that Uncle Alex hire someone to come and stay while they were gone. He said he could not afford it because there was too much for him to attend to, but they could have a sugaring-off party and invite a lot of young people. She laughed, unpleasantly, and asked him if he was still enough of a country jake to think a sugaring-off party was any fun.

And so there was no sugaring-off party. Uncle Alex went to tap the trees one day, and the next night he went alone and stayed all night to boil the syrup. I didn't mind, for even if there had been a party, I would have had to stay home to mind the baby. I was sorry for Uncle Alex, but it was too bad for Aunt Sade, too, for she was so disappointed. I gave her the bottle of White Rose perfume that Mama had kept so carefully and never used. I had meant to give it to Aunt Mary. I wished I had when I heard Aunt Sade say to Uncle Alex that night, "Wasn't that the last thing for Smith to send Olive when she didn't even know where her bread and butter were coming from? Catch me drinking laudanum for a man like that."

My yearning for Aunt Sade's love and affection began to diminish when I heard her make that speech. I had given Mama's most cherished possession into her keeping and she had not cared enough to prize it for the memory.

✻ *AUNT SADE GIVES A PARTY* ✻
THE UGLY DUCKLING

I WROTE PAPA AND TOLD HIM I WAS NOT very happy on the farm now that Grandmother and Mama were gone. I did not say anything about the perfume, but I asked him if I might go and live with Aunt Mary. I reminded him that that was what Mama wanted me to do. Papa, evidently, had the same idea that he had when he wrote to Mama that we had as much right on the farm as any of the others. He did not seem to like it that I even thought of going any place else, but he sent me twenty-five dollars which he said was to buy me some new clothes; and he wanted me to go to school in the fall.

Aunt Sade opened the letter and read it. She was very angry. She told me how ungrateful I was when Uncle Alex had been to all the expense of going to Bridgeport and bringing me home. Now when I was getting so I could really be of some help to her, I wanted to go off with Aunt Mary, who was not even a relative.

She took the twenty-five dollars and said she would see about my clothes. Twenty-five dollars seemed such a lot of money to me. I did so wish that I might choose some of the new clothes, but the joy that lay in the thought that Papa had sent me such a fabulous sum compensated for any disappointment.

I shall never forget how I felt when Aunt Sade came home from Madrid with the material for two dresses for me. One, which, she said, was for my best dress, would have been too old for Grandmother. It was a gray and black plaid wool stuff. It would wear like iron, wouldn't show the dirt, and oh, how I hated it! The other was a blue and white checked gingham for second best.

I don't know what refinement of cruelty prompted Aunt Sade to buy such unbecoming things for me. Whether she didn't take the time to think or bother and took the first things she saw, or whether she deliberately wished to add to my feeling of inferiority and humiliation. She seemed to resent the few pretty clothes I had left, and tried to show me how ridiculous it had been for Mama to dress anyone, so fat and unattractive as I, in tucked and ruffled clothes.

She brought a plain pattern home with her, cut out the dresses, and sewed up the long seams on the machine. Then I was left to finish them, and try to make them look as right as they had looked when Mama was alive. There were ruffles with the gathers bunched in one place and almost plain in others. There were button holes like pig's eyes. The blue and white gingham was trimmed with rickrack braid.

The next week Aunt Sade went to Madrid; she brought back a lovely wool challis, sprigged with tiny buds, for herself. It had the prettiest puffed sleeves and a striped sash to match the colors in the flowers. The dress had been made by the best dressmaker in Ogdensburg. There was a tiny hat to go with it, with flowers under the brim.

Some way Aunt Sade managed to make me feel my obligation to her so much that I did not have a sense of the injustice of what she did. I enjoyed her pretty clothes, and thought she looked so nice in them. I knew I was just an Ugly Duckling that would never turn into a swan, but I liked to read about the one that did. I don't know whether Uncle Alex even knew about the money. He was so harassed, trying to do the work of two men on the farm and give Aunt Sade the pleasures she demanded, that he had little time or thought for his brother's child.

I felt that the more help and the less trouble I could be, the better for everyone concerned. Mama's example had taught me that Papa must never be troubled about anything. I wrote him and said that I was getting along very nicely. Uncle Alex was very kind and the baby was sweet. I was glad to have the twenty-five dollars, and Aunt Sade had bought me two nice new dresses. But I hoped he would find a good mine and be able to send for me soon.

He wrote that Sweetwater wasn't much of a camp yet. There weren't any schools, and it would be best for me to stay on the farm where I could have advantages of schooling. He hoped I would study hard.

The apple blossoms ran down the orchard slope. A maple branch just outside my bedroom window budded and tasseled and uncurled its lacy leaves. It was warm enough now so that I could read by candlelight in my room and all the kind fairies attended me there.

The trees in the yard were not tapped that year, and I wondered if they minded not being allowed to yield up their sweetness. Grandmother's flower beds had not been banked with straw and manure as she had always had them done. Some of the bulbs, narcissus and daffodils, struggled valiantly to blossom; but the peonies did not put up any shoots. They were frozen to death. The round beds on each side of the path held nothing but weeds.

Aunt Sade went visiting a lot when spring came. I would hurry through my chores, then take the baby outside and spread a quilt under the tree. I would pretend I was a fairy or a wood sprite and dance for him. He would crow and laugh and stretch his little hands to me. Then I was a great actress, and he an enthusiastic audience, applauding. When he slept, I looked at the pictures in *Godey's Lady's Book* that Aunt Sade kept out on the table in the "other room."

The baby was getting to be a big boy and hard for me to handle, but I lugged him up to the garret one afternoon. It had not been cleaned or dusted since Grandmother and I did it together. It was draped with cobwebs and moths flew out of the corners. Aunt Sade's shiny new trunks were there. The spinning wheel was pushed back under the eaves. I tried to turn the wheel, but it was so close that it rubbed on the rafters and wouldn't spin smoothly.

I opened my trunk from Bridgeport with Papa's Knight Templar hat in it. I was afraid the moths would get into it. I got the lid up, and took the hat down and put it out in the sun. Then I brought the baby down and put the hat on his head. I played that he was a plumed knight and I was his fair lady. But the hat slid down over his ears and frightened him. He cried, so that illusion was short lived. I wrapped the hat with spices and put it away in a drawer of the big, high bureau in my bedroom.

Aunt Sade was going to have a party for me. She said we would invite my cousins and their mothers. How happy I was at the prospect. I felt she must be beginning to love me or she would not go to so much trouble on my account. She baked two sour cream cakes and frosted them. We were to have strawberries and cream, too. I dressed the baby in his prettiest short dress, and brushed his hair over my finger in a curl on top of his head. I put on my new checked gingham with plenty of starched petticoats underneath. Aunt Sade wore her pretty new dress.

The ladies were all in prints and challis, and the cousins were starched and prim and well behaved. Everyone seemed to feel rather strange sitting on the cane seated chairs in the parlor, but after awhile the mothers took their sewing out of their bags, shook out their ruffled sewing aprons, tied them on; and then it got to be quite a jolly party.

The baby was cutting teeth and was fretful. Aunt Sade said I had better take him out in the yard with the children. He was so big and heavy that I couldn't play much with the children. I had to hold him and keep him quiet. Then I had an idea. I would put

him down and dance for him like a fairy or a wood
sprite; he would forget to cry, and the children could
be my audience.

The baby stopped fretting and began to laugh and
crow and clap his hands. The cousins were quiet and
seemed to be enjoying it when Aunt Sade came out on
the porch and called to the others, "Do come here.
Did you ever see anything so funny as that great, fat,
awkward young one trying to dance?" The spell was
broken! The children began to laugh and poke their
fingers at me. I knew that in my heart I might be a
fairy or a wood sprite, but on the outside I was just a
fat, clumsy, poor relation.

The baby began to fret. I suppose he wanted the
performance to go on. He screamed when I picked him
up, and tried to wriggle out of my arms. Aunt Sade
came flying down the steps and over to me, her face
flushed, her eyes hateful. She grabbed the child out
of my arms, "She pinched him, I know she must have
pinched him. He never cries like that." She turned
on the others with an air of, "That's what I get for
taking in and mothering a thankless child!"

"It isn't true. I love the baby!" Tears of anger and
mortification filled my eyes. But Aunt Sade was a good
actress. She didn't scold; she just acted forbearing. I
knew that all the relatives felt that she was a dutiful
wife to Alex to put up with having his brother's child
around all the time.

Then we all went into the house and I helped pass
things around. My eyes were so blinded with tears
that I was too proud to shed, that I stubbed my toe and

spilled a pitcher of cream on the new pink carpet. Aunt Sade just lifted her eyebrows and shut her lips tight, as much as to say, "See what I have to endure with her!" All the ladies were terribly upset about it, but Aunt Sade said it didn't matter. She was going to take up the carpet and put it in the other room. She had seen another she liked better for the parlor.

They were quite impressed with her kindness to me; the fact that a carpet seemed to make so little difference; and that Aunt Sade could buy a new carpet whenever she wanted one.

After they were gone, I tried to tell Aunt Sade how sorry I was about all the things that had happened; that I had spoiled the nice party she had planned for me, but she only looked at me coldly and told me I could go to my room and not come down any more that day. She couldn't have selected a more exquisite punishment.

I tried to read Hans Andersen but my throat would choke and my eyes fill with tears so that I could not see the words. Uncle Alex came. I could imagine all the things she was telling him about me and how poisoned his heart would be. Even the baby, I felt, would grow up to hate me if Aunt Sade took his part against me in everything.

I rose early the next morning, built the kitchen fire, filled the reservoir and tea-kettle, and had all the dishes, that Aunt Sade had left from the party and supper, washed and put away before Uncle Alex came out to build the fire. I hated to look at him, but he said,

"Good morning, Nellie," just as if nothing had happened. All at once I realized that the sun was shining and the birds were singing, and it was such a pretty day.

☙ ST. LAWRENCE COUNTY FAIR ☙ PORTIA BRINGS DOWN THE HOUSE

THERE WAS NO CHURNING DONE AT home. Uncle Alex sent the milk to the creamery. I learned to cook some of the everyday things fairly well, remembering how I had seen it done in days gone by.

As spring work advanced, there was a hired man; and, for haying and harvesting, a hired girl came. She taught me how to make sour cream cake and soda biscuits. She cleaned up the kitchen so that it seemed more like home. I had all the care of the baby now. The weather was hot and the baby was teething and fretful. Finally, he had summer complaint and was very sick. Although Aunt Sade did not directly accuse me, she told the doctor that she was afraid that he might have gotten some of the grapes that grew on the buggy house. She had warned me to be careful; but anyone as busy as she was could not be on the watch every moment. And so even the grapes were spoiled for me until the baby got well. By that time the frost had nipped them.

One Sunday Uncle Gordon came to see me and made me understand that he wanted me to go with him to the St. Lawrence County Fair that was to open that week at Canton, the county seat. Aunt Sade said she couldn't spare me, but Uncle Alex seemed not to hear her and said I could go.

How I washed and starched and ironed to get ready. Uncle Gordon came for me in a light buggy hitched to a nice buggy team. He had a new suit of clothes.

Aunt Sade did not come out of her room that morning. The hired girl put up a nice lunch for me. I didn't think we should take it without asking Aunt Sade, but the hired girl said, "Things people don't know about don't bother 'em any," and wouldn't let me tell her.

Although Uncle Gordon couldn't talk, he was very good company. His eyes would light up when he saw a pretty garden, or a squirrel frisking his tail up a tree, and he would nudge and point and get all excited. It seemed as if he could see more things and more quickly than anybody. We drove twelve miles over country roads with the tidy rail fences on each side. Milkweed and mullen grew in the fence corners, and all the way the road smelled of sweet clover. There were beechnuts and butternuts in the woods, but they were not ripe enough to eat. They had to wait for the frost to crack their shells and mellow them, and make them sweet and nutty tasting. The woods were like a patchwork quilt made all of red and yellow and orange and golden-brown.

Uncle Gordon had been given the day off and a team to drive to the Fair, for the man who hired him had a fine bull that he was exhibiting. He wanted Uncle Gordon to take him out and walk him around the track for the judging. Uncle Gordon had had the care of the animal. He had combed and brushed him and polished his hoofs and horns, and braided his tail with ribbons.

We arrived at the fair grounds about noon. First, Uncle Gordon took me to the stock exhibit and showed me the bull. He was a handsome creature. His back was broad and flat; a man could lie down comfortably on it. That is, he could if the animal had been willing, but at that moment he was so enraged at the crowds and the unusual confinement that he was pawing the bedding straw in his pen and bellowing furiously.

As soon as he saw Uncle Gordon, he came over and rubbed his big, pink nose on him as much as to say, "Take me home, away from all these staring people. Take me home to the pasture." Uncle Gordon petted him awhile, and quieted him. Then we went around and saw the other animals. I felt so sorry for them. They had been there three days, and they all looked sick and worried. A lot of feed lay uneaten in their pens and boxes. The cows forgot to chew their cuds, but kept going around their pens trying to find some way out; and worrying themselves until their coats were all lathered with sweat. The chickens and geese kept poking their heads out and in between the sticks on the front of their cages. The race horses looked excited and sleek, but they had their own trainers with them, the men who knew how to care for them. They were exercising them in their gay, bright colored blankets. The place and the trainers smelled of the stables, and gave an exciting, horsey flavor to everything.

We found a place to eat our lunch; Uncle Gordon bought me some lemonade. Everything tasted wonderfully good. Then we went to a tent where a man out in front kept shouting, "Right here, ladies and gentlemen. Here's where you see the living skeleton and the fat woman, the best-natured girl in forty states. If you want to have good-natured wives, gentlemen, feed 'em well, and keep 'em fat like Rosy, the fat lady."

I suppose we were a strange couple. The tall, bearded silent man and the fat little girl who clung to his hand. The barker singled us out. "There's a fat little girl. She wants to see Rosy, the fat lady, I'm sure." Everyone looked at me and laughed, and I felt ashamed and proud all in one. I wanted to get away and I motioned Uncle Gordon to buy tickets, and we went into the show. The fat lady had a pretty pink and white face like a doll's, and her hands and feet were smaller than mine. She had a sweet lawn dress on, all ruffles and bows. I wondered how the lady ever got so fat, and had such tiny hands and feet. I thought she must have eaten holiday dinners all her life. The tent was hot and she kept fanning herself and drinking lemonade. The perspiration was wet in the fat creases in her neck, and I felt sorry for her just as I did for the animals out in their pens.

There was a man who ate fire and swallowed swords. Uncle Gordon was so fascinated watching him that he almost forgot about having to take the bull out on the track. But he remembered just in time, and took me to the tent where they had the exhibit of fancy work and cooking and left me there. He gave me some money and motioned for me to come to the stock pens when I was ready. I looked at the quilts and fancy work. None of the quilting was as fine as that Mama had done with her beautiful hands. The yarn, in the knitted scarfs and mittens, was not as smooth as Grandmother had spun. The salt-rising bread smelled good, and the jellies and jams were rich and luscious looking.

There were women and children here. The women looked tired, and the children were cross and sticky. I saw an aunt of mine and took her little girl, who was just walking, outside and amused her while her mother nursed the baby. When I came back, my aunt was restless.

"I don't see why the men want to stay so long," she said, "we've got the chores to do and the children to get to bed. It's time we were starting."

I thought I would buy some peanuts with the money I had, but I passed a place where a man was yelling, "Right this way for the jungle. Lions, tigers, and monkeys, straight from their native haunts. Every lady who goes into this show will be given a ring on her way out!" I thought of the animals coming home to winter quarters in Bridgeport. I wouldn't be there to see them. Besides there was the added attraction of a ring on the way out.

Inside the crowded tent were three or four cages with a lion, a tiger, three monkeys, and a leopard. They were listless and sick and discouraged looking, and even the trainer, with his whip, had difficulty in getting them to get up and pace back and forth for the benefit of those who had paid an entrance fee. I felt sorry for the animals; I did not want to watch them. I went back outside and walked up to the high platform where the man stood, and told him I wanted my ring. He said, "Why yes, sure, always glad to please the

ladies." He took up a big bell on a stand in front of
him and reached down and rang it in my face. Everybody laughed as though it was a great joke. Then I
saw the whole thing as a cheat, and my face burned
with shame and indignation.

I saw the husband of my aunt—the one who wanted
to go home—sitting in a drinking place beside a girl
with blonde hair. She was all dressed up in a red coat
and shining black boots and looked as though she belonged to the side shows.

I bought a jack-in-the-box for the baby. Then I was
tired. I went back to the pen where Uncle Gordon
was just leading in the bull. The bull had a blue ribbon
in the halter around his head. I saw he had a ring in
his nose and Uncle Gordon explained by motions that
they had to put it in because he was so mad and excited
with the crowd.

We had a nice ride home with a lovely harvest moon
coming up through the trees and shining on the yellow
pumpkins and shocks of grain in the fields. I thought
how glad the animals in the pastures should be that
they were just ordinary and not fine enough to be
exhibited in the shows, and how glad the others would
be to get back again.

The hired girl had a good supper ready for us when
we got home, and Uncle Alex asked Uncle Gordon to
stay. Aunt Sade did not come to supper and we had a
pleasant time. I told Uncle Alex about the prize bull
and the blue ribbon. He said he would have liked to
have exhibited at the Fair, but he didn't have any time
to get the animals in shape. I felt sorry that he was

disappointed and still I was glad that none of our animals had to leave their pasture. My dreams that night were a tangled parade of tight rope walkers and hurdy-gurdies, mad bulls, and sick, tired-looking animals, cross children and tired mothers, and men drinking lemonade with blonde show-women. Through them all a bell rang tauntingly and caused me to clap my hands over my ears, to shut it out.

The next day it seemed as though the Fair had all been just a jumbled dream. Aunt Sade didn't ask me about it. When I showed the baby the jack-in-the-box and it jumped at him, he was frightened. Aunt Sade said I ought to know better than to get such a toy for him. The hired girl asked me all about the Fair, and I had to tell her everything. The fat girl, the sword swallower, the race horses. She sighed and said she thought we must have had a lovely time, and that she hoped she would never be caught again working for a woman who wouldn't even let her off to go to the County Fair.

Aunt Sade didn't feel well. The doctor came to see her and he said she needed a change, so she went to Ogdensburg without Uncle Alex. When she came home, she had some lovely new clothes and a turban with plumes on it like the plumes on Papa's Knight Templar hat. The hired girl left. She said Aunt Sade was the meanest woman she had ever worked for. We did not get another girl. Uncle Alex said, now that harvest was over, he could not afford to keep one during the winter. I cried about that because I thought it meant that I could not go to school. But when school opened, Uncle Alex said I was to go. Aunt Sade stormed and said she couldn't spare me, but Uncle Alex said they would have to manage some way. And he spoke in the tone of voice that made Aunt Sade stop talking about it any more.

There is nothing like an unpleasant home to make a child enjoy school. I did my work well, not for any love for sums or geography, (I can't tell, even now, which side of the Mississippi the Middle West states are on) but to get through the necessary tasks and be able to read. The *National Fifth Reader.* I don't know who collected the fine things that went into that volume, but I have never seen another that held so much of true worth: *Thanatopsis,* Gray's *Elegy,* Lincoln's address at Gettysburg, the *Declaration of Independence,* extracts from the *Merchant of Venice,* and *King Lear,* and the *Psalms.* It was a book twice the size of a standard desk dictionary, clumsy and heavy to hold, but full of meat from cover to cover.

When the trustees came to visit the school, I was always called on to read. I did so without embarrassment because I lost myself in the fine thoughts of the printed page. I was always so earnest in school that I was never popular. I soon was known as teacher's pet, and when she left the room she would call on me to act as monitor, which did not increase my popularity.

When the nutting parties and sleighing parties were made up, I was not included; but it didn't matter for there was so much to do at home I could not have gone anyway. But it hurt not to be asked, just the same.

I seldom saw Aunt Mary. She did not come to the house because she knew Aunt Sade would not welcome her. She contrived to send me pretty hair ribbons for my braids, and I always felt nearer to her than anyone else because Mama had wanted me to be with her.

It came time for Christmas vacation. I had learned many of the fine selections in the *National Fifth Reader* by heart. There was to be a gathering in Madrid of all the schools in the vicinity. A representative from each school was to give a recitation, and, to my unbounded joy, I was chosen to represent our school. I was to give, "The quality of mercy is not strained; It droppeth as the gentle rain from heaven. . . ." The teacher trained me carefully. People did not give readings in those days. Oratory was the popular interpretation. One was not supposed to express comedy or drama without the use of the hands. So "gentle rain from heaven" must be accompanied by a sweeping gesture of the right hand toward the ceiling, and "upon the place beneath" by a corresponding gesture to indicate the earth under the floor. Sometimes a young Demosthenes became mixed like the one who recited "Cannon to right of them, Cannon to left of them" in his confusion mistaking his right hand for the left, and when he came to "Cannon in front of them" pointed to the rear.

Aunt Sade always left the dinner dishes for me, so as the days grew short, I would hurry home, arriving there when it was almost dark, to face a sink full. She would be tired of caring for the baby all day and would bring him out and stand him by a chair so that I could amuse him while I did up the work and prepared supper. I am sure if that baby is still alive, he can repeat "The quality of mercy" with appropriate gestures, so often did I recite it to him that winter.

There was the problem of something to wear for the great occasion. My gray-black best dress did not appeal to me as being quite appropriate. I longed to express myself in my clothes as well as in my rendition of "The quality of mercy." In my trunk was Mama's wedding dress. It was a bright green silk made with a long basque and polonaise. It was too small around the waist, but it was also too long. I cut off the bottom under a ruffle so it wouldn't show, and set the material into the waist leaving it as small as I could possibly squeeze myself into. I sewed nights in my cold bedroom until my fingers would get so stiff that I couldn't hold the needle, then I would hold them around the stove-pipe to get what warmth there was to be had, and sew some more.

I was afraid to have Aunt Sade discover what I was doing, for fear she would interfere. I was in a panic that last week, lest something would happen that I could not go; that Aunt Sade would get sick or the baby would get sick, or there would be a snowstorm so that the road would be blocked. But the night arrived without any untoward happening. I dawdled over the dishes and was not ready when the boys and girls came for me. I had planned to dress at the last minute, to put on the long coat that Aunt Mary had made me from one of hers, wind my fascinator around my head in my room, and rush down and out without being discovered.

Strangely enough it went off as scheduled and no one's suspicions were aroused. We went in a bob-sled with straw strewn over the bed for us to sit in, and there were lots of robes. The horses had a string of bells that ran around their bodies under their bellies and jingled merrily with every step they took. I was very happy and wouldn't have changed places with the prettiest girl in school. When we arrived and I took off my hat and coat, the other girls started to giggle, but the teacher looked at them so sharply they stopped suddenly. I wondered what could be the trouble, never dreaming that I looked queer. I felt proud of my dress, for it was silk and most of the others wore wool. The fact that they had full skirts gathered into waistbands, with sashes, did not alter my opinion of the appropriateness of my costume.

There were several recitations before I was called upon. "For I was born at Bingen, fair Bingen on the Rhine." And "Girt round with rugged mountains the fair lake Constance lies, In her blue heart reflected shine back the starry skies." With appropriate gestures. I could have coached any one of them. I knew them all by heart. Then it was my turn. I walked to the platform with all the assurance in the world. "The quality of mercy is not strained. It droppeth as the gentle rain from heaven," gesture, rip! My green silk gave way where I had pieced it at the waist line in front. Nothing daunted, I continued, "Upon the place beneath," gesture, rip! The quality of mercy was strained. The boys and girls all over the room began to titter. I stopped, humiliated and indignant. Then the words that Miss House had written in my copy of Hans Andersen's Fairy Tales flashed before me, "Never give up the ship!" I suppose the audience had expected to see me leave the stage. When I continued to stand there, they stopped giggling to listen.

The words were so imprinted on my memory that nothing could erase them. I began again, "The quality of mercy is not strained," I gestured fearlessly. There was plenty of underwear showing when I got through, but I got the prize. It was a nice manicure set in a red velvet box. The boy's prize was a copy of the *National Fifth Reader*. I traded with him, and he gave the manicure set to his best girl.

Years afterwards when I saw Ellen Terry in her great rôle as Portia I remembered the green silk that was strained even though the quality of mercy was not.

⚛ *A NOTE ON MY BUREAU* ⚛

THROUGH ALL THESE MONTHS, AL-though I had long ago given up any thought that Aunt Sade could ever love me, still I tried to please her and win her approval, counting myself repaid when I did not bring down her scorn upon me. The only time I remember her speaking kindly to me was one cold stormy night when she and Uncle Alex returned home from Madrid, bringing some chance traveler with them. When Aunt Sade had left that morning she had out-lined a program of work, besides the care of the baby, that would have made any twelve-year-old child gasp with astonishment.

It was Saturday so I had all day for it. As soon as the breakfast things were done I made a sour cream cake, the first I had attempted alone, and it rose beautifully and baked a nice even brown. Then I cleaned the buttery and scrubbed the kitchen floor, and twilight found me hanging the baby's clothes, which I had washed, on the clothes bars on the stoop. They froze almost before I could hang them out, but I finished and rushed back to get a nice warm supper ready. Aunt Sade came in, wondering, I suppose, what kind of shape the house was in to welcome a stranger, and when she found it tidy, with a warm meal all ready to put on the table, and a fresh cake to serve the guest, she was pleasanter than she had ever been to me, and said the cake was as good as she could have made, and that she was glad I had done it. But her kindness was short-lived. When the flurry of excitement over the unexpected guest died down and he went on his way, we settled again; she took to fault finding and I to drudgery.

I wondered sometimes why other girls of my age were happy and care-free and why so much unhappiness should fall to my lot, but I looked forward to the time when Papa would send for me. I studied hard as he had told me to do. I still admired Aunt Sade and clung to her, hoping that some day a miracle would happen and she would really grow to love me.

Then, one day, she did the unforgivable thing. She had told me to sweep the room upstairs that was still known as "Uncle Gordon's room." There was a rag carpet on the floor that held the dust. The bed and bureau were heavy and hard to move, the room was cold, but I swept and dusted it as best I could. Aunt Sade did not come to help or suggest. I did not know she had even looked at the room. That night when I went up to bed there was a note on my bureau. It was a short one in her very pretty handwriting which I admired so much. It said: "I am surprised that as old a girl as you are can be so shiftless. No one but a slut would leave Uncle Gordon's room as you have and think it was clean."

She had carefully underlined the word "slut."

I stood there in my cold room holding the tiny note between numb fingers and read it by candlelight. Nothing she had ever said to me, and her tongue cut deep, made me wince like that written word. A slut! I did not know the meaning of the word, but I felt it must stand for something loathsome, unclean.

My allegiance was suddenly consumed in the burning indignation that note kindled in me. All the injustice that I had suffered at her hands became the selfish, cruel thing it was, and I knew I could never forgive her. I read my Bible and Grandmother's and Mama's name over and over, but they seemed to be very far from my present needs. I prayed on my knees in the cold, but nothing changed that terrible word. Aunt Sade had found my most vulnerable spot. Words spoken hastily and in anger could hurt, but never so deeply as the crystallized written word. I opened my bureau drawer and took out Papa's Knight Templar hat. I thought it might make him seem nearer. The beautiful plumes were gone. I remembered Aunt Sade's turban!

For the first time the sound sleep of childhood deserted me. In the morning I went down to the kitchen feeling very wretched. I didn't know what to do, but one thing was very clear to me: I was not going to live with Aunt Sade any more.

I went into the buttery and looked at the medicines

on the shelf. I remember wondering if saltpeter was poison and how much of it I would have to take to put me out of my misery. I thought I would like to lie down as Mama did and never wake up.

But habit is a chain that is hard to break. There was breakfast to get and the dishes to hurry through before I could go to school. The note was not mentioned. Everything was as if it had been a bad dream. I made no plan. When I left I kissed the baby good-bye and hugged him so fiercely that he looked at me wonderingly.

I went out of the kitchen door with my lunch pail and my books. When school was out I walked four miles to Madrid to Aunt Mary's and told her the whole story. We cried together and some of my anger and bitterness was lost. She had a nice supper that night and put me to bed and told me I need never go back. She and Uncle John and Fred, their boy, were going to Dakota and they would take me with them.

Uncle Alex came to see me. He said he couldn't understand why I ran away. Poor Uncle Alex had so many troubles of his own that I am sure he never guessed the heartaches that were my portion in his home. I showed him the note. His face went white when he read what Aunt Sade had written. The next day he brought me my clothes, my Hans Andersen, and the Bible. He did not bring me Papa's Knight Templar hat.

I never saw Uncle Alex again.

Two years later in Dakota I had a pitiful letter from Aunt Sade. They had lost the farm. They were going Out West to Oregon. She had another baby, a little girl. She begged me to forgive her for having been so cruel to a homeless, helpless child. She realized how hard I had tried. She prayed that her own children might never be as cruelly mistreated as I had been. It was unbelievable that Aunt Sade could be so changed, so softened.

I cried over the letter, but there was proud flesh in the wound she had made by that word. I would not write and say I forgave her. I could not honestly tell her that I did. Aunt Mary tried to persuade me to answer the letter, but I never wrote. I did not hear from Aunt Sade again. The West swallowed her up.

You who travel across the continent in Pullman trains or fly from coast to coast in a day and a half, have no conception of the hardships a journey entailed in those days when every penny must be made to go as far as possible.

Aunt Mary and Uncle John, who had planned the journey for three, now had to stretch their resources to include me. There was no time to communicate with Papa in California. I was secretly glad, feeling that he might forbid my going. I had had no letter for several months. Sweetwater was more isolated than Bodie even, and only an occasional mail, he wrote, went in and out with a man on snowshoes. Often the carrier would be caught in a storm and have to cache his mail, trusting to find it in the spring when the snows melted.

But not only did Aunt Mary and Uncle John assume the expense necessary to take me with them, but all the time I spent in their home I was made to feel that I was a welcome visitor, very necessary to their joy and happiness.

We were in Ogdensburg again, Ogdensburg on the St. Lawrence, the hub of the universe, Ogdensburg where the missionaries had built the mission, La Présentation; where John Brown had harried the British; where Mama and I saw the sleighing and skating together; where Mama had appeared and said to me in the cold dreary station, "Be a good girl, Nellie"; Ogdensburg, where Aunt Sade got her pretty clothes and loved to come to skate and dance; Ogdensburg that now meant the beginning of the long trek out West.

How many people nowadays remember the tourist sleeping cars, the poor man's de luxe method of travel? They had cane-covered seats that were made down into beds at night. There was a cooking stove at one end of the car where the women could heat milk for the babies, boil water for tea or coffee, and cook lighter food. Everyone brought a great lunch along, enough to last till the end of their journey.

Out West in those days meant Iowa, Nebraska, Dakota, to the *St. Lawrence Republican* reading public. California was California, a land of cutthroats and desperadoes, of Indians, gold-seekers and adventurers. All of the people on our tourist excursion car were going to the Middle West, most of them to Dakota. There were families with little children, babies in arms and babies on the way; mothers who were patient and smiling in the morning, if the babies had slept well, but tired and cross by night; fathers who walked up and down the aisle with fretful children to quiet them.

When I travel on a Pullman coach nowadays and see how annoyed the passengers are if a child cries at night and disturbs them, and how they poke their heads out of their berths to ask the porter angrily and loudly if something can't be done about it, I think of that Tourist car. I do not remember hearing anyone complain because a child cried at night. I do remember seeing sympathetic fathers kindle a fire in the stove for hot water, or provident mothers offering Mother Winslow's Soothing Syrup. Everyone anxiously inquired about the child in the morning and stoutly denied having been disturbed in the night when the father or mother became apologetic.

I can see those capacious lunch-baskets with stout handles and a cover that opened on either side. The more perishable articles of food were consumed first, maybe fried chicken, or apple turnover. The bread and butter would be fresh and good, but as the days passed and the stuffy coach had its way with the contents of the baskets, the end of the journey found us consuming dry bread, hard-boiled eggs, and sliced dried beef, for canned goods were rare in those days. But there would be pound cake or fruit cake that kept the journey through, and there was great exchanging of special tid-bits. The women exchanged recipes for special dishes while the men talked of homesteading quarter-sections, half-sections, of breaking the land, of the best plows for that purpose, all eager, looking forward to better times, better fortunes in the new country.

At Sioux Falls we left the railroad for Montrose, twenty-five miles away. Sioux Falls was the center of activity for all the country round. It was here that the farmers hauled their grain over the long wagon roads that threaded their way across the prairie. There was none of the Ogdensburg gaiety. There were no trees.

Sioux Falls lay on the prairie swept by the snow-
toothed winds of winter or the blistering, heat-laden
cyclones of summer, with nothing between the town
and the empty horizon to check their progress.

We arrived in February so that land might be located
and living arranged for before it was time to begin
putting in the crops. Montrose stood on a rise that
overlooked miles of prairie, endlessly rolling like the
waves of the ocean to far distances. Four miles from
the town Uncle John located his homestead. We lived
in a dugout, afterwards our shelter from cyclones. A
short distance away ran a stream, too unimportant to
appear on any map. After the majestic sweep of the St.
Lawrence the river seemed a poor stream, but when the
prairie fires came and it was our ally in saving our home
and furnishing our neighbors with their only defense,
it became a friend indeed. A well was driven for drinking water.

There was no game except the prairie dogs that were
not fit for food, and the coyots * that made the night
weird with their howls.

The ground was too frozen to cut earth for a sod
house, and so a frame shelter was erected, plain boards
covered over with tar paper, a protection against wind
and cold. There were two rooms on the ground floor,
the kitchen and the other room. Since roofs were more
expensive than side walls, houses did not spread out on
the ground. There was one big room upstairs with
partitions dividing it into sleeping quarters for Fred and
me, and much needed store-rooms. Flimsy shelters were
built for the stock, and an outhouse that the "specialist"

* So spelled and pronounced in Dakota.

would have scorned to acknowledge. All of the shelters
stood like angular, awkward strangers on the hard, un-
friendly earth.

At last warm winds came from the south where Sioux
Falls lay and the spell of winter was broken. The sod
became responsive to the tread of foreign feet. Spring
trailed her robes over the bare land, and wild roses
covered the billowing prairie. They were a joy to the
eye, but the farmer's most persistent foe. They, with the
prairie grass, fought valiantly to keep the land for their
own. The sound of their battle could be heard as the
plowshares fought their way through roots that snapped
angrily as they gave way, blunting the plows and even
wrenching them out of the hands of the plowman.
It was slow, tedious, back-breaking work, but that has
always been the portion of pioneers.

❊ O PIONEERS! ❊ DAKOTA DAYS ❊ ASTHMA

SQUARES OF PLOWED, HARROWED, AND
planted land soon showed a tender green. Flax sent
roots into the unwilling soil and won it to friendliness.
Corn sprouted in orderly rows. Wheat grew sturdy as
the spring advanced.

Aunt Mary's kitchen became a shining place where
fragrant smells of good food always seemed to hang on
the air. The only fuel we had for the kitchen stove
was prairie grass, dried and twisted as one twists a
skein of yarn. It was necessary to feed the stove con-

stantly, and yet somehow Aunt Mary managed to perform miracles.

The other room was furnished with a rag carpet of Aunt Mary's weaving, a bed where she and Uncle John slept, a table and kerosene lamp with a red wick in its glass bowl. She put ruffled lawn curtains at the small, square windows. They made the room seem very pleasant, but from the outside they looked strange in the square cut in the tar paper.

My heart was filled to bursting with happiness. My self-respect and capacity for affection had been stunted like some plant that had been shut away from the sunlight, and as the warming rays of kindness shone into the place that had been sad and dark so long, I felt transformed.

The district school was two miles away. Every day I took my lunch pail with some surprise hidden away in it by Aunt Mary's thoughtful hand, and trudged over the prairie. There were no trees putting out their lacy leaves, no sumac bush under which to rest in the shade, no violets to surprise me on the way, but I was happy because everyone was so kind and the shadow of Aunt Sade's displeasure no longer spoiled my days.

The teacher had every grade in her one room. They were sturdy children with sunburned skin and hair, barefooted, as I was, neatly dressed and patched. We did not have the *National Fifth Reader*. All the books were more elementary in the material they offered to the pupils. Since I was so happy at home, school was not the refuge it had been under less pleasant surroundings. But Papa had wanted me to study hard. That was the reason why I could not be with him in California. There were no schools there where I could get that apparently necessary education. And since all the griefs and joys that had attended my path since he had gone away were only milestones on that long anticipated joining him there, I worked diligently at my task. His letters showed displeasure at what I had done. He enclosed no money to reimburse Uncle John and Aunt Mary. I redoubled my efforts to please him.

On Sundays we would visit our neighbors, and new and fast friendships grew lustily, fed by the common need for companionship in this lonely land whose horizons stretched so far that the homes dotting the prairie were only specks on the great canvas that nature had stretched out.

Aunt Mary was always going on some errand of mercy, to a woman in child-birth, or to help care for a sick baby, and Uncle John attended the ailing horses or cattle in the same friendly spirit. Often I was sent over the prairie to take a starter of yeast to some woman whose own refused to "come," or to mind the children while their mother went to Montrose for needed purchases.

Nature was kind that first summer. Plentiful rains came quietly when they were needed and the crops throve under their ministrations. The flax blossomed and azure fields spread like magic carpets over the land. The corn grew high above my head and whispered of plenty and prosperity. Wheat hung in heavy heads that promised food and plenty for the long winter. Fields of buckwheat put forth pink flowers whose perfume lingered on the air. The prairie grass grew tall and strong on the uncultivated land. The days were hot

and breathless. The thin houses were unprotected from
the sun, but no one complained. It was good growing
weather, and so the men toiled and sweated in the fields
and the women endured the heat uncomplainingly.
Those who lived in sod shanties were more sheltered
from the sun, but the dirt kept sifting from the sod
and the walls harbored insects and snakes.

But the crops grew tremendously. When harvest time
came there was a triumphant march from homestead to
homestead as everyone joined forces, shoulder to shoulder, neighbor to neighbor, to harvest the grain and start
it on its journey to Sioux Falls. As the men worked
together, so the women marched from shanty to shanty,
cooking the meals, taking lunch to the men in the fields.
All of the children and many of the women were barefooted, their heads protected from the heat by starched
sunbonnets, their hands rough and red, and work-worn.

High hope beat in every heart. The harvest was beyond their wildest expectation. There would be money
now for more stock and more machinery to break more
ground when spring came; more seed to plant, a greater
harvest next year. Privation does not eat the heart out
when the future promises comfort and plenty. Everyone prepared for the winter with as little expenditure
of their carefully hoarded returns from the harvest as
possible.

I started to school again. Aunt Mary had made me
some new ruffled aprons and, supposing they were only
to be worn for best, I put them away. When she told
me they were to wear to school I cried with happiness
that someone cared enough for me to make me such
pretty things for every day.

The fall was beautiful. There were long, lazy Indian summer days when the air was so still that the smoke went straight up from the stove pipes and it seemed as if the prairie stretched luxuriously in preparation for the long sleep that winter would bring. There were no trees to wave their magic gold and crimson in the sun, but the corn shocks stood proudly surrounded by yellow pumpkins, and the wheat stubble shone like gold.

There were corn huskings and impromptu dances under the harvest moon on a wooden platform that traveled from farm to farm. Barney Daugherty, the fiddler, furnished the music, and when there was a lull in the dancing he would sing that prairie classic,

> *My clothes are covered o'er with dough,*
> *I'm looking like a fright,*
> *And everything is scattered round the room,*
> *And I fear if P. T. Barnum's man should set his*
>   *eyes on me,*
> *He would take me from my little cabin home.*

CHORUS:

> *Oh, the hinges are of leather, the windows have*
>   *no glass,*
> *The roof, it lets the howling blizzard in,*
> *And I hear the hungry coyot as he sneaks up*
>   *through the grass*
> *Round my little low sod shanty on my claim.*

I don't recall the second verse, but after reciting further tribulations the song ended with

> *While I'm burning twisted hay*
> *In my little low, sod shanty on my claim.*

I was thirteen years old now and large and strong for my age. The boys began to cast sly glances at me, and I was pleased to find myself attractive in their eyes. Rhythm came naturally, and like many heavy people, I was light on my feet. I don't know when I learned to dance, but dancing was not the serious thing in those days that it is now. Quadrilles and Virginia reels, where everyone old and young took part, were carefree and jolly.

As the season advanced the days grew bitterly cold. A big heater was installed in the other room and was fed with bundles of flax straw. It gave off tremendous heat as long as it lasted, but the fuel had to be constantly replenished. Instead of a wood pile we had stacks of prairie grass and of flax straw.

While Uncle John and Fred were taking turns driving the wagons to Sioux Falls, and Aunt Mary and I had the cows to milk and the chores to do, it fell to my lot to twist the hay for the cook stove. The blades of grass were strong and wiry and sharp on the edges and cut my hands so that they bled, but no task was too hard to do for Aunt Mary's sake. I learned to milk and was glad to snuggle my hands against the cow's warm udder and watch the milk foam as I became more expert and a steady stream poured into the milk pail. The nights were very clear, and the stars shone like brilliant studs screwed into the velvet waistcoat of the heavens.

As winter closed in with its wind-driven storms, the battle against the encroaching cold in the house was constant. The wind searched every crack and crevice, the thermometer dropped to zero, ten below, twenty below. We no longer looked out on the soft falling snowflakes of New England, but on stinging particles of frozen ice riding a gale that knew no rest. Aunt Mary provided me with warm underwear, a fleece-lined hood and mittens. I wore a man's overcoat and over-shoes and leggins to school, and after battling two miles with the prairie wind, I would arrive exhausted. The odor of wet woolen garments drying all day around the schoolhouse stove during the winter lingers in my memory. A wire was stretched from the house to the barn so that Uncle John and Fred could find their way back and forth in the storms.

One day when I went to school it was so cold that my nose ached and the particles of icy snow stung my face so that tears came to my eyes. When I arrived my nose was white and the teacher had me rub it with an icicle in the entry before she would let me come into the warm room. There were not many children in school that day, and it was a good thing, for we hugged the stove, piling it with the precious wood that had been brought all the way from the railroad at Sioux Falls. The wind howled around the building like a pack of coyotes, and by afternoon it carried so much fine snow that we could not distinguish objects away from the building. It sifted like dust around the windows and doors and puddles of water began to run across the floor. After a while it grew so dark that the teacher had to light the lamps that were used for evening parties or programs held in the schoolhouse. The supply of wood in the entry grew low. Our lunches had been eaten and digested long ago. The teacher would not let us start for home for fear we would lose our way. We all realized that this was no ordinary storm but a blizzard; the winter spectre of the wind-swept prairies.

We were terrified at the thought of spending the night in the cold, dreary place. Then faint hallos came through the storm and we heard men stamping their feet in the entry. The fathers had come for their children and Fred had come for me. We drove home sitting on the high seat of the light wagon. A horse blanket covered the seat and hung down behind our legs to protect them from the wind. Aunt Mary had heated bricks and put them in the bottom of the wagon to keep our feet warm. Another horse blanket was wrapped around us. I held a lighted lantern under the blanket and curved my hands around the chimney for warmth. There was never enough snow left on the ground by the wind to form a covering for sleighing, and the iron rims on the wagon wheels jolted in and out of the hard frozen ruts. I saw a light across the prairie. It came from Barney Daugherty's sod shanty. I remembered the song,

> *"The hinges are of leather,*
> *The windows have no glass,*
> *The roof it lets the howling blizzard in—"*

I felt sorry for Barney. Once in awhile Fred would take the lantern and hold it out into the storm to see if the horses were keeping the road. Then he would warm his hands with it, and giving it back to me, beat his arms across his breast, holding the reins, first in one hand, then in the other.

Finally the horses found their way home through the storm. Aunt Mary filled a wash basin with snow. Fred pressed the snow against his frost bitten face, and buried his fingers in it. He cried with the pain. The house was not as warm as the school had been and the stove puffed smoke from every crack, but Aunt Mary baked buckwheat cakes from the batter that always was ready in a brown crock by the kitchen stove, and there was sorghum molasses to eat with them. The men, lighting the lantern that carried safely through wind and storm, followed the wire they had stretched to the barn for that purpose. They gave the horses a warm bedding of straw and brought the horse blankets into the house for extra coverings on the beds.

That night Aunt Mary had an attack of asthma. I waked, hearing her terrifying struggle for breath, and crept downstairs. She was sitting up in bed, her nostrils dilating with the effort to get air into her lungs. Her neck and chest muscles strained against the band of her high-necked, long-sleeved cotton-flannel nightgown. Her face was pinched and blue. Cold sweat stood on her forehead. Uncle John had built a hot fire, and was hunting for a powder which she had brought from the East, to burn and inhale. It seemed she had been subject to light attacks, but never one like this. It was daybreak before the spasm finally gave way, and she sank into exhausted slumber.

I had not been praying vigilantly as I used to do. Things were going so smoothly with me that my prayers had become rather stereotyped. But cold as it was, I knelt in the dawn and prayed that Aunt Mary would be spared to us. It seemed to me if I had to give her up, I would never get to Papa in California, never be able to go on. Aunt Mary soon seemed as well as ever and days passed before she had another attack. They came violently on nights when the winds were fiercest and howled mockingly at the windows. I never hear a high, cruel wind that I do not see Aunt Mary struggling for the air of which the world seemed so full. There was no doctor nearer than Sioux Falls, twenty-five miles away. There was no telephone. There was nothing to be done but use the simple home remedies and wait for the spasm to pass. Years later when I was called to my first case of asthma, and was able to give immediate relief with a hypodermic, I wished that I might have known what to do when Aunt Mary struggled for breath through those ghastly nights on the wind-swept prairie.

✤ *A PRAIRIE FIRE & A CYCLONE* ✤
PAPA SENDS FOR ME

SPRING CAME AGAIN AND MORE LAND was broken to the plow. Field by field the wild roses and tall prairie grass were torn from the land which they had claimed since time began. The precious seed that had been held for sowing was scattered over the cultivated fields. Two heifer calves and a filly arrived at the barn, giving promise of increase through the years.

Aunt Mary's asthma departed, and it seemed as if there were no clouds on our horizon. But spring winds brought no rain, and the fields turned to dust that filled our nostrils and choked our throats. The seed sprouted and languished, making a sickly growth. Irrigation, that boon to desert countries, was unheard of on the prairie. How we scanned the cloudless heavens for signs of rain! Neighborhood meetings were held and the Almighty exhorted to remember His people on the prairie farms, and send the much needed rain. Men hauled water from the river and sprinkled some of the choicest seed, hoping to save its yield for another year's sowing. Still the fields were fanned by winds that carried no moisture.

The prairie grass grew strong and tall as though to defy the creatures who sought to clear it from the earth. The faces of the men were drawn and haggard. The women forgot to sing as they went about their household tasks. Worry crept into the school and came between the children and their lessons. At recess and when we ate our lunches of bread and butter and sorghum molasses, we talked of rain; when the new moon rode through the sky with tips upturned so that it held water, we were sick with disappointment.

I finished the grade school that rainless spring. In the fall I would go to Montrose to the new high school that was being built there. I was thrilled over the prospect and drove to town with Uncle John and Aunt Mary to see the foundation laid for the new temple of learning erected to the prairie generation. Summer brought a merciless sun, blazing in a brazen sky. Only the hardiest crops survived, and those half-heartedly. Men and women saw their hard-earned savings literally crumbling

to dust before their eyes. Even the prairie grass turned
yellow, and the sharp blades writhed in the sun.

Then one day a cloud appeared on the horizon. We
watched it breathlessly for hours. But there was no
hint of oncoming moisture, only a parched heat that
grew more unbearable as day grew to noon. Uncle John
came into the kitchen, his face set and white. "A prairie
fire," he gasped, and the words struck terror into our
hearts. He called Fred and they ran to the barn, harnessed the horses to the plows and began to break fur-
rows around the acre on which stood the house and
barns. The alarm spread. Over the prairie we could
see our neighbors making hasty preparations to meet the
oncoming enemy.

The prairie grass was ripe for the invader. The air
was filled with smoke, and the sun shone through it like
a burnished shield. Men loaded all the available barrels
into wagons and raced their horses to the river for
water with which to fight the fire. The river was so
low it took a long time to fill the barrels, and still the
billows of smoke advanced. Men and women loaded
sacks, blankets, even clothing, into the wagons and went
out to battle. Children were collected in a neighbor's
home and I was left to tend them. For hours we
watched while fathers and mothers with wet sacks and
blankets and clothing fought for their homes. All hope
of saving the scanty crops was gone.

A forest fire is a glorious sight, but a prairie fire is an
ugly thing, writhing along the ground like a horde of
venomous snakes. Sometimes they would rear their
heads and leap the plowed ground around some dwell-
ing, and a spiral flame would rise to the smoke-laden

sky. Then they would fall on their bellies again and go on their devastating way.

The wind died down at sunset, and the creeping flames stopped at the river. Wild-eyed men and women, their faces grimed with sweat and smoke, their clothing hanging in rags, returned to their homes bringing with them the less fortunate ones who had nothing left but the burned-over spot on which their homes had stood. But they were thankful to escape with their lives. Tales came over the prairie of families who had been surrounded and burned, vainly trying to fight their way to safety.

One does not wonder, knowing the tragedy and hardship of those pioneer days, that the songs of the prairie were pitiful in their recitation of human woe. We no longer sang "Seeing Nellie Home" and "Jingle Bells," but songs that sought to convey something of the heartbreak that came to those prairie homes.

There is one I have never forgotten:

> *On the distant prairie when the day was long,*
> *Skipping like a fairy, light as song,*
> *Lingering in the sunshine with the birds at*
>   *play,*
> *Innocent and blythe as they.*

CHORUS:

> *Fair as a lily, joyous and free*
> *Light of the prairie home was she.*
> *Everyone who knew her felt the gentle power*
> *Of Rosalie, the prairie flower.*

The second and third verses told at length of the cold and storms of the winter and when spring came, "Little prairie flower was gone."

As far as the eye could reach, the land lay black and lifeless. Men began to figure how they could raise money enough to keep their families and stock over the winter, and get seed to sow the following spring. But with talk of ways and means, I don't remember hearing anyone mention the possibility of moving to some kindlier country. They had put down their roots into the soil of the prairie and it was home to them.

As though the fire were not enough, another calamity followed on its heels. One day, about a month later, the air was flooded with a strange light and the sky became a great copper bowl over our heads. Out of the West came a huge shadow, a roaring spiral of dust that laid waste everything in its path. We rushed to the cyclone cellar. (When an airplane comes perilously near to the house tops, I am reminded of the roaring that passed over our heads as we crouched in our dugout and waited for its fury to be spent.) Freakishly, the gale followed a path that left our house standing intact, but the wreckage of many homes was strewn over the fire-scarred land. This new disaster yielded a harvest of bodies to be buried in the acre where the long, narrow mounds told a pitiful tale of frustrated hopes and ambitions. The new high school at Montrose, finished and furnished, ready for the fall term, was picked up and torn apart as though by some giant schoolboy. Its new desks and shining blackboards traveled miles in less time than one takes in the telling.

This was a lesser and more private catastrophe. I tried
not to show how much it meant to me.

Letters came, occasionally, from Aunt Mary's friends
in Madrid. Alex MacKnight, they wrote, had lost his
farm. He had put a big mortgage on it for the expensive wedding trip that Sade made him take. He had
not been able to keep up the interest and it finally ate
him up. "Wouldn't Eliza MacKnight turn in her grave
if she knew?"

Another wrote "Gordon MacKnight is dead. He was
getting a bull ready for the County Fair, braiding ribbons in its tail. Something happened and the bull
kicked him. You know how Gordon used to lose his
temper. He was never mean to animals, but he must
have lost his head, and he went at the bull with a pitch-
fork. The man that hired him says it was a terrible
battle. The bull gored him to death. It never would
have happened if Eliza had lived. She knew how to
control him."

My childish picture of gathering at the river had
changed. The geography of heaven was not as definitely
outlined in my mind as it had been. But I felt that
somewhere Grandmother waited for Uncle Gordon; that
he would be able to hear her greetings, and his tongue
would be loosened from the spell of silence that had
been laid on it in childhood. The book of my life in
northern New York State was closed. It was as if all the
cousins and uncles and aunts did not exist, for I never
heard from any of them again.

Papa had left Sweetwater. The prospect that had
looked so good did not pan out. He was going to Inyo

County to open an assay and surveyor s office. He hoped to send for me soon. I wrote him of the prairie fire and the cyclone that had wrecked the high school.

After nine years of waiting, the dream of going to Papa in California was coming true. I could hardly believe it when the letter came. Aunt Mary was to go with me to Omaha, from there I would travel alone to meet him. He sent what seemed to me an enormous sum of money; and wrote in detail what I was to do. He sent material for two new dresses, a plum-colored wool and a blue plaid for traveling.

The news spread over the prairie. My father must be a rich man to send so much money. Why had he left me dependent on Uncle John and Aunt Mary until I was able to help them on the farm, and then sent for me when they needed me most? Women questioned whether Aunt Mary should let me go to an utterly strange man in California. The word, California, savored of all that was wild and unrighteous.

But Uncle John and Aunt Mary did not protest. Although they had never seen Papa and had heard the story of how his violent temper had been the cause of Grandfather's death, yet so loyal had Mama been to him through the years that the picture she had painted of him was the one that endured.

The dresses were made by a dressmaker in Montrose. They were too old for me in color and style, but I thought they were beautiful. Papa had sent money for Aunt Mary's return ticket to Omaha; Aunt Mary decided that her best dress would do for the trip, but she must have a new bonnet.

The money Papa had sent proved not to be so much

after all when it was divided into tickets and expense on the road. But Aunt Mary must have a new bonnet. It was finally decided that she could pay half with her egg money and I should pay half out of the money Papa had sent. I have never spent any money that gave me as much pleasure as the small amount that went to pay for half of Aunt Mary's new bonnet.

On a lovely star-lit night Fred got a buggy from one of the neighbors and took me for a ride over the prairie. He told me how much he would miss me, that he loved me and hoped that sometime, when he had made a home, I would come back and marry him. I felt very romantic. The farmer boy was transformed into a handsome lover. He put his arms shyly around me and kissed me. I was greatly touched, not so much by any real affection for him, but by the idea of going away to California and leaving a sweetheart on the prairie to pine for me.

Uncle John drove Aunt Mary and me to Sioux Falls in the light wagon. I had my trunk, the one that had traveled with Mama and me from Petrolia nine years before, the one that had gone with us to Bridgeport, and back with me alone to the farm, the one that had brought my few possessions to Dakota. It was a wooden trunk trimmed with brass nails and the lid curved over the top like a half barrel cut lengthwise. It was lined with paper that had a design of stars. In the lid was a colored picture of a lady with curls and a flowered beribboned hat. My Bible—I had filled in the record of Uncle Gordon's life—my Hans Andersen Fairy Tales, and my Fifth Reader were in the trunk.

Aunt Mary fixed a nice lunch that lasted us all the

way. We rode in a day coach because it was less expensive to travel that way, and it would only be one night. We were not happy. Aunt Mary really loved me as if I were her own child, and I knew it took all the courage she could gather to send me away from her. I hated to leave her. Now when the moment for which I had waited for so many years had arrived, the thought of going alone to far-off California to a stranger frightened me.

When we arrived at Omaha, Aunt Mary decided I had better go on a day coach all the way. She felt it would be safer. She had traveled so little that the idea of having me undress and go to bed among strangers was terrifying. I did not mind. I wanted Aunt Mary to worry about me as little as possible. Aunt Mary found the conductor and put me in his care. When our train started, she stood by the car window, smiling through her tears and kissed her hand to me as long as I could see her. I cried because Aunt Mary was going back to the burned-over prairie, to the cold and blizzards and hardships I knew so well. I wondered if she would have the asthma again that winter and wished I might be there to help her. I thought, with a great melancholy, of my sweetheart whom I was leaving behind to make a home for me, and vowed I would be true to him.

My mind was filled with uncertainty. One moment I wished I was back on the prairie, the next it seemed as if I could not wait to get to California.

While we were passing through Nevada, the conductor came and told me that he had received a telegram from my father saying he would meet me at Winnemucca, before we got to Reno. This shortening of the time before I should face the stranger who had been a kind of knight errant made my heart beat faster.

The train stopped. A strange man came into our car. His face was covered with a beard. He looked like Uncle Gordon. I knew it must be Papa. This ordinary-looking man, dressed in a flannel shirt and a mussed suit, was the plumed knight, the fairy-book prince!

YOUNG DAYS
IN THE OLD WEST

☗ *MINERS* & *MULESKINNERS* ☗
FRANCES ☗ *THE HARVEST*
FESTIVAL

THE CONDUCTOR HAD TOLD PAPA WHERE
he could find me. He came to me. Perhaps he, too, was
disappointed. He might have hoped that I would look
more like Mama. He took me in his arms. He cried
a little and trembled with emotion. It was like a scene
from a stage play.

Fellow travelers had heard the story: that I had come
alone across the continent to meet my father, whom I
had not seen since I was a baby. They crowded around.
Papa kept repeating, "I wouldn't have known her. She's
grown so!" As though he didn't realize all the years
that had passed and all that I had been through. I
don't think he ever did realize. He seemed to resent
the fact that Uncle John and Aunt Mary had brought
me to Dakota with them. He felt that I should have
been made to stay on the farm until he sent for me. We
talked about it very little. He seldom mentioned Mama.
It was hard for me to feel that he had ever belonged to

her. He seemed to be very proud of me and glad to have people know I was his daughter, just as he might have been proud of a fine animal or a valuable piece of property.

We arrived in Reno. The thing that impressed me most, as I walked around the town with my father, was the purple blossoming alfalfa that grew along the footpaths and in most of the gardens. Small wonder, after the burned-over prairie and the long trip across the desert, that a plant so green and sturdy as alfalfa should attract my attention. I learned that Reno was another hub. Here men came to take the Virginia and Truckee Railroad to the famous Comstock Lode of Virginia City. Here millions of dollars in bullion were transferred from the Virginia and Truckee to the main line, on its way to the San Francisco mint. Reno was the only outlet for all the mining and cattle country along the eastern slope of the Sierras. Here we left the main line to travel south over the Virginia and Truckee and the Carson and Colorado to Owen's Valley, our future home.

The Sierras! How they towered in magnificent grandeur, dwarfing anything I had ever known, crashing in splendor on my eyes, accustomed to the far horizons of the prairie.

When our train drew into the station at Carson City, we seemed to have plunged into the midst of some exciting social event. High-stepping horses drew fine carriages; women in fashionable clothes and well-groomed men in frock coats and silk hats exchanged greetings. What was the occasion? They were there to see the train come in! It meant contact with the world on the other side of the mountains.

At Mound House the Virginia and Truckee road swung east on its way to Virginia City. We changed there to the cramped cars of the narrow-gauge Carson and Colorado. When we arrived at the desert town of Sodaville, the train stopped to stay all night. So did we. We went to bed in the rough "Hotel and Bar." Between the oath-punctured discussions of the gambling games that were in full swing in the bar room and the yelping of the coyotes across the desert, sleep was banished. I lay awake, trying to understand this strangeness that rose like a wall between me and that Papa who had left his little family in Petrolia so many years ago.

The narrow-gauge train, apparently much refreshed by its overnight stop, started across the desert the next morning with great puffing and snorting and exhibition of renewed energy. My troubled wonderings of the night before were almost forgotten in my interest in this strangely different country. The people, too, had changed. Men wore flannel shirts and their trousers were tucked into high boots. Some of them walked behind queer little mules that my father said were burros. The wooden saddles that the burros had on their backs were pack saddles. The stout hide bags that hung on each side of the pack saddles were kyaxes. Mining supplies and food, which my father called grub, were packed in the kyaxes. The men were prospectors. They were going out to work some claim. Desert rats, my father called them. If they found "pay dirt," they were able to outfit themselves; if not, they found somebody to grub-stake them. They lived and died on the desert.

Other men drove freight wagons loaded with ore or

the soda and borax that was a valuable product of the country. The driver sat in a saddle on the wheel-horse. From there he drove the long string of mules, made up of from twenty to thirty animals. There were leaders and pointers and swing teams, held together by chains and stretchers. There were no reins. A jerk line ran to the leader. When a mule refused to perform the functions that he knew were expected of him, the driver jumped from his saddle to the ground, ran along the string of mules to the offending animal and belabored it with a short whip and a volley of oaths that made it lean into the collar. My father said the men who drove these teams were mule-skinners, and that when the mornings were cold and they knew the mules would hate to pull the load they would give each mule a beating before the team was hitched up just so they would start the day right.

The men's clothes were white with alkali dust. The car was filled with it. The sky was clear and blue. Clearer and bluer than any sky I had ever seen. The desert was covered with brush that my father said was sage-brush and grease-wood and rabbit-brush. To the west the sharp peaks of the Sierras were etched against the sky; to the east was the White Mountain range, its canyons filled with purple shadows.

We came to the monument that marked the boundary between Nevada and California. I looked firmly out of the car window while stinging tears came to my eyes. This gray, lonely desert, with the ugly red stations along the track, was California.

My father explained that we were in Mono County, the county made famous by the great mining towns of

Bodie and Aurora. He told of the old stagecoach days; how people traveled over the stage roads that ran from Sonora through a pass in the Sierras to those booming camps. Those were the days of Mark Twain and Bret Harte, the days of a wide-open mining camp when it was a mark of distinction to be a "bad man from Bodie."

Then we crossed the boundary line into Inyo County, christened by the Indians from the mountain range to the east, Inyo, the abiding place of a great spirit.

The train stopped and we got out at one of the ugly red stations. A light wagon with a fringed canopy top, drawn by a four-horse team, waited for us. The days of the stagecoach were past. We drove toward the Sierras. The sand crunched under the wheels.

Not far from the station we saw a circular stone wall, which my father called a stone corral. He said that was where Owensville, the first town in the valley, had been, and told how the settlers got together and had their first dance there in an adobe cabin only ten by twelve feet in size. When the Fourth of July came they had a celebration. There were a hundred and fifty men and seven women. The women sang and played a melodeon. There were many Southerners, but everyone was friendly, in spite of the Civil War that was going on "back home."

We crossed Owen's River on a plank bridge and climbed a ridge of sand. I saw strange huts that looked like large bowls, turned upside down. My father explained that they were Indian houses, and he called the small village a campoodie.

We reached the top of the ridge. Before us lay the Owen's River valley. As though by a miracle the desert had disappeared. My father explained that it was a miracle, the miracle wrought by irrigation. I remembered how we waited and longed and prayed for rain in Dakota. The mountains, I was told, garnered the snow and gave an unfailing water supply to the valley that stretched for over a hundred miles along their base.

We drove past cultivated fields, friendly, smiling fields of alfalfa and corn and shocked grain, to the town of Bishop, which was one of the many settlements that lay nestled in the valley.

We stopped at the Valley View Hotel and Bar. There was a harvest festival in progress and the main street on which it faced was crowded with people. They spoke a language that was strange to me. I found that farms were no longer farms but ranches; farmers were ranchers; the sod shanties of the prairies were replaced by the adobe houses of the settlers in California; unbroken horses were bronchos and a barnyard was a corral; the coyot of Dakota was the coyote here. Cowboys were buckaroos and swaggered along the streets dressed in chaps and sombreros. Twenty-five cents was two bits. Pennies were unknown. There was no paper money. Five, ten and twenty-dollar gold pieces jingled in purses and pockets.

My father introduced me. There were no class distinctions. Ranchers and buckaroos, teachers and preachers, saloon-keepers and miners, mothers and children, all gave me a cordial welcome.

The next day I met Frances. She was the daughter of a cattleman. We took to each other at first sight. She took me out behind the hotel and showed me her horse. It was saddled with a side saddle of beautifully ornamented leather. The bridle was of woven horse hair, silver mounted. I had never been on a horse in my life. Frances seemed to think that was a sad lack in my education and insisted that I get on her horse. She led him to a convenient stump and with much urging and pushing got me into the saddle. Then she led the horse around. I hung to the horn of the saddle in fear of disaster, but I wouldn't confess that I was frightened, for I was ashamed of my inexperience.

Frances had never been out of the valley, and had never been on a railroad train, yet her air of worldliness dazzled me. She rode at the Harvest Festival. She was slender and willowy. I thought she rode like a princess and wondered if I would ever be able to stay on a horse.

The Harvest Festival was very different from the Fair at Canton, N. Y. There was a circular mile of dirt road that was the race track. There were no tents. Baled alfalfa palaces held the exhibits: fine produce, apples, vegetables, grain. It all smelled so sweet and clean. There were no sideshows. Indian women whom the white people called *mahalas* were there, wearing long, full calico dresses, with gay silk handkerchiefs over their heads. Many of them carried their babies, strapped in flat baskets, on their backs.

There were horse races, cow pony races, Indian pony races, bronco busting. Buckaroos lassoed wild cattle or threw their sombreros on the ground and swooped down from madly racing horses to get them.

Frances rode with the other girls. Their long riding skirts billowed in the breeze as their horses galloped. It was all exciting, gay, care-free.

The streets of the town were like a country road, lined

with tall poplars and spreading cottonwoods—quick-growing trees that marked boundary lines and gave shelter to man and beast. Their leaves were pieces of gold in the sunshine.

Frances' father and my father decided to sit in on a poker game at the hotel that night, and I was allowed to go home with Frances. Her father was a strange-looking man, with a sandy beard and a glass eye. I never did hear how he lost his eye, but I learned later how shrewd he had been about making use of his misfortune.

When he first came to the valley, and built a ranch house and corrals to winter the stock that roamed the mountain meadows during the summer, he employed Indians to dig the post holes for fences and the ditches for irrigation.

His chief occupation and pleasure was a poker game in town. It was his custom to set the Indians to work in a ditch or along a line of post holes, remove his glass eye, place it on some elevation that commanded a view of the workers, and leave it on guard while he went into town to indulge in his favorite pastime. The Indians were so in awe of this strange, unwinking eye, that they dared not approach it but dug miles of ditches and post holes under its watchful stare.

Frances left her saddle horse in town and we drove home in her father's cart. She told me she had been born in an adobe house in Adobe Meadows, where her father owned sections of grazing land. It seemed no one spoke of acres in this country; it was a section, a half-section, a quarter-section. I learned that a section was six hundred and forty acres and seemed to be the standard of measurement.

In New York State men bought land by the rod, in Dakota by the acre, in California by the section! I seemed to have landed in a country of superlatives. Inyo County boasted the highest mountain in the United States, snow-crowned Mount Whitney, and the lowest spot in the United States, awe-inspiring Death Valley.

The atmosphere which I had come to associate with Aunt Mary pervaded that big, comfortable ranch house that was Frances' home. There were rag carpets and warm comforters, crusty homemade bread, and always a big pan of Dutch cheese making on the back of the cook stove. Supper was the evening meal in those days, and I know of no more delectable combination than a mealy, baked potato and Dutch cheese well mixed with cream, as it was served in that big ranch house.

Frances' mother was one of the most motherly women I have ever met. Perhaps the fact that she started being a mother so early in life accounted for that. It was not unusual for girls to marry at the age of fourteen in the early days in California. She came to the valley when a mere slip of a girl to visit a married sister. When the stage passed through Adobe Meadows, a man who had left the sea to amass a fortune in land and alkali cattle saw her, wanted her. He was a fascinating character, one to appeal to the fancy of a young girl, with his sailor's tales and romantic wooing. Some part of her father's adventurous life must have been reborn in Frances to give her that untrammeled freedom of movement, that touch of sophistication, which set her apart from the others.

Although Frances' father was the richest man in the valley, there were never any servants in the house, except the Indian women who came to wash and iron and scrub, receiving in payment *hogadie* (food), calico, worn shoes, an old dress, or, after many days' work, a sack of flour.

The sale of cattle went to buy more land and hire more buckaroos, to run more cattle, to sell, to buy more land, until at his death his estate was the largest that had ever passed through the courts of Inyo County.

Great corrals stood across the road from the house, and barbed-wire fences ran on all sides as far as the eye could reach. There were only a few milch cows in the corrals, for the cattle had not yet been brought down from the summer pastures.

Two or three buckaroos ate supper with us at the family table. Their faces were lean and weathered, with clean-cut jaws and piercing eyes that habitually squinted, as though peering into the distance. They wore spurs on their high-heeled boots and smoked cigarettes, which they made by rolling Bull Durham tobacco in brown cigarette papers and sealing them with a practiced lick of the tongue.

✺ *INDIANS IN THE OLD DAYS* ✺
A CAMPOODIE

I BOARDED AND WENT TO SCHOOL AT the Inyo Academy. We had splendid teachers. With gentleness and understanding they created harmony among that strange gathering of boys and girls, sons and daughters of cattlemen, of ranchers, of miners, of saloon-keepers, of county officers in a county whose area was twice that of New Jersey, and where, on election day, men traveled scores of miles to the polls.

There were pupils who were grown men. Most of their lives had been spent in the saddle or herding sheep. The spurs of their high-heeled boots clicked on the schoolroom floor.

Girls came with long riding skirts pinned over their dresses. They undid their skirts and left them on the pommel of their side saddles, which they cinched and uncinched themselves. Boys and girls from other towns, from Round Valley, Big Pine, Independence, Lone Pine, boarded in the Academy. Grace, my roommate, was the niece of a rancher and cattleman.

My father was away much of the time on surveying trips. He traveled in a buckboard, carrying transit and chains, picking up surveying crews where he might.

For Thanksgiving I went with Jessie, one of the girls who boarded at the Academy, to her home in Round Valley. Her family came from eastern Canada, across the St. Lawrence River, from Madrid, N. Y., to Sonora. They heard that in Inyo County the corn grew twice as high as a tall man and the pumpkins and squash were so large that men mistook them for sorrel horses lying down in the field. They decided to come and buy a farm.

They were the only people in that valley of ranchers that I ever heard talk about a farm. Their house was so like Grandmother's in New York State that it seemed a bit of the East set down in a fertile valley with high peaks all around. There were prim flower beds and eastern-looking barns and granaries and an orchard. There were four-poster beds in the house and old bureaus and cupboards that had been shipped around the Horn and brought over the mountains by ox-team from Sonora. There were potted plants that had to be wrapped up at night in the winter time.

Jessie's father had kind, blue eyes, and a white, neatly clipped beard. His wife's name was Zipporah. She wore starched percale dresses and her hair was frizzed on her forehead. We sat around the fire visiting that night and ate apples and pine nuts. They were smooth, brown nuts with a meaty kernel and a very different flavor from the butternuts and beechnuts we used to eat during the long winter evenings at Grandmother's. Jessie's father said that the Indians gathered them from the piñon trees in the mountains. I told him about the Indians who came in the winter to Grandmother's, in New York, and that I had a pair of moccasins, embroidered with beads, that she bought for me.

He said that those were the Huron Indians that came from the Great Lakes. The Indians living in Owen's Valley were the Paiutes. They were not so tall and fine-looking as the Hurons, but the bucks understood irrigating better than the white men and the mahalas were faithful, good servants.

Then, while we munched pine nuts, Jessie's father talked of the old days. He told how, before the white men came, the Indians snared rabbits and speared fish and gathered seeds from weeds that grew on the desert, and fat, juicy worms that they called *pe-ag-ge* from the pine trees. They made meal from pine nuts and dug taboose for its potato-like root. They feasted or starved, according to nature's moods. A few prospectors came and went through the valley, but the Indians were undisturbed until the stockmen arrived with their herds of cattle. At first the Indians tried to barter and collect tribute. This was refused and they began to forage on the herds when their food supply ran low.

Then came a hard winter. The Indians had little to eat and the cattle of the white men were a sore temptation. One day a buckaroo shot an Indian who was driving a fat steer from the herd he was watching. The Indians retaliated by killing a white man. That was the beginning of the Indian War.

Soldiers came to Fort Independence, but it was a long way from the widely scattered settlements, sixty-five miles from the house where we were sitting to the Fort. Roads were little more than trails. The only way of summoning help was by riders on horseback, who might be the target for Indian arrows and never reach the Fort.

One of the most thrilling stories I heard that night was about a party that camped at Owensville on their way through the valley from Sonora to Visalia. There were two women, a child and three men, one of them a Negro. One of the men and the women and child rode in a wagon. The other white man and the Negro were mounted on saddle animals, driving a band of horses.

The next day, as they traveled south toward Fort Independence, they saw signal fires burning on the hills. They realized their danger and left the road to ford the river and try to escape. The wagon mired in the mud in the bottom of the stream and the horses hitched to it broke loose.

By that time Indians had gathered on the bank and arrows were flying all around them. The Negro insisted that they take his saddle horse and he would lasso another. The white men took the women and child on the two horses and charged the band of Indians, with arrows whistling through the air on all sides. They escaped to the Fort. The last they saw of Negro Charley, he was running and fighting. They learned afterwards that he was taken up one of the canyons and tortured to death, which meant tying him up with willows and building a fire under him.

The settlers named a hill near which this occurred, Charley's Butte, in memory of his unselfish bravery.

Jessie's father said the Paiutes were never warriors, like the Apaches, who lived to the south, but they kept the whole valley in constant dread of their raids on isolated homes and travelers. They obtained guns from some source and, with these and their bows and arrows, hid in the Black Rocks and menaced all who traveled that way to Fort Independence. The settlers in Round Valley protected themselves, as best they could: burning the brush around their homes, moving hay so that their houses would not be set on fire by burning stacks, building corrals to protect their stock, cutting portholes in the walls of their cabins, and keeping bullets cast and their guns in order.

Zipporah told how the Indians sometimes acted like naughty children. She would be busy about her work and would be frightened dumb by a dark face appearing at her window, only to have the Indian plead, "Gimme biscuit!" They were very fond of hot biscuit, and when they obtained them might ride away without further trouble.

There were repeated encounters between the soldiers and Indians when the Indians, facing defeat, escaped into the canyons and hiding places they knew so well. Then one day the Indians killed an ox belonging to a white man and gathered for a great feast. When it was over they traveled to the south. Word was sent to Fort Independence and the soldiers and citizens who were near the Fort took up the trail and followed them. They learned that they were near the Indians when a bullet pierced the hat of one of their members.

A running fight followed, with the Indians being routed from one hiding place only to disappear in another, until finally they were driven into the open on the shore of Owen's Lake—the bitter, alkaline lake into which Owen's River flows at the southern end of the valley. There was only one way of escape. They plunged into the lake. There was a strong wind which beat them back as they tried to swim to a safe distance. A full moon rose over the mountains to the east. One by one, as its beams lighted the waters of the lake, a shot was fired and a head disappeared, until all the Indians were gone. The white men waited on the bank and counted the bodies that were washed ashore to make sure that none had escaped.

That was the last chapter in the war with the Paiutes. There were many of the tribe still left in the valley, but the story of what had happened at Owen's Lake made them "heap good Indians" from that time on.

It was difficult for me to picture a time when the women of Round Valley, which seemed so safe and sheltered, had lived in constant fear of their lives and the safety of their children, and when the gentle, soft-voiced Indians who worked in the fields and homes had fought to preserve this land for their own. But the fact that they were "heap good Indians" now did not keep me from dreaming of brown faces at the window and smelling burning haystacks as I lay in the warm embrace of a soft feather bed that night.

We had quail on toast for breakfast and roast duck and venison for Thanksgiving dinner. There was wild currant jam and ground cherry preserve. All the food held new and delicious flavors for me.

After dinner we visited an Indian campoodie. Along the trail we saw Indian women with burden baskets on their backs, going about gathering seeds by beating the pods of sand grass and weeds with a scoop-shaped basket held in the right hand. In the left hand was another cone-shaped basket into which the seeds fell. When this was filled, it was emptied into the burden basket.

The willow wickiups of the campoodie squatted in the sand and sage-brush of the foothills as though they had always been there. Children played about with only one shirt-like garment to cover their nakedness, all well enough when they stood up, but quite inadequate otherwise.

Old men, too feeble to leave camp, sunned themselves in sheltered places, and old women, whose eyes were blinded from camp fire smoke and weaving of fine baskets, sat on the sand with patiently folded hands.

Younger women, mothers of the children, were cooking on stoves set up out of doors or over camp fires; others sat at the openings in their wickiups preparing willows for weaving. Their hands were as brown as the willow bark, and small and shapely. They stripped the bark with their finger nails and scraped the willow stem with a piece of obsidian until they had the strands for weaving and the sticks for the foundation of the basket. They wove bowl-shaped cooking baskets, cone-shaped burden baskets and seed gathering baskets. A mahala invited us into her wickiup to see her treasure baskets. I stooped through the low door and entered semi-darkness. The room was so low I could not stand up until I got to the center. The inside walls were the same as the outside, willows and brush interwoven. There were two or three "store comforters" and a rabbit skin blanket thrown on the sand and a few old clothes scattered around.

The Indian woman took down a flour sack that was tied to the wall. She undid it and drew out a basket, so fine and symmetrical that it did not seem possible it had been woven from coarse willow twigs. Around the basket, woven in red and black, ran a diamond-shaped design, like the pattern on the back of a rattle-snake. The mahala explained: "I make 'em this basket—rattle-snake no bite 'em my man—my papoose." She showed us other fine baskets with zig-zag designs that meant running water or mountains and valleys, and quail top-knots that showed there were plenty of quail by the streams in the mountains and valleys.

It was a real delight to hold the baskets and run our

hands over the smooth, perfectly rounded surfaces. Jessie's father told us that the Paiutes traded with the Mono Indians and the Shoshones from Nevada, and the Tulare Indians from the other side of the Sierras for maidenhair fern and redbud bark, and dug roots for the colors with which to weave the patterns. I thought of the quilting patterns that Mama had done so beautifully. It seemed to me these Indian women traded with each other for the materials for their treasure baskets much as the women in northern New York exchanged pieces for their quilts. They exhibited them with the same pride that the New England women did their handiwork.

The treasure baskets held fine arrowheads, wampum, worn smooth by much handling, and deep collars and wide belts of intricate bead work. They told the story of the tribe, just as the New England quilts told a story of women who had worn dresses of the bright colored prints and quilted patterns that gave expression to their quest for beauty.

When we came out of the wickiup the mahalas whom we had seen on the trails had returned to the campoodie and were winnowing the grain they had gathered. They tossed the seeds up from flat baskets and the wind caught the chaff and carried it away to ride like shining arrows on the rays of the setting sun. Other mahalas were preparing supper. The men of the camp arrived on horses or driving rickety buckboards and decrepit wagons.

There was one interesting example in the valley of an Indian who had suffered life-long punishment from the Paiute tribe, because he had refused to betray the white friend of his boyhood.

Before the Indian War, a white man settled near a campoodie of Indians. A child was born in the white family. The mother died and the infant became ill, because there was no proper food for it. The father took it to the campoodie, and found a mahala who had a child of about the same age. The father made her understand that his child was ill and that he wanted her to take it and nurse it at her breast with her own. And so the Indian and white child became breast brothers, and as they grew older were close friends. The young Indian spent much of the time at the white boy's house, and they were inseparable.

Then war threatened. The white man, fearing the intimacy between his son and the Indians, sent the boy away. The Indians broke up their camp and went into the mountains. War began. So many of the tribe were killed that the young boys were forced to fight for their people, and the boy whose closest friend was a white boy was sent out to battle against the whites. He did not know that his friend had been sent away.

When they came near his old home and he realized that his friend might be killed by an arrow from his bow, he refused to fight, knowing that the penalty would be death. But perhaps because he was so young, or perhaps as a vent for their love of protracted torture, they condemned him, as a coward, to dress in women's clothes for the rest of his life. He never, apparently, tried to have the edict changed, but accepted his punishment stoically. He was known to Indians and whites alike as Mahala Jo.

Evening comes early in the mountain valleys. As soon as the sun drops behind the peaks the air becomes chilly. We hurried home, glad to be back where the cords of pine wood stood in neat rows in the yard. It was heavy with pitch and burned with a fragrant, constant heat. How I wished Aunt Mary might have a cord of that wood at her doorstep to use on nights when the wind howled and the flax-seed bundles smoked and sulked, or else roared up the stove pipe without throwing out any warmth.

Grace, my roommate, took me with her to spend the Christmas holidays on her Uncle's cattle ranch. There was a big ranch house with bunk houses for the cowboys and high corrals for the cattle. We watched the buckaroos herding the cattle that had roamed the range all summer and fall and were wild-eyed and excited from being driven so far. The cow-ponies knew as well as the cowboys what was to be done. If one of the frightened animals tried to break away from the bunch, they would turn on a space no larger than a man's hat and race after it.

The next day Grace rode with the men, helping to part out the fat steers that were to be driven over the desert and through the mountain passes to market. She was a slight, auburn-haired sprite, but she was as secure in her side saddle as the men were astride their mounts. She taught me to ride. I clutched the horn of the saddle and gritted my teeth and felt a great thrill when I was able to sit on a horse at a gallop; he was the gentlest horse they had.

There was a Chinese cook at the ranch house. I

had never seen a Chinaman before, and his shuffling slippers, his long, white smock, and his pig-tail intrigued me greatly. He was much concerned for the comfort of his "Missie" (Grace's lovely, white-haired mother) and the "Bossie man," her uncle. He showered Grace and me with gifts, silk embroidered handkerchiefs, peacock feather fans. A Chinese lily blossomed in the sitting room of the ranch house, and there was a great fireplace where pine logs crackled and sent roaring flames up the chimney.

The air was cold and crisp. Clouds gathered on the mountains and spread a snowy mantle over the peaks. But there were few days when the sun did not shine in the valley. A beautiful fir, with snow still clinging to its spreading branches, was put up in the sitting room. Grace and I decorated it. I knew for the first time the joy of a Christmas tree.

My father bought me a patent rocking-chair for Christmas, and it was in our room when we went back to the Academy. I rocked and read, and rocked and knitted, and rocked and studied, until Grace would get so nervous she would throw books at me. I was a trial to Grace in many ways. She was a nervous, high-strung creature, and little things annoyed her. She disliked apples, especially the odor, and it seemed as if I was always munching one. I suppose Grace, too, had irritating ways, but I was fat and comfortable, not a bundle of nerves as she was; and I was as oblivious of small irritations as an Indian. I adored her. Frances, tall, slender, willowy, Grace, tiny, tense and fairy-like, and Nellie, stout, round and rosy, were always together.

Jessie, older and more sedate, was "keeping company" with some "fellow." Her room was always in perfect order. Her fat feather bed was plump and smooth as a pincushion. It was great fun to dash and land plop in the middle of that feather bed.

Already the prairie was being blotted from my memory, losing its outlines in the bigness of this new country and the excitement of new friendships. Fred's love-making seemed only a pleasant, star-lit dream. Uncle John's face was growing indistinct. But Aunt Mary was just as vivid to me as ever. I planned that some day, somehow, I would bring her to visit me in this lovely valley.

A letter came from Uncle John. Aunt Mary was dead. She had passed away with an attack of asthma. I couldn't believe it! I read the letter over. The prairie lived again: the blizzards, the prairie fires, the cyclones, and through them all Aunt Mary's face, a shining benediction. I wrote to Uncle John and told him how sorry I was. I tried to express something of the love I had for Aunt Mary, hoping it might help him to bear his loss.

I wrote Fred the nearest approach to a love letter I had ever attempted. I even thought I would be willing to go back to the prairie and make a home for him for Aunt Mary's sake. But Fred answered that he was "going with" the new school teacher. She was a girl from Sioux Falls. He thought they might get married, now that he and Uncle John were left alone.

Dakota, which was a territory then, has since become

two of the great farming states of the Union. Tractors till the soil that dulled the shares of the breaking plows. Great harvesters reap and bind and thresh the grain that covers the plains where wild roses and prairie grass grew.

Aunt Mary became a cherished memory, a symbol of the great-hearted women who were the home makers of the prairie.

🕸 FATHER BREAKS THE NEWS 🕸

SPRING CAME, BRINGING BANDS OF SHEEP from Bakersfield and Southern California to the mountain meadows. They feasted as they traveled across the desert, now green with young, tender bunch grass. The fires of the sheep camps glowed in the foothills all around us. The tinkle of bells mingled with the faint bleating of the lambs. Patient Basque shepherds followed the flocks, and when they made camp in the evening there was a smell of garlic in mutton stew, and they sang as they drank their red wine, and rested from the day's herding. Faithful sheep-dogs kept the flocks from wandering, and drove away wild animals, hungry for a taste of young mutton. Burros, freed from their packs, browsed, drowsily.

Honey bees hovered over fields of clover and alfalfa, carrying their stores to hives buzzing with activity. The honey was clear and light in color, and delicate in flavor. Locust trees bloomed along country lanes, and their fragrance filled the air. Frail blossoms carpeted the desert, as if by magic, and their cups held poignant sweetness. Quail called, "Cuicado! Cuicado!" from willow thickets. Wild duck and geese flew north.

An evangelist came to town. He preached in the Masonic Hall. It was a great event. Cowboys, ranchers, Indians, mingled with the town's people in the audience. Frances, Grace, and I went every night. The preacher exhorted us to repent and be saved. He had a fine bass voice and he led us in singing, "Whiter Than Snow" and "Are You Washed in the Blood, In the Soul-cleansing Blood of the Lamb."

He was a big, blond man, with a compelling personality. Grace was convicted of sin, and went forward to the mourners' bench. I was greatly moved. I felt that I, too, should go forward and join her there. I was convicted of sin, remembering Aunt Sade's letter that I had never answered. The words of the Episcopal Litany, that I had so often heard Mama repeat, ran through my mind: "We have done those things which we ought not to have done, and we have left undone those things that we ought to have done, and there is no health in us." There was no help for me. I couldn't write to Aunt Sade. I didn't know where to send the letter.

Grace was in a beatific state. Having no sins to be forgiven, she was subject to no internal struggles. She asked me to rock and eat all the apples I wanted to. She longed to try her new-fledged wings. Grace wanted to be taken into the church, but her mother objected. She said that Grace's conversion was an emotional outburst; that we were none of us old enough to know what it really meant to join the church. And so Grace was taken in on probation.

I began to realize how alone I was. Grace could talk to her mother, and tell her all about the things she felt in her heart, and her mother sympathized with her and helped her. Frances had her mother. I had no one but Grandmother and Mama and Aunt Mary. It helped to pour out my heart to them in prayers, but they brought me no solution for present difficulties.

I could not overcome the feeling that my father was a stranger to me. I tried to recover the love for him that Mama had kept alive in my heart as long as she lived, but the wall of years of separation between was higher than I could scale. I began to resent the fact that he had left us all that time to fight the world alone.

My father comprehended nothing of this. He was glad to have me with him. His pride in me was a possessive pride. It was not the unselfish love that I had felt encircling me when Mama and Grandmother and Aunt Mary were alive. He wanted me to be with him; to learn to do all the things in which he found pleasure. The first of May came, and he arranged that we should go together on a fishing trip into the mountains. If only Frances and Grace could have gone along I would have been overjoyed, but I felt lonely going with this strange man, my father.

We had two saddle horses and a pack mule to carry our food and blankets. We took the trail that followed the willow-bordered stream into the canyon. Never had I seen such crystal-clear water. It came dashing joyously down between rocky banks to rest in quiet sunlit pools, and then flowed merrily on as though rejoicing in its freedom.

My father cast a fly on the surface of one of the pools. There was a flash of silver in the water and he landed a trout, silver-scaled, with a rainbow of color along its side. He gave me the pole and taught me how to cast. I did it awkwardly and the hook caught on a log. He replaced the broken hook and I tried again. I saw a flash of silver and felt a tug on the line. My heart missed a beat. A kind of paralysis seized me. "Jerk the line!" My muscles responded involuntarily to my father's command. I knew the thrill that prompts the fisherman to whip the stream all day. I had landed my first trout. My father built a fire and fried bacon. Then he fried the fish in the grease. They curled in the pan. We had bread and bacon grease. The fish were sweet and delicious, their flesh firm and white.

The trail led up into the forests. Pine plumes waved over our heads. Firs spread their green, silver-tipped branches. Hemlocks stood like spent giants with drooping limbs. Our horses walked on soft beds of pine needles. My father knew all the trees. He taught me to distinguish the different varieties, the two-fingered, and three-fingered, and five-fingered pines, the spruce and the hemlock.

We made camp that night in a mountain meadow. The horses and mule were hobbled. My father cut fir boughs and spread blankets on them for our beds. He made bread with flour and baking powder and cold water from the stream, and put it in a long-handled frying pan, set upright with a forked stick, to bake. He left me to tend the fire while he went off for more trout. He soon came back with some, and while they were cooking he made coffee, adding condensed milk and an egg. We were hungry and the food was satisfying. I took off my high boots and crawled between the blankets of my bed. The fir boughs were soft and fragrant. The moon rose and shone through the pine trees.

And then it was morning. All my life I have wished that I were an artist and able to paint the beauty of a mountain meadow as I saw it that morning. The stream lingered here to play with the grasses that grew along its banks. Quaking aspens held the meadow in a close embrace, their leaves now silver, now green in the sunlight. Wild cyclamen wove an orchid-colored pattern of loveliness against the tender grass. Birds, like flashing sapphires, winged from sky to tree, from earth to sky, in an ecstasy of motion. Azure butterflies floated like fairies awakened on the soft breezes of spring.

My heart was filled to bursting with the loveliness of it all. I wanted to express my emotion to someone, wanted to tell my father how I was moved by the scene, but the wall was there. Almost I could reach over it, but not quite.

It was that morning that my father told me he was going to marry again. I suppose he caught my mood and felt it would be a good time to break the news to me. My face must have shown my feeling of shocked resentment. He made excuses; he wanted to settle down, wanted a home for me. The woman was a good cook, a neat housekeeper.

I did not hear what he was saying. I only heard Mama's oft repeated words, "Till Papa sends for us," and saw her tired face. I stood there so deaf and dumb that I suppose he thought I was angry. He said he hoped I wasn't going to be foolish about it, that I was old enough to realize a man got tired of being foot-loose and wanted a home. I needed a stepmother to look after me and teach me how to cook and sew.

If he had even mentioned Mama, perhaps I could have talked with him, but he made no reference to her. He went on talking about when he would be married. He planned to bring a camp outfit and come here on their honeymoon. I could go with Grace and Frances to Long Valley for the summer.

The meadow danced before my eyes. The sun grew dark. My face must have been white. My father made me sit down on my bed. He said, "You nearly fainted. I should not have made you wait so long for your breakfast." I lay down on the couch of fragrant fir boughs. I could not look at the meadow any more. I had been so happy there. I had almost found Papa. But I was alone again, alone with that strange man, my father.

Breakfast had no flavor, but I choked it down. We broke camp. My father taught me to put the saddle on my horse and draw the cinch tight. We fished on the way home. I caught another trout. When I felt the tug on my line, I forgot everything for an instant, but when I had landed it my heart was just as heavy. It seemed to me that if my father had kept Mama's memory I could have forgiven him everything, but the gesture of putting another woman in her rightful place seemed the cruelest of all the cruel things he had done to her.

I was glad to go back to the Academy, to Frances and Grace, the only friends I knew. I told them my father was going to be married. I sobbed unrestrainedly. It was a relief. I told them about Mama, and how we had waited so long for Papa to send for us before she died. I did not tell them that she had committed suicide. Now that Grace was converted, I thought that she would feel as the preacher had about it; that Mama had sinned in the face of God.

And I knew that Bridgeport seemed a long way off. Frances had been born in the valley. She had never been away from it, and just as the valley was held in sunlight and sheltered from the storms by the mountains, I knew that Frances had lived in the sunlight of life, sheltered from the storms by her mother's tenderness and her father's protecting care. Although they loved me, it was not like the love of Grandmother or Mama or Aunt Mary. I knew I could not make them understand how I felt, and I did not try. They thought it was nice that my father was going to marry and I would have a home, and we could go back and forth and stay all night with each other.

Frances told her mother about it and her mother had her ask me to go home with her. It was a busy, happy place, and the duties were much the same as they had been in Grandmother's kitchen. There were pans of milk, covered with yellow cream. There was churning and baking, and frying of doughnuts. Frances' mother put me to work right away. She saw that I was never idle. She knew the healing power that lay in work. Before we went back to school, she put her arms around me and talked to me. She knew the woman my father was going to marry. She was a nice woman. She hoped I would try and love her and be happy there. She made me think of Aunt Mary. I was grateful to her for caring so much and trying to help me. I felt better.

The cattle were driven to the mountain valleys for the summer feed. The dust of their going lay along the roads. Anxious cows lowed to the calves that trotted at their sides, fearful of losing them in the herd. Steers bellowed, resenting the barbed-wire fences that held them from roaming over the fields. Buckaroos whooped "Ki-yi-yip-ee," and rode their ponies recklessly after frightened, straying animals.

The last days in school dragged. We, too, wanted to be away. We chafed at restraint. Most of the boys were gone, and we resented the fact that because we were girls we must stay at home. We were restive as a band of young heifers.

My father brought my future stepmother to see me. She was a small woman with a very homely face. The knuckles on her hands were enlarged and made them look clumsy. I was glad. I felt that anyone so plain as she was could never take the place of Mama in my father's affection.

They went to the county seat at Independence to be married. I was thankful that my father did not ask me to go.

☨ *COWBOYS & MOONLIGIIT* ☨ *"LET 'ER BUCK!"* ☨ *OLD CHARLEY*

SCHOOL WAS OUT. GRACE AND I RODE horseback to the mountains. Her mother rode in the cook wagon. The Chinaman was with the outfit, and he cooked our meals. We rode all day and camped at night. The next day we were on the way at dawn. We reached the top of a long, steep climb, just as the sun touched the peaks of the Sierras. Long Valley lay before us. It was another Acadian Grand Pré. The cattle grazed quietly, raising their heads to look at us in startled surprise as we came along the road. They were growing sleek and plump, and Grace's uncle said they would make as fine a bunch of beef cattle as he had ever seen.

The grazing lands held by him and Frances' father adjoined.

Grace and Frances and I stayed first at one ranch, then at the other. We were inseparable all that summer through days that were filled with excitement: horse-breaking, round-ups, branding, riding the trails that led off into the mountains.

The ranch houses were built of pine logs chinked

with adobe. There were wide porches. Heavy saddles
and silver-mounted bridles hung on wooden pegs on
the wall. There were corrals made of saplings, laid one
on top of the other and laced with raw-hide to posts
driven into the ground. They were higher than a man's
hand could reach. We were always on hand when unbroken horses were driven in off the range.

We watched them mill about, their heads high, their
eyes rolling, sensing some danger. A buckaroo rode a
saddle horse into the corral. He seemed not to be thinking about anything in particular. Suddenly a lasso
swung in his hand and cut through the air. The noose
settled over some proud head. He wound the rope
around the horn of his saddle. Then the battle was on.
The horse was led, rearing or plunging, or trembling,
to the spot outside the corral where a saddle lay in
readiness.

A blind was put over his eyes. Stealthily a saddle
blanket was slipped on his back. Then the saddle was
settled in place, very slowly and quietly. Carefully the
buckaroo brought up the cinch and tightened it. I have
never seen more infinite patience than that used by a
cowboy when saddling an animal for the first time.
Older, saddle-broken horses learned how to swell their
bellies to keep the cinch from being pulled too tight, but
these new victims knew no defense. The buckaroo put
the toe of his heavily spurred boot into the stirrup. He
swung himself lightly into the saddle. "Let 'er buck!"
There was the thrill of combat in his voice. The blinder
dropped. For an instant the animal stood still. Then
his head plunged downward, his back arched, his legs
stiffened, and he bucked and kicked and screamed in a

frenzied effort to free himself from the incubus that
threatened his freedom.

Spectators gathered. The harder the horse fought,
the greater the sport. Sometimes he was able to throw
his rider or make him pull leather. But more often he
was gradually worn down, cowed, beaten; then he was
spurred into a mad gallop over the meadows to come
home at night-fall, lathered in sweat, his head hanging
to the ground. He was broken to the saddle.

At first I couldn't bear the sight, and ran into the
farthest corner of the log house to get away. But the girls
followed me and made fun of me, and dragged me out to
see the next one—a gray "McBride" horse, the hardest
breed on the range to subdue. Grace was hugging herself with delight. This was to be her horse. Her uncle
had given him to her. He was a beauty. No other one
in the corrals held its head so proudly. He was roped
and saddled. The blinder was dropped. The rider
was thrown. The horse got away, but was lassoed and
brought back to ultimate defeat. I suddenly realized
that I was enjoying it. I was broken to the sight.

When evening came, the cowboys would sit on the
porch in the moonlight and tell stories of horses they had
broken and riders they had known, of cattle rustling,
of brands and earmarks. They sang. Strange, plaintive
songs that reminded me of the songs of the prairies. I
have never been able to understand why a bronco-bust-
ing, devil-may-care buckaroo would sing verse after
verse of the most pathetic songs and seem to find some
needed outlet in the singing.

There was one song that told the story of a heart-
broken cowboy and a letter gone astray:

> *" 'A letter nere for me?' was the question*
> *that he asked*
> *Of the mailman at the close of the day;*
> *Then he turned sadly with a sigh while*
> *a tear stood in his eye,*
> *And he jumped his horse and slowly*
> *rode away."*

These songs, like the old minstrel songs, were added to by each new singer.

I have counted fifteen verses of the "Cowboy's Lament." There were probably more.

> *"Let sixteen gamblers come handle my coffin,*
> *Let sixteen cowboys come sing me a song,*
> *Take me to the graveyard and lay the sod*
> *o'er me,*
> *For I'm a poor cowboy and I know I've*
> *done wrong.*

> *"We beat the drum slowly and played the*
> *fife lowly,*
> *And bitterly wept as we bore him along;*
> *For we all loved our comrade, so brave,*
> *young and handsome,*
> *We all loved our comrade although he'd*
> *done wrong."*

Cowboys were handsomer on their horses than they were on foot. Their legs were bowed and the heels of their boots were worn down on the outside. They drank their whiskey straight and they always respected a good woman. But flirtation was an accepted diversion. Each one of us had a favorite among them. Mine happened

to be Broncho Jim. He had a clean history of never having been thrown from a horse. His legs were as bowed as a barrel hoop, and he rolled like a sailor when he walked. His rein arm had been broken when he fell off a grub wagon and, through lack of proper attention, had knit crooked.

But in the saddle, he was a picture to stir any girl's heart. He had a fine saddle animal, which he dedicated to my exclusive use, and we rode together to the round-ups. Grace, on her tamed "McBride" gray, rode with her chosen cowboy, and all the buckaroos on all the ranches fought for Frances' attention. On a horse she was a cowboy's dream of Paradise.

One day when Grace and Frances and I were sitting on the long porch wondering what to do next, we heard a tinkle of bells and looked up the road to see two tired but determined-looking burros coming toward us. The kyaxes on their pack saddles bulged from their sides and rounded over their backs, so that we couldn't see the man who walked behind them until they suddenly stopped to grab a bite of the bunch grass that grew by the roadside. Then Old Charley appeared.

As soon as I saw him I thought of a pine tree, standing on some ridge. I had seen them with their trunks bare and curved to the prevailing wind, and with all their branches reaching to the storm-sheltered valley below. Old Charley's frame was bent the same way. His arms were long and his hands big and gnarled looking, and as much of his face as could be seen above his long, sparse beard was burned and wrinkled like the red lava wash on the side of a crater. His blue eyes shone from that setting with the same startling contrast as a blue mountain lake set in an old crater bed. His nose was hooked and pushed to one side, as if he had run into something in a blinding storm. His eyes mirrored the kindliest possible smile, as he indulgently left the burros to enjoy the sweet, juicy bunch grass and came to sit down on the edge of the porch and talk to us.

"You see," he said, "them two jinneys are just like human wimmen folks. They'll go along, patient an' willin' an' lovin' for months and then all at once they'll git their heads turned by some durned bit of bunch grass along the road an' all you can do is stop an' wait 'til they eat their fill, an' then drench 'em if they git the bloat.

"I'm headin' for Pine City," he said in answer to our questions. "Used to mine there when the boom was on. When it petered out I took Jinny and Joan and started travelin'. We've been a lot o' places: Idaho and Montanny and back through Nevada and down South, lookin' for the old Peg Leg, and then I thought we'd take a run at the placer diggin's. I was around Placer County an' the Feather River country. But I'm a rock man. Washin' sand don't interest me. I'm gettin' along, an' all the time I was travelin' round I kep' thinkin' of Old Pine City an' Lake Mary. I hain't seen as purty a place anywhere as that is.

"I know there ain't nobody there any more, but there's some old cabins an' I can always take out enough rock to keep me in beans an' bacon, an' there's plenty of grass in the meadows for Jinny an' Joan. I've decided to go back there an' build me a little arastra an' work those old tunnels an' settle down to rest an' ruminate."

Grace and I evidently jumped at the same conclusion at the same time. We looked at each other and Grace nodded her head in the direction of the kitchen, and disappeared. She soon returned and invited our porch visitor to camp by the cabin for the night and have supper with the family and buckaroos at the long table in the ranch house.

"I'm mighty obliged to ye," Old Charley said. "Ye see, that just lets Jinny an' Joan think I decided to stay of my own accord. Otherwise I'd uv been kinda' obliged to urge 'em along an' we'd uv had one of them kind uv days a man an' his wife has when they're barely on speakin' terms an' wish they wasn't."

He unloaded the shovel and pick and gold pans and the loaded kyaxes from Jinny and Joan. "I always pack my choosiest things on Joan," he explained; "Joan's the steady one. She's as sure-footed as a mountain goat. She never turned a pack saddle under her belly in her life. No matter how ornery she may get, she always carries her pack straight."

While we all sat on the porch that night and joined in singing the cowboy songs, Old Charley volunteered, "I know a song they sing around the Feather River country. How about a miner's song for a change?"

His voice quavered on the high notes, but he sang the song to the tune of "A Life on the Ocean Wave." *

> *A life by the cabin fire,*
> *A home in the northern mine,*
> *We'll make a pile and retire,*
> *Won't that be charming fine;*

* Printed by request in *Overland Monthly*, June, 1892.

We'll roam the Sierra Nevadas
And kill the grizzly bear
And send the fur back to the ladies
For overcoats how it will wear.

··We built us a cabin so fine,
And got grub to last us a while,
Commenced in the morning to mine,
But at night fell short of a pile.
We soon had a row in the camp,
For no one was willing to cook,
We kicked out a miserable scamp
And we did it as neat as a book.
The doctor would give us advice
And the lawyer would argue the point,
But we couldn't get rid of our lice
No matter how often we'd oint.

We hung on a kettle of beans
The diet we miners admire,
'Twas the last of the grub, and our means,
And they tipped over into the fire.
So then we divided the tools
And each took a different route
Concluded we'd acted like fools,
But none of us died of the gout.

The doctor and lawyer combined
And 'twas agreed the doctor should kill
And the lawyer came on behind
To collect the exorbitant bill.

The preacher could not make a pile
For the gospel he came out to preach;
He fiddled and grumbled a while
But money kept out of his reach.

The cabin's no longer in sight
That stood on the western slope,
We left it for nothing but spite,
For that was our only hope.
The rest of the party went home
Disgusted with what they had seen,
While I was left behind to roam,
Oh, wasn't I wonderful green.

That night Old Charley threw down his blankets, took off his boots and crawled in. He let the burros roam. We asked him if he was not afraid they would stray away.

"I got them burros hog-tied," he said. "I always give 'em a lump o' sugar at sun-up, an' they never fail to be there. I sometimes think some husbands might take an old miner's suggestion an' hand out a lump o' sugar every day. Wimmen won't stray too far, even after bunch grass, if you'll just remember to give 'em a lump o' sugar every day."

When Old Charley got packed up the next morning and started off, he urged, "Now you girls ride up to Pine City some day in a couple o' weeks an' I'll show you how to run an arastra."

After he was gone, Grace and Frances and I went to join the buckaroos at the round-up. I have never taken part in any sport as exciting as parting out the cattle—

separating the calves from their mothers at branding time. We would ride quietly to the edge of the band. Then, at a signal, two by two, we spurred our horses and dashed into the herd. The horses knew as well as we did what was to be done, and eagerly entered into the game. Side by side we rode down a bewildered calf, our horses dodging in and out among the other stock, until finally we had the creature clear of the herd and raced it triumphantly to the branding place, where a fire kept the branding irons hot.

Then came one of the cowboy's favorite pastimes: roping and throwing and branding. It took skill to single out a calf from the milling bunch and unerringly throw a rope over its tossing horns. The animal was thrown, branded with the triangle *R*, or the cross-bar *X*. If it was the triangle *R*, they were dulaped; if it was the cross-bar *X*, their ears were slit—the dulap and ear marks for long-distance recognition, and the brands for closer inspection.

PINE CITY, *A GHOST TOWN*
AN OLD MINER'S TALE

WHEN THE TWO WEEKS WERE UP, Frances and Grace and I went to see Old Charley. We rode across the flat meadowland and then began to climb an old mining road that wound up through manzanita, with its flat, green leaves shining against the smooth red bark of the strangely sprawling bush, to higher levels of young pine and fir groves. Pine City lay still higher. The country grew more rough and huge boulders were across the wagon road that had once led to the camp. But there were always trails that wound around the fallen trees or rock slides back to the road.

We came to a rise that looked out over a flat basin at the foot of high peaks where the snow lay in great glistening drifts. Through the pines and firs and spruce trees we saw the sparkling blue waters of Lake Mary. For the first time that piece which I had learned from the old *National Fifth Reader* in the little country school at Madrid, meant something to me:

Girt round by rugged mountains the fair Lake
  Constance lies
In her blue heart reflected shine back the starry
  skies,
And watching each white cloudlet float silently
  and slow
You think a piece of heaven lies on our earth
  below.

All along the neglected road there were old log cabins, some with the roofs caved in and meadow grass growing around them as though no paths had ever led to their doors. In a grove of firs we saw a well preserved cabin, and there were evidences about the place that Old Charley had taken up his abode there.

It was the prettiest spot imaginable. Wild roses blossomed on bushes that grew behind the cabin where the sandy hillside started up from the meadow. There were red columbine along a stream that gurgled by. Pine birds, deep blue as a shadowed mountain lake, flew from tamarack to fir and pine trees. A striped-backed chipmunk on a flat rock in front of the cabin door sat on his hind legs, nibbling something that he held in his tiny paws.

We heard a clatter of loose rocks and looked up. Jinny and Joan, with Old Charley behind them, were coming down a trail that led from the mouth of a tunnel high up on the mountain side.

We rode across the meadow to meet them. Old Charley seemed happy and Jinny and Joan were sleek and fat and had lost that determined look. Their kyaxes were filled to bulging with rock. They were on the way to the arastra, and we went along. Old Charley had dug a round pit, deep enough so that the top came to my waist when I stood in it, and twice as far across as I could reach.

The bottom was of large, flat rocks and Old Charley showed us how he had left big cracks between and filled them in so that they were still below the surface of the rocks. He poured quicksilver into these cracks. Then he emptied the kyaxes into the pit. He hitched Jinny and Joan to the tamarack sweep from which other flat rocks were suspended, so that the ore would be ground between them and the rocks on the bottom of the pit. He turned in a stream of water that he had brought from the creek which ran near the cabin, and started Jinny and Joan pulling the sweep around and around the pit. There was a great commotion as rock attacked rock, and Old Charley said the quartz would be ground to powder and the gold would be grabbed by the quick‹ silver that lay in the cracks, to form amalgam. A stream began to flow from a pipe on the down hillside to a muddy mass that Old Charley said was the tailings pond.

We left Jinny and Joan plodding round and round the circle, as though they had never dreamed of bunch grass. Old Charley told us where to find a wild strawberry patch, and said he would make a short cake and we would have a picnic. The berries were small and sweet and of a flavor unknown in cultivated berries. Years later in Paris I saw berries like them sold at exorbitant prices and remembered Old Charley and his strawberry patch in the mountains.

When we returned, there was a fire going in the ruins of an old fireplace where a cabin had once stood. Old Charley was making frying-pan bread, and trout that he had caught in Lake Mary that morning were sizzling over the fire. They were so fresh that they squirmed in the bacon grease in which he cooked them. We had a stump for a table and rocks for chairs. The frying-pan bread was cut through the middle and the mashed berries put between the crisp layers. Old Charley brought dishes and beans from his cabin. He said no miner's meal was complete without beans. That was the kind of picnic one never forgets!

While he ate, Old Charley told us of the time when Pine City had been a camp of ten thousand people. There had been Fourth of July celebrations on Lake Mary, and the flat that we saw covered with the new growth of pine and fir trees had been a clearing where there were cabins and stores and saloons and gambling houses.

Then we went to look at Old Charley's cabin. There was one room, built of logs, and a lean-to shed-kitchen.

A rough pine bedstead stood in one corner, and a wood box as big as the bed hugged the fireplace. There was a pine table with the top worn smooth and so soaked with bacon grease that it looked as if it had been rubbed with wax. There were shelves with mining supplies and a black kettle with a spout, which Old Charley said was a retort. The fireplace was wide enough to take great pine logs.

Old Charley said he had found everything in the cabin. The wood box was even filled with logs. It happened that the cabin stood in a sheltered spot where the weight of the snow had not been as great as in other places.

While Old Charley smoked his corn-cob pipe, he told us more about Pine City in the days when he was a young man.

"You know," he said, "folks shake the dust of a busted mining town like rats desert a sinking ship. They walk out an' leave everything, furniture and beds an' dishes on the table, maybe, like they had et an' run. I suppose that's the reason they got the name of 'ghost towns.'

"When the mines are running and freight teams hauling ore an' bullion out, it's easy enough to get in furniture an' fixin's, an' some of these cabins was done up real purty. Men had their families come an' the wimmen put paper on the walls an' lace curtains at the windows. An' then the mines closed down in the fall an' every one ran like scared coyotes to get out before the snows came.

"There was a fellow in camp that had been a kind of pardner of mine, off an' on, up around Feather River and over in Nevada in early days on the Comstock.

He'd got married an' brought his wife up to the camp at Pine City.

"We thought we had a lead in a tunnel that looked as though it might break into a pocket any time, an' we decided to hole in for the winter an' maybe do a little work if the snow wasn't too heavy, an' be here on the job when spring broke.

"He'd ought to have sent his wife out, but she was a purty thing an' they was terribly in love. She was young an' strong an' was all for stayin' an' spendin' the winter with us. We had one of the biggest storms I ever saw in these mountains an' before it stopped the snow was six feet on the level and drifted over the roofs of the cabins in lots of places. The nearest settlement was a hundred miles away an' there wasn't any way to get out except on snow-shoes.

"One day my pardner and I thought we'd go out an' kill some snow-shoe rabbits an' have some fresh meat. We were cleanin' our shot guns an' somehow a shell got jammed in my pardner's gun barrel, an' while he was tryin' to get it out the gun went off an' shot his wife.

"I've been through some bad times in rip-roarin' mining camps, but never anything like that. My pardner was beside himself. I was afraid to leave him alone a minute. We couldn't bury his wife. There was no place to dig a grave. All we could do was to make a hole in the snow an' keep her there till spring.

"He wouldn't go away an' leave her. At first he raved like a maniac. Then he took sick an' I had to nurse him an' keep drivin' new stakes in the snow that kept driftin', so as we could find her body in the spring before the coyotes did.

"My pardner got well after a while an' when the snow melted off on the flat down there we took his wife down an' buried her. She came from back East an' she had always dreamed of havin' a house with a picket fence around it, so nothin' would do but we must put a picket fence around her grave. It took us quite awhile to do it with the tools we had, but we did a good job. I was noticin' the other day, that fence is just as strong an' straight as 'twas when we put it there.

"My pardner an' I moved into another cabin and started workin' that tunnel in the spring, but all the deserted cabins, with the dishes on the tables an' maybe a baby's crib or a rag doll lyin' around, got on our nerves an' we left to find new diggin's."

Old Charley's story seemed to bring back the shades of all those people who had made the shores of Lake Mary echo to their voices. We felt as though he had forgotten us, but he reassured us with his kindly smile and continued:

"You know, I felt mighty bad at the time all this happened but I came to see that maybe it was for the best. That little woman was taken when she was soft an' warm an' care-free an' gay as a kitten, dreamin' of her little home with a picket fence.

"There's nothin' more forlorn than a woman in a minin' camp longin' for back home. The mountain peaks and the forests get to be walls holdin' 'em back an' keepin' 'em from gettin' where they want to go. They just can't see a view or a beautiful sunset for the Down East frame houses an' picket fences that get in their way.

"If you'll ride off the road a little way down on the flat you'll find that grave with the picket fence around it."

Old Charley put his pipe away.

"Now," he said, "I guess you'd like to hear about something more cheerful."

He took a flat canvas sack from a box in the corner.

"You know," he explained as he undid the buckskin string that tied the package, "I've seen a lot travelin' around an' I like to keep a record of things. Sometimes I get 'em out and look 'em over. It's like meetin' an' shakin' hands with old friends."

He laid the contents of the sack on the table. There were programs of celebrations on Lake Mary. There were poems and menus and stories of tragedies and comedies. There was a bill of fare from the Eldorado Hotel in Hangtown. Frances hunted around and found a stub of a pencil and some paper and copied it:

Soup

| *Bean $1.00* | *Oxtail (short) $1.50* |

Roast

Beef, Mexican (prime cut)	*$1.50*
Beef, Upalong	*$1.00*
Beef, Plain	*$1.00*
Beef, with one	
potato (fair size)	*$1.25*
Beef, tame, from	
the States	*$1.50*

Vegetables

Baked beans, plain	$ .75
Baked beans, greased	$1.00
Two potatoes (medium size)	.50
Two potatoes (peeled)	.75

Entrée

Sauerkraut	$1.00
Bacon, fried	$1.00
Bacon, stuffed	$1.50
Hash, low grade	.75
Hash, 18 carat	$1.00

Game

Codfish Balls, per pair	.75
Grizzly Roast	$1.00
Grizzly Fried	.75
Jack Rabbit (whole)	$1.00

Pastry

Rice Pudding (plain)	.75
Rice Pudding (with molasses)	$1.00
Rice Pudding (with Brandy Peaches)	$2.00
Square meal with dessert	$3.00

Payable in advance
Gold Scales on the end of the Bar

"I aint never seen the Palace Hotel in Frisco, but it's got to go some to beat the old Eldorado at Hangtown," Old Charley assured us. He handed us a poem that seemed to be miles long. "I suppose you've hearn tell of Bret Harte and how he was the poet of the miner," he said. "Well, he was all right, but he never did know the miners an' their real lingo like that fellow De Groot that used to write about 'em."

The verses were printed in the Golden City newspaper and at the top was the statement "The poem is very long and cannot all be printed here. We just give enough of it to serve as an illustration."

"Now," Old Charley volunteered, "you girls might like to take that poem home with you. I might talk for days and I couldn't picture how us old prospectors has traveled around as well as that poem does. But you be careful with it. That's next to Jinny an' Joan in my affections."

We had been so absorbed in what Old Charley was showing us that we had not realized that the sound of breaking rock and slushing water that came from the arastra had stopped. "Well," Old Charley explained, "Jinny an' Joan have just decided that they're through for today. I never argue it with them. When they're through, they're through an' that's all there is to it. But they always play fair an' get a lot done before they quit. Now I'll go up and turn them out on the meadow, an' you best be makin' tracks for home. But before you go, there's one piece of rock I want to show you. You never saw jewelry any purtier than that rock." He went back to the box in the corner and took out a tin coffee can.

When he undid the cotton wadding that held his treasure, I couldn't believe my eyes.

He held up a white nugget with wires of pure gold hanging from it. My thoughts flew back to Mama, when she took the nugget with its wires of gold from the Christmas package, back in Madrid. I remembered the White Rose perfume for her and the Jockey Club for me. My throat ached and my eyes filled with tears. I went outside to my horse quickly, so that the girls and Old Charley wouldn't notice.

On the way home we found the grave with the picket fence. It was covered with a soft pad of pine needles. The sun filtered through the trees and the air was filled with piney fragrance. It was very peaceful. Perhaps Old Charley was right.

Mama, too, might have lived to see her dream shattered.

✼ DR. DE GROOT'S POEM ✼

D URING THE SUMMER GRACE AND Frances and I had great fun committing Old Charley's poem, *The Colloquy of The Old Timers*,* to memory:

> *"Hello!" "Hello!" "Why, Jim!" "Why, Dan!"*
> *"Good Lord!" "I want to know!"*
> *"Well, well, old fell, give us your hand."*
> *"But, Jim, how does it go?"*

* First printed in the Golden City newspaper; reprinted, September, 1893, in the *Overland Monthly.*

    "Oh, sometimes gay and sometimes rough—
    And how's it go with you?"
    "Well, times jus' now's a little tough
    Up here in Idaho."

    "But where ye been, Jim, ever since
    We left the Stanislaw
    And pulled up stakes down there at Dent's
    Now eighteen years ago?"

    "Wal, since the time that we put out
    On that stampede with Stoney—
    Been mos' the time knockin' about
    Way down in Air-e-zony.

    Only been back a month or so
    And thought I'd take a tramp
    Through the old diggin's long with Jo,
    Who stops at Nigger Camp.

    Started from Alpha on our trip,
    And passed up the Divide,
    Through Tangle Leg and Let-Her-Rip,
    Red Dog and Whiskey Slide.

    Then after leaving thar we went
    Down by the Tail-Holt Mill,
    'Cross Green Horse Mountain to Snow Tent
    And up to Gouge-Eye Hill.

    From Gouge-Eye down to Esperance
    Slap Jack and Oro Fin;
    Through Dead Wood over to Last Chance,
    Root Hog and Lost Ravine.

From Petticoat to Shirt-Tail Flat
And on by Murderer's Bar
'Crost Bloody Run and through Wild Cat
To Poker and Lone Star.

From Angel's Camp down by Rawhide
We took a run one night
Through Chinese Roost and Satan's Pride
Across to Hell's Delight.

Then came along to Poverty,
Dead Broke and Battle Ridge,
By Hangtown, Poorman, and Lone Tree,
Garrote and Smash-up-Bridge.

Through Nip and Tuck and Old Bear Trap
Coon Hollow and Fair Play
Along by Scorpion and Fir Gap
Kanaka and El Ray.

We stopped one day at Never Sweat,
Another up at Ophir
Then moved our boots on to You Bet
And struck across by Gopher.

To Sucker near Grass Widow Bend
Where as 'twas getting late,
We brought our journey to an end
Down by the Devil's Gate."

"Well, Jim, you must uv seen a heap;
I'd like to make the rounds
As you have done, and take a peep
Through the old stamping grounds."

"Y-a-s, but I tell you what it is,
The times they ain't no more
In Californy as they was
'Way back in Fifty-four.

Hit's swarming with them Chinese rats,
Wots tuk the country, sure,
A race that lives on dogs and cats
Will make all mean or poor."

"But 'bout the girls and Schneider's frau
And Kate and Sal McGee?
I 'spose they've all got married now—
Leastwise they ought to be."

"Married? You can buck high on that
Some of them two, three times;
First fellows they just had to get—
They didn't have the dimes."

"Well! Well! Do tell! Is that the way
The gals is goin' on?
But how's the boys and Old Man Ray,
And Ike and Steve and John?

And whas become of Zaccheus Wade,
Who run the big mule train?"
"Wall, Zach he made his pile, they say,
And then went back to Maine.

And so did old Pop Ray and Steve
And Ike and Johnny Yates,—
All made a raise at least I b'lieve,
And went home to the States."

"And Slater, him that took the trip
With us to Yazoo Branch?"
"Wal, Slate he kind o' lost his grip
And settled on a ranch."

"And Jackass Jones that came about
With Whisky on the Bar?"
"Wal, Jackass, he too petered out
And went—I don't know whar."

"And tell me, where is Jerry Ring,
Who kept the Grizzly Bear
Jes' down forninst the Lobscouse Spring
And kilt the Greaser there?

That Greaser, Jesus, don't you know,
That stabbed Mike at the ball;
The time we had the fandango
At Blood and Thunder Hall?"

"Oh, Jerry didn't do no good,
Got crazy 'bout a woman
And tuck at last to drinkin' hard,
'Cause she got sort o' common.

Y-a-s was by nature low inclined
And went clean to the bad
Which worked so on to Jerry's mind
Hit almost made him mad.

Dick went one day up Pike Divide
And there lay Jerry, dead,
A navy pistol by his side,—
A bullet through his head."

"Tight papers, them, on Jerry Ring,
But, Jim, as sure as you live
Them women is a dreadful thing
For a man to have to do with.

But Plug Hat Smith that kept a stand
Sold pens and ink and sich?"
"Wal, Plug he helt a poorish hand
And never struck it rich.

Got sort o' loony and stage-struck,
Cut up a heap o' capers
And final went below and tuck
To writin' for the papers."

"And Jolly Jake that drove so long
There on the Lightnin' Line
And afterwards from One-Horse Town
To Webfoot and Port Wine?"

"Got hurt on Bogus Thunder Hill—
Throwed on his horses' necks,
Was carried up to Coyoteville
And there hant in his checks.

'Twas kind o' queer, but these, they said,
War the last words of Jake,
'Wal, boys, I'm on the down hill grade
And cannot reach the break.'"

"And Butcher Brown that used to boast
He'd killed so many men?"
"Ah, Butch, he met his match at last,
Van Sickle settled him."

"But, Dan, how has it been with you,
Off on some wild goose chase?"
"Yes, too, a trip to Carribo
And over on the Peace.

Stayed there three years and then turned South,
Came back to Camp McPhail,
And soon on down to Quesuelle Mouth
And 'cross the La Hache Trail.

To Kamloops and Okinagane
And through the Grand Coulé,
By way of the Samilkameen
Clean round to Kootenai.

Stopped till I made a raise again
Then started out anew
And striking 'cross for Coeur d'Alène
Came on to Idaho.

I'd a close call at Tête l'June
In May of fifty-seven,
A little more and there'd have been
Another saint in heaven.

A half-breed Brule, a vicious set,
There—with a fishing spear—
The broken point is in me yet
The scar—you see it here.

A well aimed shot from Johnny Lune
And at a single bound
That savage passed from Tête l'June
To the happy hunting ground."

"*Well, Dan, you've been about some, too,*
But tell me if you know
What has become of Ned McGrew
And whar is Sleepy Joe?

And Poker Pete and Monte Bill
And—I forget his name—
What used to run the whisky mill
And keep the keno game?"

"*Well, as for Ned, can't 'zactly say*
But 'bout the t'other three
The last we heard, were up this way
A hanging on a tree,—

Went into the Road Agency
Along with Texas Jim,
The Vigilants of Montanny
Likewise also got him.

Sleepy was drowned at Upper Dalles
And so was Al LaTour—
Went in a skiff over the falls
And we didn't see 'em no more.

Some think that Ned was eat by bears,
And I must think so, too,
'Cause didn't one gobble up Nick McNairs
On the trail to Carribo?

Cold up North! I've known a name
To congeal in my mouth
And that is how the saying came
About the frozen truth.

Yes, and I've seen still stranger feats;
You know, Jim, I'm no liar;
The flames freeze into solid sheets
As they rose up from the fire."

"Sure, that's right cold, but tell me, Dan,
How goes the mining game,
And what's the chance here for a man
To strike a paying claim?"

"Well, jest 'bout here it's rather slim,
But I've got one that pays,
So pitch right in here with me, Jim,
And when we've made a raise

We'll put off North with a good rig,
For yesterday I seen
Gus Gape who said they's struck it big
High up on the Stickeen.

Or, if you rather like the South,
Why then it's South we'll go,
The only drawback is the drouth,
Down that ar way, you know."

The next we hear of Dan and Jim
May be on the Yukon
Or in the forests damp and dim
That shade the Amazon;

Or, what's more likely still, we shall
Hear of them on their way
To the diamond fields beyond the Vaal
In Southern Africa.

And if there be no mines up there
For them to prospect, then,
They'll surely leave the heavenly shore
For the Pacific Coast again.

𝕏 *AN INDIAN FANDANGO* 𝕏
STEPMOTHER 𝕏 *MY*
CAREER

THE FROST CAME EARLY IN LONG VALLEY. The cottonwood trees looked like an army marching down the canyons with shields of burnished copper. The call of the cock quail, *cui-ca-do, cui-ca-do,* had an anxious note. Wild duck and geese, flying in wedge formation, were dark shadows against the sky and their honking echoed in the early morning stillness.

The Indians gathered for the pine nut harvest. We saw them arriving: loudly protesting wagons that carried the old men and women, young bucks on ponies that shot by like an arrow, fat mahalas with their papooses on their backs and their voluminous skirts bunched around them, astride patient, raw-boned horses. The father of the family rode ahead with the rest of the children mounted before or behind him. They brought burden baskets and cooking baskets and winnowing baskets. Tall, erect Shoshones and fat Washoes came from Nevada; short, well-fed Indians from Tulare journeyed through the passes of the Sierras.

We rode out and watched them knocking the cones from the piñon trees, heaping them over a slow fire, covering them over with dirt, so that the pitch would be burned away, and beating them to release the smooth brown nuts.

Then, one moonlight night when the harvest was over, we took the trail to the camp to watch the Indian fandango. We came to a large, circular enclosure built of sage and rabbit brush, on the bank of Hot Creek. Outside this rude corral were the wagons and stock; inside the Indians feasted, danced, mourned, gambled, slept. They were preparing to feast when we arrived and there were many family camp fires around the inside of the enclosure.

The odor of burning sagebrush and barbecued meat mingled with the fragrance of the pine nuts which the old women roasted by dropping hot coals into cooking baskets filled with nuts and keeping them in constant motion. There was deer meat and butcher meat (young, fat steer), sage hen and quail and fish, with gray looking acorn mush in bowl-shaped baskets.

Children frolicked with dogs, or clung to their mother's skirts, their chubby faces and big, brown eyes glowing with merriment under the thatch of straight, black hair. And those were skirts to cling to! Yards of bright red or yellow or sky-blue figured calico, gathered to the waist above wide hips. Many of the women were barefooted, but they all wore beautifully patterned, cape-like collars of bead work hung from a band fastened around their necks. The lining of the collar band might be unbleached muslin and the buttons that fastened it, those salvaged from cast-off underwear of the whites, but the bead work was inconceivably fine and intricate.

When the feast was over, shy young squaws, whose faces were painted in the marriage pattern, and Indian wooers in overalls, gay shirts and red bandanas drifted toward the center of the enclosure. Soon two circles were formed, the squaws joining hands to make the inner one, the young bucks in the outer one.

Then both circles began to move with a sidewise shuffling of feet, around and around, interminably, while they chanted: *"Ah-te-me-ne-es-go-in-e-wah in-e-wah in-e-wah in-e-wah,"* breaking forth occasionally into what seemed to be an invocation: *"Ai-hi-u-y-nah! Ai-hi-u-y-nah!"*

The children crawled between blankets and slept. In one corner of the camp old women, their faces blackened with pine pitch, squatted in a circle, throwing ashes over themselves, rocking back and forth and wailing for the spirits who had passed to the happy hunting grounds since the last gathering of the tribes. In another part of the camp men gambled, shaking sticks between their palms and throwing them into a flat placque-like basket placed on the ground between them.

Older men and women joined the circle of dancers until it grew wider and wider. They invited us to dance with them, and Grace and Frances and I shuffled and sang with the rest. There was something hypnotic about that ceaseless shuffling of feet and that rhythmic repetition of strange syllables that made us want to go on and on.

But it was time for the war dance. Indian men who looked wise and old as the desert appeared. They were dressed in buckskin garments embroidered with beads and wampum. Their head-dresses were of eagles' feathers, and each one carried a quiver of arrows at the waist. Their faces were made menacing by war paint.

They made the men in overalls and store shirts look commonplace. With bodies bent forward and eyes on the ground, they ran as though following the trail. Suddenly they stood erect, shading their eyes as though peering into the distance, and then shouted and leaped into the air in triumphant abandon. It was pitiful to see the old men trying to reconstruct for the younger ones something of the vanished prowess of the tribe, when men had followed the warpath in the glory of their unbroken strength and spirit.

I remembered the story of how the Indians were driven into the bitter lake till the waters closed over their heads, and realized the moving power that dance had had over the Indians who fought the intrusion of the white man into the valleys that had been theirs to wander at will.

But I was not afraid. The power of the white man was unquestioned. Bows and arrows were only playthings, and the white man's fire-water was a gift worth everything he had taken away.

And yet sometimes the Indians took justice and punishment in their own hands. A Chinese restaurant in Sodaville was burned. The bodies of two Indians were found in a cellar under the building. They had been too dead with whiskey or opium to get away. But two other Indians, not so oblivious to what was happening, escaped. Not long afterwards the train, arriving in the confusing desert dusk, ran over a Chinaman who lay on the tracks. The Chinaman, when extricated, was dead enough, but he didn't bleed, showing that the placing of the body on the track had been a kind of afterthought in relation to his previous demise.

Later, a Chinaman, selling pickled pork to the Indians, was so negligent as to let an Indian get a peep into his pork barrel. The barrel was nearly empty, but an Indian foot still remaining in the brine left no question as to the origin of the pork.

The Chinaman was promptly arrested and held for trial at Bridgeport, the county seat of Mono County. As if they had sprung out of the ground, over five hundred Indians appeared at the jail and demanded the prisoner. Awed by their number and their evident determination, the sheriff and his henchmen delivered the quaking Chinaman into their hands.

Then began a strange procession. The Indians marched their victim down the main street of the terrified small town, and literally carved him to pieces as they advanced,—an ear, a hand, a nose, an arm—until he was mince-meat when he reached the end of the street.

A few days after the Indian dance we went to see Old Charley make a "clean up." The muddy mass in the pit of the arastra was allowed to run off into the tailings pond. Old Charley scooped up the amalgam that lay in the cracks, between the flat rocks in the bottom of the pit, and put it in a piece of chamois skin and wrung it until all the quicksilver possible had passed through the interstices of the chamois. The mass left was dry amalgam. He put this in the funny black kettle that was a retort, and placed it over a fire in the old out-of-doors fireplace.

We had another picnic and each of us repeated scraps of *"Hello!" "Hello!" "Why, Jim!" "Why, Dan!"* to Old Charley's huge enjoyment. Then Old Charley opened the retort and showed us the button of gold and silver in the bottom. It seemed so small for all the time and trouble it took to get it! But Old Charley said he would send it to the mint in San Francisco and get enough out of it to buy beans and coffee and flour and bacon for the winter. He had cut the grass on an upper meadow to make hay for Jinny and Joan. He hadn't got to the pocket in the mine yet, but he was sure he would find it soon.

So we left Old Charley and followed the boulder-strewn road down from the mountains, where we gathered wild strawberries and rode over trails to tree-fringed mountain lakes and found high meadows where tiger lilies and lark-spur grew above our heads.

Grace was back-sliding. A young suitor from town, whose attentions her mother did not endorse, came to see her and she met him "on the sly." I was shocked that any girl could so deceive her mother, and begged Grace to go and make a clean breast of it. I reminded her of her conversion and her promises to walk the straight and narrow path. She said that for any one who read poetry as much as I did, I was certainly lacking in imagination, and besides she wasn't sure whether or not she wanted to join the church.

The night before the last round-up there was a big dance, in Frances' father's bunk-house. All the bunks were taken out and two Mexicans came out from town to play the violin and the guitar. A lot of people who were camping in the mountains came, too. Grace wanted to dance, but her mother reminded her that she could not if she was going to join the church.

The caller started, "Take your partners for a quadrille!" Right there Grace back-slid clear to the end of the room and asked her favorite cow-boy to dance with her.

The caller kept time to the music with his foot while he sang:

> *First lady swing with the right hand gent,*
> *Right and around; right and around;*
> *Next lady swing with the right hand gent,*
> *Lady in the center and all hands around.*
> *Lady swing out and gents swing in*
> *All join hands and circle once again*
> *Swing 'em around and don't be afraid*
> *Al-a-mand left and all promenade.*

We had a wonderful time. Bronco Jim's crooked arm got in the way of the other dancers sometimes, but all together it was great fun. He rode with me to the triangle *R* ranch in the moonlight. We walked our horses most of the way. He said sweet things to me and told me how he would miss me when we were gone. He looked so handsome on his horse that I felt it would be easy to love him, perhaps to marry him and settle down on a cattle ranch and cook and raise a family. But when we were home and he got down to help me from the horse, I realized I could never really love a bow-legged man.

I had expected Grace would be overcome with the sin she had committed, dancing when she was on probation to join the church. But she was gay and happy and appeared relieved that she would no longer be held to her convictions. She seemed as irresponsible as I had been when I kicked my heels on the floor and cried for a red plush bonnet.

I envied her. Life was such a serious matter to me. I thought of my new stepmother and dreaded to go back to the home that she was to make for us.

I soon found I had no reason to dread my stepmother. She came from Boston. She had been an "old maid." I suppose her unattractive face explained her spinster-hood in a country where there were so many more men than women.

Her bachelor brothers, who ran a small hotel, had sent for her to come West and manage it for them. I suppose they thought she was so homely that they were not likely to lose her by marriage. But my father felt that he could acquire, at little expense, those home-making qualities for his own.

In these days when "women bachelors" hold them-selves proudly and the epithet "old maid" seems as an-tiquated as long flannel underwear, it is hard to understand why women in the Eighties rose so eagerly to any bait that offered the title *Mrs.* I am sure that my father's wooing was neither long nor arduous. He and my stepmother were installed in a neat little cottage when I returned to Bishop. She welcomed me with an open-heartedness which I could not deny.

I am sure she had already found that "Mac," who was known to his acquaintances as a pleasant, genial man, was really a person of violent and uncertain temper, who felt that the marriage ceremony had made her his, body and soul. I never knew a woman who put forth greater effort to win the love of her husband and her stepchild. She had a magic touch with food. The Boston baked beans and brown bread of national fame became a delicious reality in our home. Boston cream pies melted in our mouths. The batter for crisp, brown buckwheat cakes stood in a crock by the stove, as it had at Aunt Mary's. Instead of maple syrup or sorghum, there was strained honey to eat with them.

I had come to realize that my father, the man who had married this woman, was not Papa; and I put Mama's memory away with the memory of the Papa whom she had taught me to love, and so I reconciled myself to the presence of my stepmother. We were soon drawn together in a common bond of fear of my father's displeasure, his unwarranted suspicions and unreasoning jealousies.

It all seems such a pity when I think of it. I admired my father in many ways. He was a genius in mathematics. His maps, accurately drawn and beautifully colored, and lettered in a firm, round hand that was as legible as print, still remain the outstanding guides to the boundaries and mineral deposits of that region. But his word was law in the house. No pleasures, no desires, no ambitions were fostered, except as they contributed to his comfort, his pleasure, his personal vanity. And that personal vanity became centered in me with a jealous intensity that was demoniacal.

In spite of all the sorrows and hardships that had fallen to my lot, I was a normal, healthy, happy girl, craving the pleasures and companionships of girlhood;

but I soon came to feel that I was a prisoner. I was like the cattle, held to the road by a barbed-wire fence. My only outlet was school; not that I was so passionately fond of books, but there I found the companionship otherwise denied.

My father bought me a gun, and together we went quail hunting. He taught me to shoot, but I never found any pleasure in killing the prettily marked birds with their graceful top-knots. My lack of enthusiasm was a disappointment to him. He was an epicure, and would never allow the birds to be skinned, because of the sweet layer of fat that lay underneath. I learned to pick the tiny feathers carefully from their dainty bodies, only one of the many distasteful tasks that I was called upon to do.

When the duck season came there were always wet, sad-eyed hunting dogs in the house, and ducks to pick and prepare for roasting. If I found courage sometimes to say that I didn't want to go hunting, there would follow days when my father ignored my presence, as deaf and dumb to me as Uncle Gordon had been, only lacking Uncle Gordon's friendliness. And so that wall that had begun with infinitesimal particles grew wider and higher between us.

When visitors came, or Grace or Frances spent the night with me, my father would be so different that I could scarcely believe it was he. He was genial and smiling. The pretty, well-kept home and delicious food made my friends envy me for being able to live in town and not having to board at the Academy.

But it was a rare occasion when I was ever allowed to

go home with them—so rare that its importance was magnified in my mind, and when my father refused to allow me to accept an invitation I was sick with disappointment.

We lived across the road from the Academy. Naturally that was the center around which revolved all the activities of the young people of the country. It was here they met to go on hay rides, or to the light-hearted country dances. I was never allowed to join them, but I had the exquisite pain of watching the preparations and seeing them drive away, shouting and calling happily to each other. Then I would go to bed and cry my heart out with loneliness. At first my stepmother tried to interfere, to make my father realize that it was only natural for me to want to go. But his sullen silence was her answer. She soon learned to express her unspoken sympathy through some pretty gift that she would make for me.

We never discussed my father with each other. We were both New England women, steeped in the tradition that never questioned the authority of a husband or a father, or thought of disobeying his wishes. Women were inarticulate. They shouldered their crosses and bore them as best they might.

Youth is wonderfully resilient. Fortunately, I was acutely responsive to the beauties of nature. The grandeur of the mountains, the lure of the streams, the enchantment of the forests, the dainty loveliness of the meadows never lost their power to charm away my secret hurts and disappointments. Frances used to say that I stopped at every irrigating ditch and acted as though

I wanted to pick it up in my arms and hug it. But she had never lived on the prairie.

I must have inherited some of this love of nature from my father, and in spite of my loneliness for other companions, we were never so happy together as when we went with our pack outfits into the mountains. We never lost our way; once having located a mountain peak, my father recognized it from every angle.

The second summer we packed into Yosemite Valley, through Long Valley, past the burned-out craters of the Mono Basin, along the shores of Mono Lake, that strange, alkaline, inland sea, with its islands where Mark Twain gathered gulls' eggs; over the Bloody Canyon Trail, through Tuolomne Meadows to the head of Yosemite Falls.

There, from a rocky ledge, we looked down unbelievable distances to the floor of the valley, where the houses were like doll-houses and the roads were only ribbons. Then we followed the setting sun down the trail, wet with spray from Yosemite Falls, as they leaped from crag to crag on their way to join the quiet Merced River.

Not for a trip to Europe would I relinquish my memory of Yosemite, before the days of automobiles and crowded tourist camps. But, like all vacations, this one came to an end and we returned to the vexations and misunderstandings that always seemed to beset us when anything came between me and my father's possessive hold on me.

There were respites for my stepmother and me when my father was called away on surveying expeditions.

Looking back, I don't know how we could have gone on living if these respites had not been allowed us. We grew very close to each other, and her homely face was no longer homely in my sight.

Denied the usual pleasures and distractions of youth, I became more and more engrossed in my studies. I stood at the head of my classes, and my father's pride in me increased. I began to feel that this pride was an instrument in my hands with which I could carve my way to freedom. My father had said that I could go away to school! When I graduated from the Academy as the valedictorian of my class, I was seventeen years old. It never occurred to me that my father would insist on any other than a classical education. Ever since the days of the *National Fifth Reader,* I had dreamed of going to college to learn intimately of those great minds that had revealed themselves through the written word. I hoped some day to follow, however feebly, in their footsteps.

But my father had other plans. Just as he had insisted that I should learn to camp and fish and carry a gun, he now declared his intention to educate me for the practice of law or medicine. I could make my choice.

My teachers argued with him. They had become interested in my literary efforts, and felt that I should be encouraged to go on with them. But my father was deaf to argument. He had decided. If I wished an education I must abide by his decision.

My only knowledge of the law was of "the quality of mercy." My only picture of a woman doctor was that of Dr. Mary Walker, dressed in men's clothes and endeavoring in every way to disguise the fact that she had been born a woman. That I should choose neither was unthinkable. It was my only way of escape.

Then all at once everything was clear. I thought of Grandmother and the typhoid-breeding cistern. I remembered Mama with that gesture to the back of her head and her repeated insistence, "There must be something, Doctor, that you can do with medicine." I saw Aunt Mary fighting for air in the mean little prairie shanty, and I felt as if called by God through that strange man, my father.

I was allowed to go to Frances' home to stay all night with her and Grace. They were both engaged to be married; Grace to an energetic fellow who had a hardware store in town, Frances to a young giant, who had been raised in the saddle and whose father owned wide acres of rich grazing land, over which great herds of cattle roamed.

I felt lonely. Life seemed so settled, so patterned, for them. I had no sweetheart. Every time a boy paid any attention to me, my father, in jealous rage, would place unthinkable interpretations on our innocent enjoyment. He made me sex-conscious, and I became diffident and shy in the company of boys.

Grace and Frances could not understand me. It seemed very strange to think of my going away, the other side of the mountains, to study medicine. They laughed and teased me, and called me a blue-stocking. They never knew how lonely and outside their charmed, snug, little world it made me feel.

But nothing ever changed the sincere affection we had for each other. We were sad at the thought of parting, so we tried to be very gay. When we went to bed, Frances and Grace started singing, all in a joking mood, looking very silly and sentimental:

"I hear from this valley you're going,
I shall miss your blue eyes and bright smile,
For, alas, you will take all the sunshine
That has brightened my pathway awhile."

My throat tightened; their voices faltered, but they went bravely on with the chorus:

"Then consider awhile e're you leave me;
Do not hasten to bid me adieu;
But remember the bright little valley
And the girl that has loved you so true."

We were all crying before they finished. We threw our arms around each other, and sobbed at the thought of being separated.

I hated to leave my stepmother most of all. She had realized long ago the cruel fact that my father had married her, not for any love he bore her but to satisfy his selfish desire to have a home for himself and me. I never knew what romantic dreams that had lain so long in an "old maid's" breast were shattered, but I comprehended the cruel years that lay ahead for her, alone, with my father, in the house where he had brought her to make a home for him.

It seemed unbelievable that I was to be released. I looked ahead, not with any dread of the strange, unfamiliar studies that I was to plunge into with such

scant preparation, but with a steady, unflinching joy in
the knowledge that the barbed-wire fences were down;
the fields were mine to graze.

✠ THE STORY OF VIRGINIA CITY ✠ MARK TWAIN ✠ THE BIG FOUR & THE BONANZA KINGS

MY FATHER AND I STARTED FOR SAN
Francisco. We traveled north over the desert to Sodaville, where the train stayed all night and passengers
and train crew enjoyed the hospitality of the Sodaville
Hotel and Bar. When every one was ready the next
morning, we journeyed on to Mound House, where, instead of going to Reno, we took the Virginia and
Truckee road, east-bound to Virginia City.

When we boarded the train I heard some one say,
"Well, hoist my bucket, if here ain't old MacKnight!"
A dusty looking miner, with hair so long it brushed the
collar of his flannel shirt, came up and slapped Papa
on the back. Papa turned. "Well, Sandy, what happened to your red hair? You're gray as an old badger."
I had never seen Papa so glad to see anybody. He
almost forgot to introduce me in his excitement. The
man looked at me as though he thought Papa must be
joking. "Your daughter, Mac? Well, I'll be gol
darned! Who ever knew you had a daughter in the
good old Bodie days?"

As he talked he kept looking at me in a puzzled

way and I realized what a small place Mama and I occupied in Papa's life during those full, adventurous days
that their reminiscences recalled so vividly.

I remembered Mama, always writing a letter to Papa,
in Bodie. Mama, working in the corset factory, waiting
for Papa to send for us to come to him in Bodie.

But in spite of those memories, I was fascinated by
the spirit of the old West that seemed to come back at
their bidding. While the wood-burning engine puffed
up the winding road that was built by Sharon, past
stunted piñon trees and outcroppings of rock, they began to recall the stirring days of the Comstock Lode
and to name the men who amassed fortunes there.

They talked of how the placer miners, when they first
came to prospect on the slope of Mount Davidson, were
puzzled by the blue-black stuff that interfered with their
primitive methods of washing for gold and clogged their
arastras and rockers.

Bit by bit I picked up the pieces of information they
let fall and pieced it together until I had the story of
Virginia City.

The versions of the first real discovery varied. One
was that Henry Comstock, "Old Pancake," ran his hand
down a gopher hole and grabbed a handful of ore, rich
in gold and silver. Another ran that two Irishmen,
prospecting where the famous Ophir mine was later developed, took out a rocker of ore which they washed at
a spring owned by Comstock, and made a "clean-up"
that opened their eyes. "Old Pancake" immediately declared himself in on the find, the ore having been washed
at his spring, and bluffed it through to carve his name
on the Comstock Lode. The black stuff that the placer

miners had cursed assayed four and a half thousand dollars in silver to the ton!

Then "Old Virginia," partner of "Old Pancake," after the camp was well started, having been on a spree, fell down in front of his cabin and broke his bottle of whiskey. He got to his knees and swinging the bottle above his head chanted: "I baptize this ground Virginia Town." So the infant was christened and grew to Virginia City, where miners toiled and sweat underground to build fortunes for men whose names went ringing down the pages of the history of the Pacific slope.

Machinery and supplies came around the Horn or across the Isthmus of Panama to San Francisco, on river boats to Sacramento, where the mule skinners, driving twenty-mule teams with their jerk-lines, loaded them on wagons and trailers and started the trek across mountains and desert to the Comstock.

Everything had to be hauled in; timbers to stope the tunnels in the mines, lumber to build houses, food, furniture, mining supplies of all kinds.

"Old Pancake" and "Old Virginia," not comprehending what they had discovered, sold out for a few thousand dollars and faded from the picture.

Six-horse stages brought passengers by way of Placerville and Downieville; one line, the Pioneer, that ran through Placerville carried twenty thousand passengers a year. And so the curtain was rung up for the second act—the crowning of the king of the Comstock, and the entrance of the fool who proved to be a wise man.

My father and his Bodie friend drew a vivid picture of Sharon, the white-handed, blue eyed, dapper little man who was born of Quaker parents and came over the emigrant trail in '49 to San Francisco. He made a fortune in real estate and lost it in stock speculation before he was sent to Virginia City, by the Bank of California, to open the first bank on the Comstock Lode.

With the power of the San Francisco Bank of California behind him, he started operations on a scale that eclipsed anything even dreamed of by the men who had watched the Comstock grow. The names of Ralston and D. O. Mills, coupled with his own, spelled a force that ground lesser holders between the wheels of their enterprise, and Sharon became the acknowledged King of the Comstock.

He built great stamp mills and forced the owners of other properties to run their ore through the company mills. The shafts went down in the mines to lower and lower levels. Men sweat and panted in the stagnant air underground. Water ran into the mines and had to be pumped to the surface. Ore was hoisted from greater and greater depths.

But a fly appeared in the ointment with which Sharon was anointing his white hands. Adolph Sutro, a hardheaded, intelligent German Jew, dared to question the methods of the sovereign. This stocky, well set-up young fellow had a small amalgamation plant at Dayton. As he rode horseback to and from his mill to the mines of Virginia City, the busy brain behind his high forehead noted the contours and formation of the country.

He conceived the idea of running a tunnel to tap the Comstock Lode, with the result that ore now being hoisted could be run on an incline out of the tunnel, water being pumped could flow out the tunnel, circulation of fresh air would be provided, and greatest of all, in the minds of the miners, the terrifying hazard of fire that caught and trapped them in the tunnels would be eliminated.

My father was in Virginia City when Sutro placarded the camp with great posters showing a fire underground, leaping and devouring the men who were caught in the trap. They were invited to come and hear him speak at Piper Hall that night.

It was probably one of the first poster campaigns ever made and it brought results. The miners thronged the hall. Stereopticon pictures of the mines on fire, with men being rescued through the tunnel, were thrown on the screen. In answer to Sutro's dramatic and convincing appeal, the miners emptied their pockets to start the work on the Sutro Tunnel.

It seems unbelievable that a project that promised so much should have met with real opposition. But with an indomitable will Sutro besieged capital in Europe and at home to finance his plan.

The King of the Comstock spoke lightly of "Adolph's coyote hole." Sutro responded with remarks about "Sharon's crooked railroad." So the contest was not without its moments.

Then the Irishmen who had been understudying the part took the stage for the third act and climax of the great drama. James Fair, of County Tyrone, crossed the plains to work with shovel and rocker in the Placer diggin's of Angels Camp. He drifted to the Comstock and by diligent application became superintendent of the Ophir Mine, and the "Slippery Jim" of the Bonanza Kings.

John Mackay arrived from the auld sod by way of the

Isthmus and started as a mucker at four dollars a day, to rise from timberman to shift boss to mine superintendent.

No other men on the Lode knew the workings that burrowed under Virginia City and Gold Hill as did those two.

Meanwhile, James Flood, a master mason, and William S. O'Brien, a ship chandler, were amassing a fortune, tending their own mahogany bar in their saloon in San Francisco. They kept a high-class establishment where the great men of the mining world moistened their throats while they discussed the manipulation of the latest strikes on the Comstock Lode. With Irish receptivity, Flood and O'Brien learned more over their mahogany bar than they would have known had they been in the tunnels with pick and shovel.

They became the financiers and Fair and Mackay, with their greater knowledge of the mines than either Sharon or Sutro, the men on the ground of that combination known as the Bonanza Kings, were to wrest the throne from Sharon and take two hundred million dollars from the hidden treasure of Virginia City and Gold Hill to spend them magnificently in San Francisco, the City by the Golden Gate.

As my father and Sandy talked, they seemed to radiate something of the bigness, the ruthlessness, the high adventure, that moved men in those days. The knowledge that they had lost while others won seemed to hold no bitterness for them. The fact that they had contacted the vein was sufficient.

As we came near to Virginia City they pointed out the Belcher and the Yellow Jacket mines. We crossed

Crown Point bridge with the Kentuck and the Crown Point mines in the canyon below us, past the Old Homestead, to Gold Hill and the city that grew on the Comstock Lode, in the shadow of Mount Davidson, which the Indians called Sun Peak.

We were in a great mining camp. It straggled up and down the steep hillside from C Street, the main street of Virginia City. We went to the International House. We saw the famous Crystal Bar, where opaque, flowered glass doors, set in heavy mahogany frames, swung at the entrance. Shining rows of crystal glasses were reflected in the plate glass wall behind the polished bar with its hospitable brass rail. A great chandelier, terraced with prisms of crystal, was suspended from the center of the room. Fine oil paintings decorated the walls.

There were photographs of that famous day when General Grant had visited Virginia City. Sandy told me of witnessing the parade. A famous stage driver, Curly Bill, drove eight black, plumed horses hitched to a phaëton in which General and Mrs. Grant, Jim Fair and Mrs. Mackay rode to the International House. There were brass bands in the parade and the Virginia Engine Company was out in full regalia. Above the Crystal Bar was the Washoe Club, where Mackay and Fair had hobnobbed with the millionaires who came to the Comstock.

We went to the old offices of the *Virginia Enterprise* where Mark Twain, a reporter on the paper, wrote a thrilling murder story.

He told how a man at Dutch Mick's on the Carson River cut his wife's throat and those of his nine children. After this diabolical deed he got on his horse, cut his own throat from ear to ear, and rode three and a half miles to Carson City and fell dead in front of Pete Hawkins' saloon.

Although the thrilling story stated that the family lived in a little cabin at the edge of a great pine forest, and everyone knew there was not a pine tree within ten miles of Nick's, and although a man would scarcely be able to ride horseback three and one-half miles with his throat cut from ear to ear, the subscribers to the *Enterprise* swallowed the story, hook, line, and sinker. When they found that the whole thing was a hoax, they were terribly let down, and Mark Twain nearly lost his place on the paper over the affair.

We were lowered in a cage, 2,900 feet underground, to the lower level of the C. and C. mine. It was hot. Miners worked, stripped to the waist. The sweat glistened on their skins, much as did the moisture that oozed from the rock they had gouged out to form the tunnels. We saw the sump being pumped into the Sutro Tunnel. I heard the story of the last stand of the owners on the Comstock against the man who fought them for years. When his tunnel was completed, they still refused to pay the toll that Sutro demanded. The Savage Mine flooded with water. In the emergency the owners turned the water into the Sutro Tunnel. Sutro threw a dam across the tunnel and the mine filled. The Savage owners came to terms and from that time on the owners on the Comstock Lode paid tribute to the man who had triumphed in the face of every obstacle.

Above-ground the mountain side was a labyrinth of trails that led to tunnels and workings and mine dumps and mills and shafts and chimneys and flumes. In places where the underground workings had been abandoned, Virginia City was already sinking into the grave whose digging had contributed over three hundred million dollars to the wealth of the nation.

The hey-day of the great Comstock Lode was over. The people were living in a glorious past—a past of the days of Sharon, Fair, Mackay, Flood, and O'Brien. I heard their names coupled with dazzling stories of the wealth they had amassed and the prodigality of their spending. People might smile over the news that Mrs. Fair, she that was Theresa Rooney, was planning the finest wedding ever seen on the coast for her daughter, and that Mrs. Mackay, who used to be a good boarding-house keeper, was now entertaining the aristocracy of Europe in her salon in Paris and had picked out a count for her son-in-law—but it was a good-natured smile.

Some had won. Others had lost. But it had been a great adventure. Life is a gambling game. How different it might have been for Mama and Papa and me if the vein in the Nellie Mine had not pinched out. . . .

We left Old Sandy in Virginia City, outfitting himself to strike out for a new camp. My father bade him good-bye as though he expected they might bump into each other soon again. There was never any finality about parting in the Old West.

When we took the Union Pacific west from Reno I learned from my father that the building of this railroad was the work of another big four. A Big Four who came across the plains, around Cape Horn, and across the Isthmus, to meet in Sacramento where they established small businesses, trading in miners' supplies and general merchandise.

When they conceived the project of building a railroad to connect the shores of the Pacific with the Central Pacific railroad at the Nevada line, it seemed inconceivable that a quartet of small tradesmen could accomplish such a stupendous undertaking. One of the group, when warned of the tremendous amount of hard work connected with the project, replied: "I don't work hard; I work easy!" Perhaps he gave the keynote of their success in that terse sentence. The first ground was broken in Sacramento in 1863, and Collis P. Huntington, Mark Hopkins, Leland Stanford and Charles Crocker began writing their names indelibly into the history of California.

In 1869 Charles Crocker, who nineteen years before had taken one hundred days to cross the plains from the Missouri River to Sacramento, made the same trip in his private car in one hundred hours.

The wood-burning locomotives and the rails for the road were shipped around the Horn in sailing vessels, which grew to a fleet bought by the "Big Four" for that purpose.

It was estimated that the total cost of a rail, delivered at San Francisco, was $143.67, to which it was necessary to add the cost of transfer from the ships to river boats, which landed them in Sacramento. Hay to feed the stock along the line of operations cost a hundred dollars a ton and oats fifteen cents a pound. Ties were hewn out of the mountain forests at tremendous expense. Tracks were laid by Chinese coolies, who bent their backs to the grilling task like the galley-slaves of old.

Herds of buffalo were sacrificed to provide meat for the workmen, who swarmed over the mountain and desert.

San Francisco went wild when the Pacific Railroad Bill was passed. The people realized that rail communication with the East, for which they had waited so long, was to be accomplished, and that the Pony Express which had carried the mail at the rate of five dollars a letter and the Wells Fargo stages, beset by highwaymen, would soon be relegated to a romantic past.

A great celebration was held. The streets were thronged with revelers. Transparencies proclaimed the joyful news: "Cape Horn be blowed! Salt Lake City the half-way house." "The locomotive! His prow is wet with the surge and foam of either ocean. His breast is gray with the sands of the desert." "Chesapeake Bay Oysters! Six days from the water!"

From the Union Pacific railroad which they had built, we caught a glimpse of Donner Lake and I heard the story of the Donner party who came that way over the Oregon Trail, to be caught in the terrible grip of a mountain storm at Donner Lake. It was a heart-breaking tale of men who tried to push ahead on snow-shoes and became snow-blind, of men who died and were eaten by their starving companions, of women who singed and scraped green hides and cooked them into a jelly to nourish their famished children, and gathered bones and boiled or burned them for their slight food values; of one woman who, when a rescue party finally came, would not leave her sick husband, who could not be moved, and so stayed to perish with him.

And now, over the way that had been beset with such dangers, we rode in luxurious comfort.

Ever since coming to live in the High Sierras I had heard of "the other side," of "God's country," of "the Bay," of San Francisco, the city by the Golden Gate. When we emerged from the snow sheds, that protected the track from the storms that had heaped twenty feet of snow above the sufferers at Donner Lake, I found that the desert was left behind. Tall ferns grew under the forest trees. The mountains rose less abruptly and undulated towards the coast in friendly foothills. The bay reached a silvery arm north to meet us at Benecia, where our train ran onto a boat to be ferried across to Port Costa.

And then we were at the Oakland "mole," and took the ferry for San Francisco. San Francisco has many moods, but none lovelier than the one we found her in that day. Soft gray fog banks were drifting in from the ocean, and against them the city swept proudly up from the waterfront to squander her beauty on the hills. She was mysterious, uplifted, as though she would say to those who would find her heart: "First you must scale the walls."

Although San Francisco, viewed from the deck of the ferry boat, seemed aloof, we found her waterfront a bustling, colorful place as we glided into the slip at the old ferry sheds in 1890.

It was all exciting and a bit terrifying to me. We were besieged by runners for the hotel, who greeted us: "OCCIDENTAL *HO*-tel!" "RRRRR-USS HOUSE!" "PALACE *HO*-tel!" "LICK HOUSE!" Each one tried to outdo the other in the vehemence with which he shouted the words and the energy with which he endeavored to relieve us of our baggage. Outside the ferry sheds the omnibuses were drawn up. The names of the hotels to which they offered to deliver us appeared in large lettering along the body of the bus.

I should have been quite distracted had I not known that my father had already decided we would stay at the Russ House. Hotels fell easily into classes those days. Ranchers and cattlemen and small mining men stayed at the Russ House. Mining men of wide interests were found at the Lick House. The Occidental Hotel was headquarters for the Army and Navy people, while the socially and financially élite, ambassadors, diplomats, and even kings, stopped at the Palace.

We were deposited with our baggage in the Russ House bus. The driver climbed to his seat, cracked his whip, and the horses' hoofs and the omnibus wheels clattered over the cobblestones up Market Street, passing on the way the cable cars that clanged along the Slot.

I soon learned that this Market Street Slot had come to be a social dividing line, and that people were rated by the fact that they came from north or south of the Slot.

There were a few rooms in the Russ House with running water and stationary bowls, but mine had a familiar wash-bowl and pitcher. My father instructed me at length about lighting the strange gas jet, and told me when I turned out the light I should always test it with a burning match to be sure no gas was escaping. I would have been much more comfortable with a coal-oil lamp or a candle.

My father met some mining men whom he knew and we went out with them to the other hotels that night. As we entered the Occidental Hotel lobby, we found that a party of Englishmen had just arrived. They were talking about their "luggage." I had never heard the word luggage before and I looked the foreign-looking baggage over curiously.

There was one piece that especially attracted my attention. It looked as though it might be a large, high-backed armchair with no legs. My father's friends explained that it was a sitz bath tub. He said that the English carried their bath tubs with them, either a high backed sitz tub or a hat-bath tub, which was like a huge, inverted hat with the part that would be the crown designed to hold the bath water.

The Englishmen were having an argument at the desk and we found that they were protesting against being assigned to rooms with running water and stationary bowls, as they were afraid of sewer gas. They were finally sent happily on their way with their luggage and sitz bath tub, to rooms furnished with a satisfactory bowl and pitcher.

I was much impressed by the military uniforms of the officers at the Occidental and the elegant, bustled costumes of the ladies. The brilliance of the Palace Hotel court, where carriages drove in to deposit beautifully gowned women and men in evening dress, seemed like the realization of a Hans Andersen fairy tale to me. I had never seen men and women in evening dress before.

My father and his friends wanted a drink, so they went over the connecting bridge to the Grand Hotel Bar. It was said to be the finest in San Francisco, but drinks were only half the price that they were at the gorgeous Palace.

I sat in one of the galleries that surrounded the court

and waited for them, glad to be left by myself, free to feast my eyes on such undreamed-of splendor. Of all the men I saw that night, one type, which seemed to be most in evidence at the Lick House, represented to me the men of affairs of those days.

I saw such a man recently. I took an early morning Powell Street cable car which runs over Nob Hill, past the Fairmont Hotel to Market Street. When we made the California Street stop, several men, evidently from the Fairmont Hotel, boarded the car. They were well groomed and prosperous looking. Some of them carried golf bags in evident anticipation of a game after office hours.

But one man of that group might have walked out of the old Lick House, or the old Palace, instead of the modern Fairmont. He was tall, big-boned and powerful looking, with iron gray hair. His face was brown and his eyes held a zest for living. His clothes fitted comfortably but not too well, and he wore a large felt hat. His cravat pin was an opal, as large as my thumbnail, surrounded by diamonds, and he had two large rings set with magnificent diamonds.

I know it sounds terribly flashy; but it wasn't. That man's fine personality pervaded that car like a breath of the Old West. You could just picture him walking up to some one in distress with a hearty hand-shake, and a genial, "Hello, stranger!"

My father lighted the gas in my room for me when we returned to the Russ House that night. I was glad that, like the Englishmen, I, too, had a safe bowl and pitcher. When I was ready for bed, I turned off the gas and lighted a match, and in fear and trembling, applied it to the jet to see if there were any leaks. There were none!

The next morning we took the horse-car on Kearny Street and rode out to Washington Square, and then walked over Stockton Street to the Medical College.

A STUDENT IN
OLD SAN FRANCISCO

❦ *LUCY WANZER'S BATTLE* ❦
TOLAND HALL

W HEN I SEE THE BURDEN OF PREPARA-
tion that is placed on young men and women nowadays
before they can reach the threshold of one of the professions, I smile to think of the inexperienced country
girl, with only the old Academy behind her, who
knocked so fearlessly at the door of Toland Hall in
San Francisco.

In the days when Dr. Toland built this Hall at the
North Beach end of Stockton Street, I am sure it never
occurred to him that such a phenomenon as a woman
knocking for admission would ever be seen.

Dr. Toland left a "munificent practice" of sixteen thousand dollars a year to cross the plains, journeying from
Independence, Missouri, the railway terminus, to San
Francisco, in seventy-six days, the shortest time on record. He was in quest of adventure and gold. He
found both, not in the mines, but in the practice of his
profession where the need was great, and the fees for

medical service exceeded a doctor's Arabian Night's dream.

Those were the days when physicians had their offices in tents, when two ounces of gold dust, thirty-two dollars, was paid for one visit, and quinine was the cure-all for disease. Records tell us that an old-time physician sold his supply of quinine at auction at sixty-four dollars an ounce. Laudanum was priced at one dollar a drop, in the days when boots cost forty dollars a pair, blankets a hundred dollars, and potatoes one dollar a pound.

Dr. Toland established offices on Montgomery Street in San Francisco, and never moved from that location. He often saw as many as four hundred patients a day, besides the bed-side cases. He became a millionaire, a man respected and honored in the medical world, and in 1872 built, at an expense of seventy-five thousand dollars, Toland Hall, a school where young men might receive instruction in the art of medicine.

One pauses to wonder how far seventy-five thousand dollars would go today toward building a medical school and equipping its laboratories.

In 1873 Lucy Wanzer—who was to be the first woman to graduate in medicine in California—made application for admission to Toland Hall. Dr. Toland must have felt himself well out of it when he listened to the controversy that arose. She was firmly told that a medical lecture hall, a dissecting room, and clinics were not proper places for women. She was advised to go East to some woman's college in Boston or Philadelphia.

Nothing daunted, she laid the matter before the Board of Regents of the University, much to their consternation. For months the Board of Regents and their attorneys wrestled with the problem. Finally they reluctantly affirmed: "It is an organic law of the state that male and female shall have equal chance in the university in all its departments."

Lucy Wanzer appeared before the Dean of Toland Hall, handed him the decision which she had received from the Board of Regents, and paid her entrance fee.

The Dean's perturbation is shown by the fact that he announced to his students that a woman would attend the classes the following day. He advised them to haze her. He said: "It's the old story; women want to get in everywhere. We have to accept this woman student, as she has the best of us. The law has been decided in her favor, but you can make it so uncomfortable that she cannot stay. We will get rid of her in short order. Of course she will complain, but we will say we are very sorry but we cannot lecture to two classes. With just one woman we will make short work of it."

But these men had not reckoned with the spirit of the woman who was struggling to gain for women the right to study medicine and surgery in California. One incident illustrates the many trying situations Lucy Wanzer encountered. When she was present at an eye clinic, the professor in charge stated: "A woman has no business to study medicine. If she does, she ought to have her ovaries removed."

She quietly replied: "If that is true, the men students ought also to have their testicles removed!"

Lucy Wanzer persisted, in spite of the taunts of the professors, ignoring the hazing by the students, which reached its greatest emphasis in the dissecting room where she found the genital organs of the subject, on which she was making a dissection of femoral hernia, arranged, by the aid of a catheter, in a most suggestive manner, for her discomfiture and embarrassment. She graduated in Medicine; a beacon light of indomitable courage and self-respect for those women who were to follow in her footsteps.

When I entered Toland Hall, although seventeen years had elapsed since Dr. Wanzer had forced the University Regents to make their decision, the attitude of many of the professors and students toward women in Medicine was not greatly different from what it had been in her day. She was still, in their eyes, an experiment and something of a joke.

The course had been lengthened from two to three years, but the only requirement for entrance was an elementary examination in English, which I passed without difficulty. This allowed me to enter the preliminary term, which gave me three months to demonstrate whether I was capable of being enrolled in the regular term, as a student of Medicine.

My father stayed a few days and went with me to the lectures and dissecting room. I shall never forget my first sight of that old dissecting room. Bodies in all stages of preservation and decomposition were placed on rough board tables with zinc tops. Maggots were not infrequent denizens of those "stiffs" which had been carelessly handled, and only the smoke from the pipes of the students made it possible to stay in the room.

Shanley, the janitor, had charge of the pickling vats in the basement, and subjects for dissection were supposed to be drawn alphabetically. Many were the wiles practiced on Shanley to insure a well muscled, well cured "stiff" for those who were in his friendly services.

My father showed signs of weakening when he saw the room. He glowered at the young medical students who cast curious glances in my direction.

I remember an outstanding woman of meager education but great intelligence, who went out from our mountain valley to meet with some woman's club, hoping, through its influence, to obtain the beginnings of a sorely-needed library. One of the women, looking her over from her superior heights, remarked: "You come from the interior, do you not?" The country woman replied, with a twinkle in her eye, "Yes, you can undoubtedly tell that from my exterior."

My exterior too was an open book that told a tale of inexperience, and lack of common knowledge of the world, that made me seem and feel as foreign as any immigrant who arrived at Angel Island in San Francisco Bay.

We looked about for a place near the college where I could room and board, and found a white house with green blinds snuggled on the slope of Telegraph Hill. There was a tidy garden where geraniums and fuschias and, most miraculous of all, calla lilies bloomed. And heliotrope. The blessed fragrance of that heliotrope after a morning spent in the dissecting room! We pulled the modest porcelain knob of the door bell and heard it jangle in the back of the house. A young, pleasant-faced Irish girl came to the door and ushered us into a parlor as familiar as though I had always known it, with its horse-hair furniture and the hair wreath in its deep mahogany frame on the wall. The landlady was summoned. She was dressed in heavy black crape and spoke with a rich brogue. We learned that her husband had been a foreman in the Union Iron Works and that they had built this home when he was strong and able to work. Now, left a widow, she was obliged to take the young medical students to board, and she left no doubt in our minds that this was a sore cross.

I learned afterwards from Katie, the "hired girl," that the fact that they had put a bell in this house, as though they always had a servant, and installed the only bath tub in the neighborhood, shut them off from the comradeship of their old neighbors on the Hill, who now looked on our landlady's fallen fortunes in the light of a just retribution.

But the thrilling experience of bathing in that bath tub justified any extravagance in my eyes. It was the first one of my acquaintance.

My father took me to the Grand Opera House on Mission Street, where I heard my first opera, *The Bohemian Girl*. I was deeply stirred by the sad, sweet music and the poignant appeal of "I Dreamt I Dwelt in Marble Halls," and "Then You'll Remember Me." I cried into my handkerchief in a luxury of unhappiness over the sad story.

Then it came time for my father to go back to the valley. I crossed the ferry with him and waited for his train to pull out. My throat ached with the effort to hold back my tears. Notwithstanding all the heart-break and disappointment I had known through him, he was Papa. Papa, whom Mama had taught me to love.

Papa, whom I had looked forward to knowing all through the years of my childhood and young girlhood. Papa, of the plumed hat and the golden quest!

Poor as the realization of my fancies had been, yet he was the only relative in the world of whom I had any knowledge. Although I knew his love for me was a selfish, cruel substitute for what I had expected to find, yet it was something that kept me from being entirely alone.

I took the ferry boat back across the bay. I got some bread from a friendly steward and fed the gulls, who swooped down with shrill cries to receive my offering. We passed Yerba Buena Island. Already the romantic Spanish names of my new home caught my imagination. I liked to say them over: *Dolores—Vallejo—Potrero—Laguna*—names that rolled softly from the lips and seemed to give a luster to the streets.

Italian musicians played the tunes of their far-away country on a harp and violin. What old San Franciscan does not wish them back again on the ferry boats?

I came back through Washington Square. Dark-eyed children of the Italian families who clustered at the foot of Telegraph Hill were romping under the graceful weeping-willow trees, or playing hop-scotch on the sidewalks. Their grandmothers, wrinkled old crones, and their Madonna-faced mothers gossiped on the benches. There were shops with overhanging eaves and wide balconies where festoons of spaghetti and macaroni hung in the windows; through the open doors of the homes I could see tables set with food and straw-covered bottles of wine and smell the pungent odor of garlic. It made me think of the sheep camps in the valley.

Men went along the streets with a torch, lighting the gas in the street lamps, and soon ribbons of light ran up and down the hills.

I went to my room in the boarding house and lighted my gas jet. Already the room was beginning to seem like home. There was an oak bedstead with a head-board that reached to the high ceiling. There was a bureau to match, with a bureau scarf and a heart-shaped pincushion occupying the place of honor. An ingrain carpet, somewhat worn in front of the bureau and wash-stand, covered the floor of the room, and a gaily decorated wash-bowl and pitcher invited cleanliness.

The fog horns that sounded on the bay at night, instead of filling my room with loneliness, always lulled me with a sense of watchful security and the promise of a safe harbor. They made me think of Grandmother and the beautiful river.

I burned the midnight gas industriously, and many a time our landlady would come to my room in the morning to find me asleep with my Gray's *Anatomy* clasped to my breast and a skull beside my head on the pillow. She was a Catholic and it took much telling of beads and punctilious attendance at Mass to relieve her mind after such experiences.

At first I was utterly confused by the strange, meaningless words that fell from the lips of our professors. They spoke in an unknown tongue and the tantalizing syllables buzzed at my ears until my head swam with the fruitless endeavor to understand. But I soon found that a clavicle was only a collar bone and a scapula was only a shoulder blade; that the sterno-cleido-mastoid was a muscle that ran from the breast-bone to back of the ear, and that acute gastro-enteritis was commonly known as a stomach-ache.

And so I groped slowly through the maze of Osteology, and Physiology and Medical Chemistry, in which the freshman class seemed hopelessly lost. There were thirty-five students in the class. Three of them were women. The other two were older than I. They had been teachers, who, catching the spirit of the new woman's movement, had decided to go into the profession, to take their places in the sun, to stand shoulder to shoulder with the men.

Having completed the preliminary term satisfactorily, I appeared before the Dean to enroll as a regular student. Doctor McLean, our Dean, had been a protégé of Dr. Toland. He was a thin-faced man with a sparse beard, piercing eyes and long, slender hands and fingers. He used to say, "No man can be a surgeon who does not have eyes in the ends of his fingers." His fingers did seem to have magical qualities. He was driven in his carriage from lecture room to hospital to bedside, with a pile of medical books on the seat beside him. Every moment was spent in study. He died at forty-five, a great surgeon who had given his life to science.

The Medical Department of the University admitted women. There was nothing to do about it! But I left his office with the feeling that I was just one of the petty annoyances to be endured. He evidently concurred in the views of an eminent practitioner who said in 1875, speaking of women in Medicine, before the State Medical Society:

"Taken as a whole they will probably never amount to much unless the experience of the past belies that of the future. While this is so, yet no person of extended views or liberal ideas can desire to see the doors of science closed against them."

Many of the professors always resented our presence in medical college. Some of them treated us with cold indifference. Others seemed to take an unholy pleasure in shocking every feminine sense. They told ribald jokes. Many of them I did not understand, but I felt disgraced as I had when Aunt Sade left the note on my bureau.

In the evening I would climb to the top of Telegraph Hill. When San Francisco was in her gayest moods, the sea was a scintillating sapphire jewel for her adornment. On days when she wrapped herself in misty veils of fog the waters became a jade green brooch to hold her draperies. I watched the ships, lying at anchor, the masts of the sailing vessels swaying with the wash of the waves, the steamers and white-sailed ships that went out through the Golden Gate with the evening tide.

Telegraph Hill was a jolly place in those days. Wallace Irwin caught the spirit of it as old San Franciscans knew it:

> *O, Telygraft Hill, she sits proud as a queen,*
> *And th' docks lie below in th' glare,*
> *And th' bay runs beyant her all purple and green*
> *Wid th' gingerbread island out there,*
> *And th' ferryboats toot at owld Telygraft Hill*
> *And th' Hill it don't care if they do,*
> *While th' Bradys and Caseys av Telygraft Hill*
> *Joost sit there enj'yin' th' view.*

For th' Irish they live on th' top av it,
And th' Dagoes they live on th' base av it,
And th' goats and th' chicks and th' brickbats and
    shticks
Is joombled all over th' face av it,
Av Telygraft Hill, Telygraft Hill,
Crazy owld, daisy owld Telygraft Hill! *

☡ *AN OLD SEA-CAPTAIN'S TALE* ☡
TEACHERS, TRIALS &
TELEGRAPH HILL

SUBJECTS, BODIES FOR DISSECTION, WERE
divided into five parts—the head, two uppers and two
lowers. By some ironical twist of circumstance, the first
dissection assigned to me was a lower. The dissection
of the pelvic organs was to be done in company with the
young man who was assigned to the other lower. It
was a male subject.

The two other women of the class were doing their
dissection together. There was no way out. Nothing
to do but face the music. I waited as long as possible,
putting off the evil day. The young man waited, a bit
cynical, wholly amused. It came time for the quiz section in anatomy. The quiz master was a dapper young
graduate, much impressed with himself and his authority.
He was of the group who hated the incursion of women
into what he considered the distinctly masculine territory of medicine.

* Used by permission of Wallace Irwin.

I had studied my anatomy assiduously, but neither the young man nor myself had touched a scalpel to the subject. We met in the dissecting room. All the other subjects were in position and had had more or less work done on them. The quiz master walked over to our dissecting table.

He turned to the young man. "Why has nothing been done on your subject?" he questioned.

The young man hesitated, glancing at me.

The quiz master turned on me. "Have you the other lower on this subject?" His words were like a steel file.

"Yes," I replied, the blood rushing to my face.

"Do you expect to graduate in medicine, or are you just playing around with the idea?"

"I hope to graduate." I tried to make my voice sound firm, but instead I realized it sounded ridiculously weak and feminine.

The group around me were "all eyes," some friendly, some hostile.

"If you have any feelings of delicacy in this matter, young woman, you had better leave college and take them with you, or fold them away in your work basket and be here, on your stool, tomorrow morning. We don't put up with any hysterical feminine nonsense in men's medical schools."

He turned away. The group followed him to be quizzed on another subject where the dissection was well advanced. I bit my tongue and held back the tears. I was trembling with shame and indignation. I clenched my fists and joined the group. When the quiz master asked me a question I was able to answer it clearly and intelligently. I had lived and dined and slept with Gray's *Anatomy*.

I left as soon as the quiz was over and started up Telegraph Hill to let the fog lay soft, caressing hands on my burning face. On my way I passed a house with a ship's walk on the roof. I had often seen a man dressed in full captain's uniform, with a captain's cap on his head, standing there, looking out to sea through a telescope. He rolled as he walked, as though he had a ship's deck under him instead of a roof.

As I passed the house this day, he halloed: "Ahoy, lass! Drop your anchor and I'll come down to you."

He came rolling down the steps of his house. He had warm brown eyes and a weathered face. His long, gray moustache drooped over his chin and he twisted it as he talked.

"I've seen there's something troubling you, lass," he began. "Now I'm a friendly old sailing man and I thought I might throw you a rope!"

He started walking up the hill with me, and we found a sheltered spot and sat down together. I couldn't resist his good-humored friendliness. I told him about medical college and how I climbed the Hill to forget about it and to have the wind blow the smell of the dissecting room out of my nostrils.

He chuckled as though it was all a great joke. "Shiver my timbers, if you haven't run into the same kind of a sand bar I used to hear the old sailors tell about when our ship docked down there at the foot of the Hill in what used to be Yerba Buena Cove.

"I was splicing ropes and working for my able-bodied seaman's papers. When the sailors had shore leave we used to go up to the plaza and dance with the señoritas. The old sailors would tell us what a soft bunk we had and how different it was in their day, when they shipped on vessels that traded in hides and tallow. As soon as they were sighted coming in the Golden Gate the station on top of this Hill would signal the news and what vessel it was. By the time they anchored in the cove the ox-carts, most of them driven by Indians, would be on their way to the landing, loaded with hides. The sailor's job was to get those hides on the ship.

"The hides had been stretched and pegged down to dry and when they were piled on the landing they were as stiff as boards and wide across as a man's arms could reach. Some of 'em weren't half cured. Talk about smell. Those old sailors used to describe those stinking hides till you could hardly stay in the room.

"They had to load the hides on their heads and wade out to the ships. I've seen the Scotch caps they used to wear to keep the smell out of their hair. If the wind was blowing those stiff hides were like sails and the sailors would be blown over and knocked around trying to get them on their heads. But they kept their sea legs and lived to a good old age to tell the story.

"Keep your sea legs, lass! When the smells get too bad, come up on old Telegraph Hill and let the winds blow them away.

"I was about your age," he continued, "when I first made this port. The bay came up to where Montgomery Street is now. Portsmouth Square was a trading post. There was a minty smelling vine that ran all over the sand dunes. The Spanish settlers used it for a medicine and they named the place Yerba Buena, meaning the good herb.

"There were three settlements in those days. One in the hills to the south, where the Franciscan Fathers had converted the Indians and taught them to make adobe bricks, and built a mission church on a stream which they called Arroyo de los Dolores, because they first saw it on the day of the Mother of Sorrows. They named the church the Mission Dolores.

"At the north, overlooking the channel that runs out to the Golden Gate, was the Presidio, where the Spanish had established their military post. Then there was Yerba Buena, the trading post.

"It was built around a plaza, or square, the way the Spanish always built their towns. The main street was called La Calle de la Fundacion. There were no wagons in those days, except the ox-carts the Indians made. The caballeros and señoritas all rode horseback. There were trails all over the hills, and scrub oak and chapparal made a cover for the quail and grouse.

"The Spanish were fond of sports and dancing and every time a ship came into port there would be a celebration. They would send boats to all the ranchos around the bay, and gather all the people. The caballeros and señoritas came from the Presidio and we danced in the adobe houses at the trading post.

"There were ships in the port from all over the world, whaling vessels, trading vessels, and all kinds of adventurers. Men from Russia and France, Germany, and New England danced with the lovely señoritas and lost their hearts to them. I forget my old age and rheumatiz when I think of those señoritas with their dark eyes shadowed by their cobwebby lace mantillas.

"I sailed away and when I struck this port again Captain Montgomery from the United States sloop *Portsmouth* had taken over Yerba Buena and named it Portsmouth Square. And the settlement was called San Francisco for St. Francis to whose honor and glory Father Junipero had dedicated the mission.

"There was a school house and a post office and a customs house and a bank on the old plaza. I sailed away again. When we were in our home port, the news came that gold had been discovered in California. I'd gotten to be a ship's mate by then, and we came back to San Francisco. The ships were so thick in the harbor we could hardly find a place to cast anchor.

"Most of the sailors deserted the ships as soon as they got into the harbor. The vessels lay there at anchor with no one to sail them. But I was never a land man, so I put to sea again.

"After awhile I got to be captain and ran my own vessel into this port o'call and stayed at the What Cheer House for many a year. It's the most beautiful harbor in the world! So when I was too old to follow the sea, I came here to live and built me a ship's walk on top of my house so as I could look out the Golden Gate."

Twilight was creeping across the bay and the lamplighters were out with their torches before the Captain had finished his story. He rose stiffly to his feet.

"I'm not quite as spry as I was when I danced with the señoritas. Kind of hard to hoist my sail sometimes.

But when I get under wind I'm all right," he said as we went down the hill. "Keep your sea legs, lass! Keep your sea legs!" he kept repeating as he bade me goodnight. Somehow his words braced my courage.

The next morning I entered the dissecting room with every nerve tense. I expected to meet a score of mocking eyes. The place was deserted. Our subject was in position, ready to begin work. Rubber gloves and a dissecting case and Gray's manual were placed conveniently near. There was a note on the table. "You had better go ahead. We can't be here for a day or two. We'll show up for the next quiz."

The quiz master came in after his lecture. He hadn't forgotten. I was perched on my stool, working busily. He asked me what had become of the others. I told him I didn't know. The note was tucked securely in my smock. I put my hand in my pocket and felt it. It was as reassuring as the handclasp of a brother.

Something of the difficulties that I encountered must have crept between the lines of my letters to my father. I had never written anything about them. Perhaps the thought of the dissecting room as we had seen it together stimulated him to allow me to give up medicine for something more pleasant. He may have felt that I could not make a success in a profession that was distasteful to me, thereby causing his pride to suffer a fall. Whatever the motive, a letter came quite unexpectedly, saying that I could go across the bay to Berkeley and enter the University proper if I cared to do so.

I was surprised to find that I had no wish to change. I really liked the study of medicine. I wanted to go on with it more than I wanted anything else in the world. I wanted to win out. I wanted to keep the respect that I felt had prompted those young men to do what they had done that morning. I wanted to demonstrate that a woman could be just as good a sport as a man.

From that time forward when the professors told risqué jokes or made scornful allusions to the encroachment of petticoats, I wrapped the cloak of their respect around me and felt secure in its folds.

Dr. R. Beverly Cole, our professor of Obstetrics and Gynecology, was a man of the old school who delighted in being a thorn in the flesh of the women who attended his lectures. He was a slight, wiry man with a moustache through which he spat tobacco juice into the cuspidor, which often, as he strode back and forth in the pit of the amphitheater, was a precarious distance away. He never missed. He wore a Prince Albert coat and a black skull cap covered his bald pate with its fringe of white hair.

He used to say, "Female doctors are failures! It is a fact there are from six to eight ounces less brain matter in the female, which shows how handicapped she is! Ladies should grace homes." His opinions were just as pronounced regarding other innovations in medicine as they were regarding women. He taught, "Listerism is unnecessary if you use soap and an open faucet. Cleanliness is next to Godliness. A dirty woman is the dirtiest creature in all God's creation." He held that antisepsis had not reduced the mortality rate in obstetrics.

He was a brilliant and daring man in the operating room, but he was never in better fettle than when, in the pit of the amphitheater, he demonstrated the proper

procedure when attending a patient during accouchement.

He insisted that no gentleman ever removed his coat
in the presence of a lady, but he took off his detachable
cuffs, rolled back his sleeves, and with the aid of a much-
worn leather pelvis and baby illustrated the malpositions,
malformations, and emergencies that confront the obstetrician when assisting the mother to bring her child
into the world.

He always carried a crystal of alum, about the size
of an egg, with a string attached to it in his vest pocket.
He proudly exhibited this as his world-renowned treatment for uterine hemorrhage. One writer describes him
as "brilliant, rather than profound, with a contagious
joviality and a mischievous wit." This wit he used to
impress his lessons on the students. The fact that there
were women present added a certain zest to the performance.

It seemed cruel and unnecessary to me in those days,
but I realize now that those risqué illustrations fixed
certain facts in our minds as nothing else could have
done.

I cite one of his less riotous stories to show how, when
confronted with a certain difficulty, the young doctor
would hark back to the days of Dr. Cole and, remembering one of his stories, know what to do. He was
lecturing on the difficulties the obstetrician encountered
when he found a hand presenting instead of the normal
head presentation. He claimed that, when in an examination he asked one of his students what to do under
such emergency, the student replied: "I'd take that little
hand in mine and say, 'Good-bye, baby,' and send for

a doctor." Whenever I encountered that emergency in my practice, I would hear Dr. Cole telling that story and remember how he demonstrated on that worn leather pelvis with the shabby leather baby what to do about it.

One entire lecture hour was given to the making of the bed for the patient. Sheets and blankets were provided and the lecture table became a lying-in couch, where Dr. Cole illustrated the proper kind of mattress to be provided for the event, how the sheets must be drawn tight with the wide hems to the patient's face, how there must be two single blankets instead of one double one, in case the patient became too warm and one thickness must be dispensed with, how the draw-sheet should be placed and pinned.

Another lecture hour went to the dressing of the leather baby. A complete layette was provided, even to bassinet, somewhat worn from much use, but still fulfilling its purpose. First, we were instructed in the proper scorching of the old piece of linen to be used with lycopodium for dressing the cord. Then a binder was pinned around the child so tightly that he could snap his finger on its taut surface. Then came the shirt and flannel pinning blanket. Then the long flannel petticoat, then a long, white, ruffled petticoat, and then a long white dress!

Then Dr. Cole took the leather baby in his arms and pictured that thrilling moment when the doctor should present the child to the happy mother. He insisted that a nurse should never be allowed to perform this rite. It meant the cementing of the bond between the patient and the accoucheur.

The whole process was accompanied by witty comment that gave it more the atmosphere of a stage performance than a medical lecture. It would seem like a puppet show to the modern medical student, but many a time, in my country practice, I looked back in gratitude to Dr. Cole for the homely, housewifely, nursing hints I carried away from those lectures.

The Old West furnished a picturesque background for a man with such dramatic propensities. Many amusing stories are handed down—one in connection with the celebrated murder of James King of William.

I often puzzled over the name, James King of William, that was so heroically written on the pages of the early history of California. It had a royal sound. When I read that James King was born in Georgetown, D. C., and upon reaching maturity, found so many James Kings in the vicinity that he annexed his father's given name to his own, as a means of identification, the name lost something of its luster. The zealous courage of the man and the tragedy of his murder, avenged by the swift and terrible justice of the Vigilantes, still had the power to stir one's blood.

Dr. Cole was surgeon-general of the Vigilance Committee, and the first surgeon to treat James King of William. Later the wounded man was placed under the care of Dr. Toland and his confrères.

When James King of William died, Dr. Cole appeared before the State Medical Society and voiced his wrath. He stated that there had been gross negligence in the treatment of the case and that the wound was not at all dangerous, and with ordinary care and judgment there would not have been the slightest danger to the life of the wounded man. He claimed that a sponge was left in the wound five days, and dramatically hurled accusations of malpractice right and left. Much indignation and a vigorous display of legal pyrotechnics followed this outburst.

The squabble among the surgeons led to some amusing comments by the press of the day, among them a facetious poem:

> *"Who killed cock-robin?"*
>   *"I," said Dr. 'Scammon,'*
> *"With my chloroform and gammon,*
>   *I killed cock-robin."*
>
> *"Why was it given*
>   *In a smothering dose, by Heaven?"*
> *"I refuse to say,"*
>   *Replied Dr. Gray.*
>
> *"Who put in the sponge?"*
>   *"I," says Dr. 'Lunge.'*
> *"They did me impunge,*
>   *So 'bedad' I left in my sponge."*
>
> *"Who found the sponge in the body?"*
>   *"I," says (clever) little Bertody,*
> *"I found it in the body."*
>
> *"Who took it out?"*
>   *"I," says plucky Stout,*
> *"I took it out."*

> *"Who blabbed the whole?"*
> *"I," says Dr. Cole,*
> *"It lay on my soul*
> *And I blabbed the whole!"*

But we have evidence that everything was settled amicably in the fact that Dr. Toland appointed Dr. R. Beverly Cole as the first Dean of Toland Medical College, and that he held the chair of Obstetrics in that institution until his death.

Medical journals record that: "In 1859, before the California State Medical Society, Dr. Cole, speaking of the pioneer women of California, removed at the most critical periods of their lives from the healthful advice of their mothers, stated that 'three out of four of those ladies, both married and single, who have reached the age of fifteen are no better than they should be.' He compared them to a certain woman of Babylon as being the victims of dissipation and fashionable life, yielding to the solicitation of the opposite sex and finding themselves in a short time a prey to disease."

Eastern papers commented at length on the statements made by Dr. Cole and added reflections on the morality and chastity of the women of California.

Dr. Cole became the center of the violent storm which arose. He was threatened with expulsion from the American Medical Association, but was finally exonerated of any "evil intent to defame the character of the women in the state, although there can be no doubt that the language of the report in question was very loose and improper."

He lived to become president of the same organization

and return from the eastern convention where that honor was bestowed, to the students who gave him a great ovation in old Toland Hall.

✕ *RAMBLES ON THE WATERFRONT* ✕ *NOTES ON THE GOLDEN NINETIES*

THE OTHER TWO WOMEN STUDENTS OF the class lived in San Francisco and studied together. They were kind to me and often invited me to their homes. One, of Irish descent, lived in the Mission, that old part of San Francisco where people settled before cable cars made the hills and the view accessible. Her parents were fine, thrifty people of pioneer stock. Their daughter was an indomitable worker and the most brilliant student in our class. What her brain lacked in weight it certainly made up in quality.

The third woman was a Jewess. I shall never forget the luxurious home where she lived nor the huge dining table, loaded with delectable food unheard of in a Telegraph Hill boarding house. The atmosphere of domestic serenity and genuine hospitality which pervaded that home has always been associated in my mind with the Jews of San Francisco.

Kind as they were, those women were older, more experienced than I, and absorbed in their work. They probably thought me too young and irresponsible to finish the course. But after the dissecting room incident, I was received in the students' boarding house on Telegraph Hill as one of the group. It was my privilege to sit around the big table in the study room, where some part of a skeleton was always suspended from the gas chandelier in the center, and share in the quizzes and discussions. They accepted me in brotherly comradeship and took me with them on their explorations of San Francisco.

It was a real adventure to take a cable car that jerked up and down the steep hills. We sat up in front in the out-of-doors seats that ran along either side, and when the grip-man shouted: "Mind the curve!" we dug in our toes and braced ourselves to keep from being hurled into space. It was much the same sensation I had experienced when sliding down hill in Grandmother's orchard. At the end of the line we transferred to the steam cars that ran to the Cliff House. The cinders that we accumulated in our eyes on the way interfered somewhat with our enjoyment of that part of the trip, but it gave us an opportunity to show with what dexterity we could turn the eyelid of a fellow student inside out and extract the offending body.

I am told that the old Cliff House, with its spires and turrets and towers, was a glaring example of the worst possible architecture, but there has never been a Cliff House that has seemed to me one half as beautiful.

From the promenade, overhanging the ocean, we watched the waves of the Pacific lazily lapping the sand. We heard the plump, shiny seals barking as they slid into the water from Seal Rocks, frolicking like happy school children. We laughed over the story of the Englishman who exclaimed when he saw them: "By Jove, those seals must be wonderfully tame, you know, or their owners wouldn't dare to let them loose right out in the ocean!"

We climbed to Sutro Heights where the man who had built the Sutro Tunnel to tap the Comstock Lode sat in his unpretentious home and derived the keenest pleasure from watching the people come and go in the gardens that he had planted for their enjoyment.

Friday was the best time to see the fishing boats come in and when a holiday fell on that day, we made a grand tour of the waterfront, starting at Meigg's Wharf soon after dawn. The boats came swarming into the harbor— Italian feluccas, some painted white with blue gunwales and blue or pink decks, others white with green trimmings. Their three-cornered sails filled to the fresh ocean breeze and they rode the waves like graceful, homing gulls. The throaty commands of the Italian skippers sounded across the water and the sails folded like birds' wings.

The fishermen in gum boots, shabby trousers, bright sashes, and checked flannel shirts came into view. There was a rattle of chains as they cast anchor. Their catch was scooped from the deck into baskets and landed. Everything on board was made snug. They ate their breakfast on deck from a big bowl of stew, accompanied by bread and claret wine. Then they cleaned their nets, or if they had been trawling, they coiled the lines in circular baskets and pressed the hooks into the rim.

The wharf was a busy place. The rays of the rising sun glistened on the sides of flounders and striped bass, red rock-cod and salmon, mackerel and crab, sharks and starfish, octopus and devil-fish with their squirming arms lined with little cups. The choice of the catch was loaded into boxes, stacked for the market, and carted away in big wagons. Hucksters with broken-down carts bargained for the less desirable portions. Chinamen, with baskets swung on flexible poles that rested on their shoulders, departed with shark's fins, dogfish, squids, clams and shrimps.

The wharf settled to the routine of the day. Decks were scrubbed, nets mended and festooned along the wharf to dry. Gulls gathered for the feast of small fish that were thrown from the nets. A whale that had followed in the wake of the fishing fleet spouted off shore.

We talked with old fishermen, who told us that Meigg's Wharf had once been a fashionable promenade and that the landing covered the site of Clarke's Point and India Dock where the old clipper fleet, the finest ships of their day, had discharged their cargoes.

Following east along the waterfront, we saw four-masted sailing vessels riding in on the breeze that brought them through the Golden Gate like winged clouds. The wharves were crowded with shipping, steamers and trig schooners and Chinese junks, squatty and foreign-looking. Into the docks at Washington and Jackson Streets came river steamers, loaded with fruit and vegetables. Their clumsy stern wheels churned the water to foam. The fruit dealers were there to bargain for their share. The canners departed with their loads of "cots" and "toms" (apricots and tomatoes).

The government steamer docked and landed officers and soldiers on shore leave for the day, picking up others, to continue its way to the Presidio and to Alcatraz Island, the military prison, that rose, grim as some pirates' fortress, from the smiling waters of the bay. Farther along were the coast steamers, from Alaska, from Puget Sound and San Diego. Stout tugs like busy bumblebees tooted with importance. Across the street were the sailors' harbors: "The Fair Breeze," "Snug Harbor," and the beer halls where Jack had a riotous time as long as his leave or his money lasted. To offset these were the Mariner's Church and the little band of Salvation Army workers, who welcomed him to a safer if less exciting harbor.

There were fascinating odors of tea and spices, sugar-cane and hemp, coffee and tropical fruits. We went on board a sailing vessel from Mexico and while the students drank Mexican mescal with the ships' officers, I teased the gaudy parrots who swore at me in the language in which "Dios" and "Diablo" can never be made to sound profane. One of the mates was quite taken with me and gave me a Mexican shawl and a dried porcupine fish, which I treasured for years.

Then we came to the old ferry sheds and successfully dodged the hacks and express wagons and escaped the peril of the clashing cable cars, to follow along by the lumber yards and Tar Flat, the Limehouse of old San Francisco. Next came the lumber schooners and the coal bunkers, and then the China Basin, where lay the great ocean-going passenger ships flying the flags of every nation. Beyond them huddled the tramp schooners, with their patched sails, riding close to their more fortunate sisters like a squadron of poor relations.

We passed the Union Iron Works with their ship-building yards, the sugar refineries, and then came to the little horse-car that ran to the Potrero, to the tune of its jangling bell. The Potrero—the pasture land of the old Mission fathers. It seemed strange to think of pasture land in this busy city by the Golden Gate.

All this time I had no girl friends, so I used to go down to the kitchen and visit with Katie and hear all the gossip of the neighborhood. I would listen while she haggled with John, the Chinaman, who came shuffling to the door in his felt-soled slippers with his baskets of fresh vegetables and fruit swung from his shoulders. John would stand there, in his blue cotton coolie coat and his pig tail, blandly listening while Katie vociferously told him that his wares were not fit to eat.

When she had finished John would pick out the fruits and vegetables which had met with her greatest scorn and put them on the kitchen table. "How muchee you pay?" he would ask in his calm, unruffled way. Katie would name the sum. John would accept it as though bestowing a favor and go shuffling on his way.

Katie had a friend, Gussie, who worked in the canneries. Gussie was a dark-eyed Mexican girl, with a pretty face but her hands were always sore and swollen from the raw cuts that came from peeling the "toms" and "cots" in the canneries. They made me think of Mama's hands and the time she ran the machine needle into her thumb in the corset factory. But Gussie was very happy. She had a lover who worked in the Union Iron Works and that made a great difference.

One day Gussie took me home with her to dinner. She lived near Portsmouth Square and there were shops all around with strings of red peppers, and yellow gourds and queer shaped brown and yellow pottery in the windows. We had Mexican beans and tostodas, and enchiladas for dinner. They were hot with chili pepper, but it was a cold, foggy day, and they tasted wonderfully good and gave me a warm, pleasant feeling all over.

They were a gay, happy family with many children. After dinner Gussie's lover came and they played the guitar and sang old Spanish songs, and Gussie put on a short, red skirt and shook a castanet in her hand and danced a fandango. I had not realized how pretty Gussie was until then, but her dark eyes flashed and her cheeks glowed with color. I envied her the big family and the gay, care-free life they seemed to have together, and I envied her her lover.

After a while we walked over to Portsmouth Square. The queer, pagoda-shaped roofs of the buildings of Chinatown were outlined against the sky on the farther side. There were trees and paths and benches in the square. Men were sitting on the benches, and Gussie's lover said they were mostly tramps from all over the world, some of them sailors, some of them men who had lost their money in the gold fields.

He said that Robert Louis Stevenson, the writer, used to board near the Square with Mary Carson on Bush Street, and that he sat on the benches and listened to the stories these old men told, and then put them into books.

I remembered the story the old Captain had told me of Portsmouth Square when it was Yerba Buena. The fresh breeze blew the smells of the city away and the minty odor of the Good Herb, that trailing vine with its tiny lavender blossoms, was in my nostrils.

Although California had contributed Yerba Santa, Grindelia Robusta, and Cascara Sagrada to the U. S. Pharmacopoeia, that fact did not illuminate the dry as-dust study of Materia Medica. The diagnosis of disease and its treatment by drugs, as set forth by our professor of the Practice of Medicine, became very tedious at times and seemed remote from actual experience. But the unique personality of the man who delivered those lectures enlivened many a dull moment.

I can see him now, driving up to the door of Toland Hall in his splendid barouche, dressed in a frock coat, striped trousers, a silk hat, white kid gloves and spats. Two fine hounds always followed his carriage.

He arrived in the lecture room precisely at the appointed hour. He removed an immaculate, fine linen handkerchief from the upper, left-hand pocket of his coat, shook it out, brushed the end of his nose, returned the handkerchief to its place, shook down his cuffs, cleared his throat and began. I never knew this program to vary.

He had an attack of gout at the time we were to undergo the final quiz of Materia Medica. It was arranged that we should go to his home and that the quiz should be conducted there. It was a trying ordeal.

He sat, clad in a handsome dressing gown, enthroned in a great chair, with the offending foot, wrapped in lamb's wool, on the stool in front of him. Woe to the student who ventured too close to that stool!

His charming wife and daughter took pity on us and served raspberry sherbet when the gruelling test was over. I had never tasted sherbet before. They lived in one of the fine old homes of San Francisco. The red plush furniture may have been, as the interior decorators of the present day tell us, "simply atrocious," but it was cheerful and comfortable, and I thought it was the acme of luxury.

Architects are very scornful now when they recall the mill work and the bay windows of the Gay Eighties and Nineties. But there was something very expansive and welcoming about those windows. They reminded me of some stout, benevolent gentleman, smiling complacently above a well filled stomach and a gold watch chain. And how those bay windows did lend themselves to the elaborate social functions in vogue at that time! After the momentous evening spent in the home of our professor, I was able to picture the scenes so vividly reported in the newspapers of the day.

There were receptions where "the receiving party occupied a position in the bay window of the library, between marble busts of the host and hostess, and beneath a canopy of verdant foliage fringed with masses of lace, which was arranged to represent drifted snow."

Dancing clubs met in private homes and the decorations were given in detail in the society pages of the *San Francisco Argonaut.* The report of one of those functions read: "In the bay window was a lever or beam of bamboo not quite in equipoise, the scales being laden with Bon Silène and Perle du Jardin roses. Diminutive vases, full of pink and yellow roses, graced the étagère, while the oil painting in the corner on its easel of beaten brass was draped with pink silk and vines and had a cluster of roses and ferns at the top."

The newel post and the hat rack also received the attention of the decorators, and I read that "the newel post at the foot of the staircase was robed with verdant foliage kept in place by a scarf of pistache green surah silk. A band of pale green silk was diagonally draped across the mirror of the hat rack, and the wood-work was deftly concealed by foliage."

Those were the days when that dashing bachelor, Ned Greenway, led the cotillion and the beaus and belles danced the figures, "Grand Right and Left," "Gliding Lines," "Royal Arches," "The Basket," "Reverse Circles." There was one very daring figure called "Over the Garden Wall." In this the gentlemen were masked and a sheet represented a wall. The gentlemen placed their hands on the wall and the ladies chose their partners by that thrilling device.

The favors, as described in the columns of the *Argonaut,* were "porcelain slippers, hand-painted blotters, silk sachet bags, and other articles, handsome and ornamental"!

Even that greatest of all social events of the "Gay Nineties," the Fair-Oelrichs wedding, took place in the embrace of a bay window. "The nuptial bower was in the main saloon. It was arranged at the end of the room, with the curtained bay window as a background. Here were the prie-dieu of white satin and before it the altar rail of sweet-peas and ferns joined by ropes of corded silk, while above all was the beautiful bower."

San Francisco buzzed with the details of that wedding. "Mrs. Fair issued seven hundred and fifty invitations to the reception, and one hundred and fifty cards to the wedding. . . . Miss Fair's trousseau was made in Europe under the supervision of Mrs. John W. Mackay. . . . The bride appeared charming in her wedding dress, which was very elegant and one of the most expensive ever worn in America! . . . The dress was of cream white satin and the court train was three yards long. . . . Senator Fair presented the bride with a bank account of $500,000 and a monthly income for life of $1,000.00."

The *Argonaut* was enthusiastic in its approbation of this marriage of a California heiress with one of New York's most eligible bachelors. Evidently they felt American fortunes should be kept in America.

Their comments on other alliances were somewhat acrid: "The number of American girls who have bought titled husbands and the enormous prices they have paid for them make pertinent the inquiry: 'What is the cash value of a title?' The price paid by Miss Huntington for Prince Hatzfeldt was $200,000. . . . What Mrs. Mackay paid for Prince Colonna and Mrs. Hammersley for the Duke of Marlborough cannot be estimated with any degree of accuracy. . . . In some cases, of course, value has been received and the purchase money has not been excessive. For instance, Miss Jerome obtained a prize in Lord Randolph Churchill." While all this was happening I was still going to medical college, dressed in shabby, unsuitable clothes. My father had selected them and outfitted me when we arrived in

San Francisco and I endured them as best I might. I remember especially a coat of checked woollen material in plain brown and some kind of mixture. The checks were at least two inches square, and I weighed one hundred and seventy-five pounds!

Women were not reading *Eat and Grow Thin* or *Counting the Calories* in those days, but no one wished to appear like a young mountain. When I see the slim, starved young women on the campus nowadays, I think what a riot it would cause if I turned out in that brown checked coat.

In spite of my clothes, I had admirers among the students. There was Tom, who always had an eye out for business. He felt that a partnership with a wife who could be a help-meet in a business way would be a most desirable arrangement. Although he cloaked his underlying motive in a formula of ardent love-making, I realized that he was offering me a sugar-coated pill.

There was Clarence, with the big, soulful eyes and the interesting pallor.

Then there was Paul, protecting as a brother. I loved him as I knew I would have adored my own brother had he lived. I felt very miserable and romantic when I told him I could not marry and go on through the years with him as he had planned. I cried into my pillow that night, feeling that I had ruined his life, broken his heart. I feared that my rejection of his love might drive him to some desperate, despairing deed. But Paul survived the ordeal very well, and afterward mended his broken heart quite satisfactorily with the help of another girl.

There were many happy, care-free days spent with
men of the class, when friendships that asked nothing
more were welded. None of us had money to squander, but there was always the old Tivoli Opera House,
the first house in the United States to present opera
every night of the year. Seats were fifty cents. The
audience of the old Tivoli was the first to recognize
the rare gifts of Tetrazzini. I was there the night that
Alice Neilson found her first stepping-stone on the
way to success. Alice was in the chorus, but she had
understudied the rôle of the leading soprano, Tille
Sallenger, that buxom blonde who was the idol of Tivoli
habitués, hoping that chance might cast her in it some
day. Her opportunity came, and San Francisco took
her to its heart. That was a distinguishing trait of the
city by the Golden Gate. It never waited on the approval of New York or Paris or London. Many an
uncut diamond has been taken away from the Tivoli by
managers who had dropped in to see the show.

There were dinners at the Poodle Dog or the Fly
Trap, or Techau's or Coppa's, or any one of the places
where 3 for 2's (three dishes for two-bits) were to be
had with a glass of red or white wine; or seven course,
fifty cent meals, with a pint of wine; or more elaborate
repasts, where each course was a chef-d'œuvre, with a
pint of wine, for one dollar, catered to every appetite
and pocket book. "When half the town was restaurants
and all of them were good."

What a mercy we were not bothered about calories
those days, but could enjoy Italian ravioli, Mexican
enchiladas, French bread and salads with plenty of
olive oil in the dressing, green turtle soup, juicy planked

steaks with rich sauces and ambrosial fried cream, golden brown with burning rum—to the accompaniment of soft Italian or Spanish music.

☙ *A CHINATOWN ADVENTURE* ☙
FATHER JUNIPERO'S
MISSION

SAN FRANCISCO'S NOB HILL ALWAYS HELD a peculiar fascination for me. There stood the houses of some of the Bonanza Kings; palaces built with the fortunes that came from the ore of Virginia City or that started in the glory hole of Bodie. I knew that the building material for one of those homes, a brown-stone front, had been transported all the way, by the Isthmus, from Connecticut. Mama and I had worked in a corset factory in Connecticut on the chance that some day we, too, might live in a palace.

The tales of the splendor in which the Bonanza Kings and the railroad magnates lived on that hill were told as one might tell the story of Aladdin and his lamp. It is said that by 1890 there were probably more mil-lionaires in San Francisco than in any other city of equal population in the world. Even the men, them-selves, it seems, were so awed by the enormity of their wealth that they endeavored to keep the public in igno-rance of its real extent. The story was told of how, when Leland Stanford bought some beautiful and expensive diamonds for his wife, the incident and an estimate of the value of the jewels got into the papers, and he was reprimanded by the apparently more frugal members of the aristocracy of wealth for allowing the public to know the sums that had been spent.

Huntington wrote Colton regarding the affair: "The higher a monkey climbs a tree the more apt he is to expose himself, especially if he is painted sky-blue."

From his mansion on Nob Hill the owner of the brown-stone front could look down to the corner where he had tended bar in his own saloon, and to Pauper Alley, that strange street behind the Stock Exchange where the Mud Hens lived. In the boom days of Virginia City and Bodie, Pauper Alley was crowded with adventurers and gamblers who had access to the Stock Exchange, the bucket shops, and the broker's offices from the Alley. Now that those days were past, the people who had been the camp followers stayed on. They had landed in the tailings pond of the Big Bonanza.

Prosperity had a way of climbing the hills. Even the "ladies of pleasure" climbed, not to the heights, but part way up; or sank to the level of old Dupont Street, according to whether fickle fortune smiled or frowned upon them. One of the famous ones died not so long ago, and the following tribute appeared in the *San Francisco Chronicle*: "One more bit of the San Francisco that was has drifted off to that uncharted Sargasso that holds the old Barbary Coast, the Poodle Dog, the Silver Dollar, the Bank Exchange, the Mason Street Tenderloin, and those other gay haunts that made San Francisco famous throughout the seven seas.

"To a post-war generation that knows only speakeasies, jazz and automobile petting parties the name of

Tessie Wall means nothing. Before a State law closed the doors of places where men gathered, everyone knew who Tessie Wall was. A traveling man you met in Indianapolis, a sailor you encountered on the Shanghai Bund, might not be able to tell you who was Mayor of San Francisco, but he could tell you about Tessie Wall."

Stories were told of how she used to attend the policemen's ball, dressed in a flowing white satin gown and a jewelled tiara, and how she would throw a thousand dollars on the bar and shout: "Drink that up, boys! Have a drink on Tessie Wall!"

Recently the newspapers announced an auction: "Tessie Wall's Treasures, the jewels, the furs, the ornate furnishings, the accumulation of her gala, golden years, closing the career of one of San Francisco's famous characters."

I went. The rooms that had been arranged with the brocaded damasks, the gold mantel, the crystal fixtures, the luxuriously upholstered furniture, held a curious throng. There were sharp-nosed old women who may have found Tessie Wall a menace to their youthful dreams; there were pouchy-lidded old men who poked about with canes, and stopped before some painting or piece of statuary as though recalling the gift and the youthful giver.

In the midst of the display, I thought of one day when I had walked home from the clinics to my boarding house on Telegraph Hill. I had chosen to go out Dupont Street, not knowing that the name was a byword on every tongue. I came to a row of shabby houses springing, bare and unlovely, from the sidewalk. On the doors were names—Nellie, Marguerite, Lillie. I read them curiously, not comprehending. Then I came to an open door. There was a glimpse of a room lighted by a red lantern. Descending a narrow stairway into the room I saw a rather slatternly woman, about whom clung a faded beauty, dressed in a gay but flimsy Mother-Hubbard that came only to her knees. Her feet and legs were bare. All at once I knew.

Those unfortunate women on Dupont Street and the glamorous Tessie Wall were sisters under the skin—sisters, too, of the "good-time women" of Barbary Coast, and of their neighbors, the slant-eyed slave girls, who looked out from the barred windows of the balconies of Chinatown.

Chinatown, where the commercial value of a rare porcelain bowl depended on its antiquity, and the commercial value of a slave girl's body on its youth. Chinatown with its hands tucked up its sleeves and its guileless smile. Chinatown with its writhing dragon parading through the streets on feast days and funeral days to the sound of clashing cymbals and screeching Chinese fiddles. From it came the most faithful servants that ever ministered to the comfort and pleasure of their "Missie" or "Bossie Man," and the friendly coolies who shuffled to the door each morning with fresh and delectable fruits, vegetables, and fish. To it went men and women too weak to resist the lure of the opium and gambling dens and the pleasures that lay behind those barred windows.

But in spite of its sinister background, Chinatown was a fascinating place. I loved to roam through the streets, brushing the sleeves of the gentlemen merchants in their brocaded silks of gorgeous hues, watching the children dancing in and out of those sinister alleys, gay as butterflies in their costumes that held every color of the rainbow, wondering about the preserved eggs and strange vegetables and varnished meats in the open markets, admiring the jade and carvings and the lustrous silks displayed in the shop windows.

Most interesting of all to the young medical student were the windows where the Chinese doctors displayed the dried lizards and snakes, the pickled toads and queer-looking herbs, the powders and ginseng root, that went to make up the pharmacopoeia of the dignified, bespectacled gentlemen who dispensed those gruesome-looking remedies.

Later on I spent one of the strangest nights of my career in Chinatown. While I was an interne in the Children's Hospital, a woman physician, who was on the visiting staff, invited me to go with her to attend a confinement case on Spofford Alley, one of the most notorious places of Old San Francisco.

The Chinese preferred American women doctors to attend their women in confinement. At that time no respectable Chinese woman or "family girl" was allowed on the streets and the alleys of Chinatown were no place for a white woman to be seen alone at night. But the black medicine case that the women physicians carried insured safety. They were never molested. Just the same, the strange odors, the shadowy figures that shuffled along the streets and alleys, the weird screeching of Chinese fiddles, and the wailing of oboes, all gave me a feeling of dangers.

We climbed stairways where slant eyes peered through

peepholes and heavily hinged and barred doors were opened to us. We were ushered into a room where gorgeously embroidered panels hung on the walls, elaborately carved teakwood tables held priceless ornaments and our feet sank into soft rugs of exquisite design. There was an altar to Joss and incense was burning before the shrine where Chinese lilies bloomed.

The prospective father, a wealthy Chinese merchant, received us. He was wearing a mandarin coat stiff with embroidery and a round, black cap with a jade button set in the top. Chinese women attendants in wide trousers and wide-sleeved coats of somber hues padded about noiselessly. The mother-to-be lay on a bed of red and gold lacquer; on the floor beside it stood her tiny, high-heeled, embroidered slippers. She was one of the beautiful ladies whose feet had been bound since childhood. Her hair was securely glued to form an elaborate head-dress and was ornamented with jade. On her fingers and arms were beautiful jade bracelets and rings. A dainty brocaded coverlet was on the bed and she lay between paper sheets, soft and fine as silk.

She did not understand or speak English, nor did her attendants. The husband was our interpreter. As the labor progressed, the doctor realized that the woman was about to give birth to an acephalous child—a terrible monstrosity. We had no chance to talk over the situation. That imperturbable Chinaman was watching every move.

The doctor knew the danger to us. She knew that the Chinese considered a deformed child a curse upon the house, and that the doctor was held responsible for any deviation from the normal. But she was a match for that imperturbable Chinaman. With perfect calm she faced the difficult task of preparing the father for the tragedy that was about to occur in the room that had been prepared so ceremoniously for an auspicious event.

I shall never forget that night. The smoke of the incense stung and blinded our eyes and choked our lungs. The only relief we could find was to put our heads out the window, which must be hurriedly closed again, and inhale a few breaths of fog. The cries of the mother, about to be disgraced by her offspring, the stoical, sinister calm of the father, and the soft padding feet of the attendants were the only accompaniment to what seemed an endless labor.

The child was born. Fortunately it took only a few breaths. Then the father sent for his friends. When they came there was great gesticulating and high-pitched argument. We knew they were discussing how far we were responsible for the monstrosity and what should be done. It happened that the doctor had been away on a vacation during a certain period of the prospective mother's pregnancy and the consultation resulted in the decision that the woman who had attended the patient during the doctor's absence was responsible for the condition.

The doctor restrained them from throwing the child out into the alley, as they wished to do. She insisted that the birth must be recorded and the child buried. We were told that in China such children were thrown out to be collected by the street scavengers, but the father finally reluctantly consented to do as she directed.

I have never been more thankful to get away from any

place than I was to leave that house where the prayer
papers fluttered from the windows as we left Spofford
Alley in the early morning.

Up and down the streets of Chinatown today go boys
and girls from public schools, and from the universities,
most of them in modern American clothes. Donaldina
Cameron, in the mission on the edge of Chinatown, is
devoting her life to the rescue of slave girls. But the
plump matrons go to market in their wide trousers and
loose coats and the strange foods that they purchase are
the same as they were in the days when only slave girls
went abroad on the streets.

The Chinese newspaper is still brushed in black characters on the old, red walls, and the shops hold rare,
beautiful porcelains, jades, and embroideries, while the
incense continues to burn before the altars in the Joss
houses, and John Chinaman's attitude is the same as
when expressed in that famous commentary overheard
in a street car: "I no like Flenchman; no like German;
no like Ilishman. Melican man ve'y good. Not many
Melicans in Melica!"

There is a Chinese interne, Dr. Deng, now at the
Children's Hospital. She graduated from a women's
medical college in Shanghai. She was not allowed to
attend the co-educational medical school in Peking because her grandmother, the head of the family, objected
to co-education for women.

The Children's Hospital in San Francisco, open only
to women internes, offered an opportunity for practical
experience. She is at present Resident Pathologist there,

doing most creditable work in her chosen field. There are two Chinese women physicians practicing medicine in Chinatown. I called on them recently. They are fine, intelligent women with well equipped modern offices. Dr. Wong is a graduate from the Women's Medical College of Philadelphia. Dr. Chung obtained her medical degree from the University of Southern California.

Dr. Wong seems to have remained close to her people. She is married and raising a Chinese family in Chinatown. Her professional card is printed in English on one side, and on the other in Chinese characters.

Dr. Chung's card is printed only in English. Her offices are on the ground floor of one of the old buildings that face what was once "China Street." Next door is a regulation herb doctor's shop with snakes in jars, dried lizards and toads and all the ingredients of a witch's broth, displayed in the windows.

When I rang Dr. Chung's bell a Chinese girl in white, starched uniform admitted me. She spoke perfect English. She asked me to be seated in the waiting-room. My eyes rested on lovely old Chinese furniture and rugs. I was invited into the inner office. There was a modern, very practical-looking desk, but the large, worn volumes of her medical library were shelved in a beautiful red and gold cabinet.

The doctor is a fine-looking woman, poised and dignified. Her hair was combed straight back in the Chinese fashion, but she wore a white linen uniform, horn-rimmed glasses, and flat-heeled American shoes. She explained that she interned in the Santa Fé Hospital in Los Angeles, and did post-graduate work in Chicago, that she did not care for Pediatrics or Obstetrics and decided to practice Surgery.

She located in Chinatown in San Francisco, expecting that most of her practice would be among her own people. Contrary to that expectation, she says that 97% of her patients are white people. She explained this by stating that the Chinaman who clings to the ancient teachings and customs prefers the old Chinese herb doctor, while those who have adopted American ways and institutions feel that if they use American drugs they might better have American doctors.

My first year in Medical School was drawing to a close. In October I went with my Irish landlady to witness the celebration of the day of the patron, Saint Francis, at the old Mission Dolores. Castilian roses climbed over the crumbling headstones that marked the graves where the men and women of pioneer days lay in the shadow of the redwood cross erected by the padrés. There slept Don Luis Antonio Arguello, first commandant of the Presidio. There were good Irish names, Patrick and Michael, Bridget and Katherine, from County Limerick and Tipperary Parish, from Roscommon and County Down.

Michiele Gargurevich
Nativo di Raguso
Provincia di Dalmazio

rested beside

Jacques Emmanuel
de Vergille
né à St. Malo, France

and James Noonan from Sydney, Australia, and Luis Casanneva from Santiago de Chile, lay side by side.

The names of Felicidad Carillo de Castro and Doña Joaquina brought back the days of dark-eyed señoritas and lace mantillas. The dates ran 1850-54-60. Henry Valley, born in Verchère, Lower Canada, had lived from 1812 to 1854.

One headstone read:

> *Sacred to the memory of*
> *the late deceased*
> *James Sullivan*
> *who died by the hands*
> *of the*
> *V.C., 1856*

> *"Thou shalt bring my soul out*
> *of tribulation, and in thy*
> *mercy thou shalt destroy mine*
> *enemies."*

John Baptist Burwood Cooper, a native of England, must have been a seafaring man, for he left the legend:

> *"Though Bora's blows and Neptune's waves*
> *Have tossed me to and fro,*
> *Yet by Heaven's decree*
> *You plainly see*
> *I'm harbored here below with many of our fleet*
> *In hopes our admiral Christ to meet."*

The monument to James P. Casey, who killed James King of William and became a victim of the Vigilantes,

had been erected by the Crescent Engine Company and
bore the significant lines: "May God forgive my perse-
cutors." The headstone of Michael Mann, a native of
Ireland, county of Tipperary Parish, bade those who followed in his footsteps to:

> *"Remember man as you pass by*
> *As you are now so once was I*
> *As I am now so you will be*
> *Remember man Eternity."*

An aged Spanish woman in an old-fashioned dress,
with a black shawl over her snow-white hair, knelt by
one of the graves where she had placed fresh calla lilies
and bright geraniums. She raised her head: *"Buenas
tardes, Señora, Señorita,"* she greeted us. In her deep-
set eyes there still glowed a smoldering fire.

We entered the church, where the rough-hewn,
crudely decorated beams of the ceiling were lashed together with raw-hide. Old women knelt far back on
the floor, muttering over their beads and touching the
worn tiles with their foreheads.

A ray of sunlight fell across the blue smoke that lay
in the air from the burning incense and rested on the
baptismal font, where Doña Concepción Arguella, that
tragic figure of the romantic days of Yerba Buena who
waited in vain for the return of her Russian lover,
Resanov, was baptized.

We walked the tiles to the altar, where the saints
looked down on a carpet of roses spread before a ship
of flowers that carried the prayers of those who knelt
before his shrine to the patron saint of their beloved
Mission.

When the great earthquake and fire destroyed so many of the landmarks of old San Francisco, the new church that had been erected by the side of the old adobe building fell, but the Mission stood, firm as the faith of that saintly padré, Father Junipero Serra, who founded it.

⚛ SPEAKING OF OPERATIONS ⚛ THE DEAN CHANGES MY NAME

THE SCHEDULE OF THE MEDICAL COLlege was different in those days. Our vacation fell during the winter months. I went home. My father paraded me through the streets as if I were some choice exhibit at a county fair, and I felt like a prize animal. I resented his possession closing in on me, causing me to lose the sense of liberty that I had been steadily gaining. I knew how little the fact that he was my father had had to do with shaping my life, and I was grateful that it was so.

Grace and Frances were to be married in the spring. They bubbled with excitement at the prospect and talked continuously of their respective grooms. They questioned me about the young medical students I had met, and when they learned that I was not engaged they seemed to feel sorry for me and thought that my time had been wasted.

My father, too, questioned me, trying to find out if I had fallen in love. I could not tell him of the wholesome friendships that I had grown to prize so dearly, for I knew he would misinterpret anything that I might say.

My stepmother was not well. She looked thin and her homely face no longer held its cheerfulness. I felt great pity for her, knowing that although the "Mrs." had released her from the stigma of "old maid," it had bound her to a life full of cruel perplexities.

Soon I started back to college. A day's trip on the Carson and Colorado, a night's stop at Sodaville, another day on the Carson and Colorado and the Virginia and Truckee, and at last Reno, where I took the through train for San Francisco.

I moved to Geary Street, for our time was now divided between the clinics on Howard Street, the old City and County Hospital in the Mission, and Toland Hall at North Beach.

When I see a modern efficient medical college and realize that the students have eight years in all to grasp and perfect their knowledge, I am astonished to remember that we completed the medical course in three years, spending part of this period on horse cars traveling from the Mission to North Beach and to the clinics in between; and I wonder how our equipment compared with that of the present graduate. The science of medicine has traveled far since those days, with sterilization, immunization, radium, ultra-violet and X-ray; and yet future generations will doubtless look back on these graduates as they look back on us and wonder how they ever dared to practice medicine and surgery, knowing so little as they did.

Our class had the first course in Bacteriology that was given in the University Medical School. Our instructor was a veterinary surgeon who affected loud checks and a diamond horse-shoe pin. Our equipment was most meager; the whole idea was really on trial. But I can recall the breathtaking experience of using acid-fast dyes and through them being able to see the tubercle bacillus under the microscope.

We may smile now to read an extract from the *Pacific Medical Journal* of 1892. It is taken from an article commending the Medical School for having introduced the study of Bacteriology: "In conclusion we wish to impress on all our readers that Bacteriology, while yet an infant in swaddling clothes, has a great future before it. As a science it will amply repay cultivation, and the material is well-nigh inexhaustible."

From our class came a man whose knowledge of Bacteriology, gained in that poorly equipped laboratory, saved this country from a devastating plague epidemic brought in by rats on ships from the Orient and harbored in San Francisco's Chinatown. He headed the valiant fight of the medical men against the city fathers who tried, ostrich-like, to deny the existence of plague for commercial reasons, and the denizens of Chinatown, who dreaded the activities of the Health Board more than they did the devastating disease. Wallace Irwin describes this time perfectly.

> *"Hey, boss, quick! d'ye see 'im duck*
>   *Under the curb by Sun Mok's stall,*
> *Long tail, bead eye rat—bad luck!*
>   *D'ye see 'is color? It's green, by all*

That's dead! Some Chinaman's time has struck
    And the plague's a-creepin' along the wall.

Call me 'hop-head,' 'dope-stick' bum,
    If ye will—but I know that green is green
And the old Bubonic's bound to come
    And set the health board sweepin' clean
To put the microbes under the thumb
    Wit' chloride o' lime and quarantine.

Somewheres up in the balconies
    Priests are howlin' their heathen songs,
Dippin' down on their hands and knees,
    Smudgin' incense and bangin' gongs
To fumigate the devil and please
    The Health Board God, the dread o' the
        Tongs." *

At the same time that our newly fledged bacteriologists were waging the good fight in San Francisco, Pierre and Marie Curie in still another poorly equipped laboratory in Paris, and under circumstances that only the stoutest hearts could have mastered, were conducting those experiments that led to the discovery of radium.

Little did I dream in those days that my daughter would graduate from the same university which offered my class that beginning course in Bacteriology, and major in that subject, receiving a foreign fellowship in Bacteriology to study in Canada and Belgium.

But with all our modern equipment, it seems to me

---

* From *Chinatown Ballads,* by Wallace Irwin. Reproduced by permission.

that some of the intuition of the early physician has been lost. Laboratory findings have replaced the "eyes in the ends of his fingers." While grasping the new, we have lost something of the old.

It was interesting to read of bones and muscles, and their functions in health and disease, but it was thrilling to observe them in action in the human economy. In the clinics down on Howard Street we had our first medical contacts. We dosed out calomel and castor oil; swabbed throats and set bones. We learned to know an ear drum when we saw one, opened the boils of Madonna-faced mothers and put drops in the eyes of their black-eyed bambinos. Soft-tongued señoras, Irishmen down on their luck, flotsam of Barbary Coast and the left-overs from every land came to the clinic. We began to feel the joy of service and to realize that the science which had seemed so fixed and definite in the lecture room was constantly upset by the most surprising departures in its application.

Surgery was not as commonly resorted to in those days as it is now. It was the most spectacular and remunerative branch of medicine. Every young graduate felt himself an embryo surgeon. One was not out of style without an operation to talk about, but he was certainly an object of interest and admiration if he had. In those days people held on to their teeth, their tonsils and their appendices, and if they got a heart disease or died of inflammation of the bowels, their passing was ascribed to a lamentable act of a Divine Providence.

People dreaded the anesthetic even more than they did the operation. The thought of losing consciousness, not knowing whether one would ever regain it, was the

spectre that stalked every surgical patient. And well
it might. At the City and County Hospital chloroform
was the generally used anesthetic, and the mortality was
high. There was no nitrous oxide gas with which to
induce slumber, and internes and nurses held the patient
pinned to the table until he or she succumbed to the
fumes from the liquid that fell, drop by drop, on the
mask that covered the nose and mouth. The internes
who administered the anesthetic were usually as frightened as the patient, and often the drop would become a
splash in their shaking hands. Many a big brute of a
stevedore fought them, and it was a fine lark for the
students to be called in to help hold the patient while
the interne gave him a knockout blow.

But when the patient was brought to the operating
amphitheater, he was out cold, and his fate lay in the
hands of our surgeon, the Dean. Next to being a
surgeon himself, the student dreamed of being an assistant to Dr. McLean. To hold a retractor in a wound
for him till one dropped dead of exhaustion would have
been to cover one's self with glory, but to let that retractor slip a fraction of an inch was to bring a rebuke
that sizzled like a white-hot cautery.

I have a vivid mental picture of that old City and
County operating amphitheater, which was heated by a
big stove with the stove-pipe rambling all over the place
until it found an outlet near the sky-light. My first experience there made an indelible impression on me. The
patient was brought in. Dr. McLean, in shirt-sleeves
and a butcher's apron, looked like a priest about to perform a sacred rite, surrounded by his acolytes.

Trays of gleaming instruments glistened in the radiance that fell from the skylight above the operating table. There was the sickish, sweet odor of chloroform, the pungent odor of carbolic acid, the penetrating odor of iodoform.

The patient was to have a mastoid operation, at that time looked upon as most critical, requiring great skill. The sight of the unconscious patient, the array of instruments and the combined odors were most disturbing to the novitiate. I was conscious of an uncomfortable feeling at the pit of my stomach. Dr. McLean picked up his knife. Blood followed his first incision, made behind the ear over the mastoid process. My upper lip was moist with perspiration. He inserted retractors in the wound and gave them to his attendants. He picked up another instrument. It was a chisel. Another. It was a mallet. He struck a blow. The chisel grated on bone.

I knew the anatomy of that mastoid process, knew that the plate of bone that lay between those mastoid cells and the palpitating brain beneath was as thin as paper. And yet he was wielding that mallet and chisel with the apparent recklessness of a schoolboy cracking hazelnuts.

Things began to get black. I set my jaws and swallowed my stomach. Then I looked at a fellow boarder. His face was as white as the aprons of the operators. He rose from his seat, stumbled up the stairs and left the amphitheater. I felt sorry for him, ashamed for him, and resolved that I would see it through.

The surgeon talked as he worked. He described the

blood supply, the nerve supply, the vessels that must be avoided, the paralysis that would follow if he invaded the sacred precincts of the facial nerve. Chip by chip he removed the bone cells, but the gruesome spectacle had been magically transformed into a thrilling adventure. I forgot that I had a stomach; forgot everything but the miracle that was being performed before my eyes, until the last stitches were placed, the last dressings applied. My initiation was over.

We followed our professor of clinical medicine through the wards; saw hollow-cheeked patients, delirious with fever, picking at the bed-clothes; studied the charts and the effect of remedies. I watched the typhoid patients, remembering Grandmother and the tragic havoc that disease wrought on the farm in northern New York. Coal tar derivatives had recently been discovered and were hailed as a panacea for fever. It was magical to note the effect of those anti-pyretics, but soon the dangers that go hand in hand with every medical advance were apparent in the weakened hearts. We learned the need of following the maxim: Remember, young man, when you practice the art, the condition of the nerve, the blood, and the part. We began to realize that to practice medicine successfully one should have caution as his hand-maiden and courage as his guiding star.

We visited wards whose patients after spending "a night time with Venus" were doomed to spend "a life time with Mercury," and wards whose patients, suffering from the "white plague," saw a new star of hope arising in the tuberculin of Koch. A star that became a falling star before those hopes were realized.

Three years seem long when youth looks ahead, but the sands of time run quickly through the glass. As graduation drew near the young men of the class grew lusty beards, that were supposed to give them an appearance of age and experience. We passed through the agonizing ordeal of examinations. We were ready for graduation.

I was called to the Dean's office. I went in fear and trembling. I must have flunked some course! How could I ever face my father if I was not going to graduate?

The Dean looked severe. He rarely smiled. "How do you wish to have your name appear on your diploma, Miss MacKnight?" he asked.

I was to have a diploma! I was so relieved that I wanted to hug him, but he was not that kind of a man.

He was waiting for me to answer. I did not understand. I had been christened Nellie Mattie MacKnight. I had been Nellie MacKnight all through college. What other name could appear on my diploma? I told the Dean that my name was Nellie Mattie MacKnight; that I supposed it should go on my diploma that way.

I remember he wore a coat with long tails. He folded his hands together under those coat tails and strode back and forth across the room in a perfect fury.

"Nellie Mattie—Nellie Mattie—" he kept repeating. "How do women ever expect to get any place in medicine when they are labeled with pet names? Can't you find something more appropriate? What would you think if we were to graduate a Doctor Willie or a Doctor Tommy with the class?"

Faced with the necessity of re-christening myself, I tried to remember the names from which that pet name, "Nellie," had been derived. I had had an Aunt Ellen. There was Helen of Troy.

"You may write in Helen M. MacKnight," I said.

"That's better." The Dean stopped pacing the floor. He was inclined to friendliness. "Helen M. MacKnight. I'll see that your name appears that way on your diploma. And also—" those piercing steel gray eyes were fixed on me, "see that it is Helen M. MacKnight on your shingle!"

My father arrived. I had looked forward to his coming, hoping that by some miracle we might have been drawn closer together by the separation. I wanted to love him, wanted to let him know that I appreciated what he had done for me, tried to see him as Mama had pictured him. But the love of a child for a parent is not a matter of the head but of the heart. The wall was there. He was suspicious of the fact that I wanted to take a year's internship. He felt there must be some other motive for my wishing to stay in San Francisco.

I had coveted the appointment, worked for it, and felt I needed the training it would give me. My father said he had spent all the time and money on my education that he intended to, that he had signed a note for my last year's expenses, and that I should come home and help him pay off the money that he had been forced to borrow.

Back of it all, I could feel the raging fear that I was

out from under his control. The things that he said
did not move me. I decided to stay. The interneship
offered a living and a pittance besides. I could manage.
My diploma would not be officially recognized until I
became of age. I could not obtain my license until I
was twenty-one years old. My father acceded grudgingly.

The graduation exercises were held in the old Baldwin Hotel, built by "Lucky" Baldwin, who owned a
famous stable in the days when men and women of
fashion drove in tallyhos to witness the sport of kings.
I had a brocaded black wool graduating dress, with a
discreet bustle. There was a pocket in the skirt, which
I was sometimes able to find. The dress had sleeves
enormously puffed above the elbow and skin-tight below. There was a boned high collar that sawed my
chin. Over the dress was my gown and a mortar-board
rested on my pompadour.

My name was read. The parchment roll was placed
in my hands. I felt a new dignity settle on me like a
mantle. Nellie MacKnight, of the post borough of
Petrolia, Pennsylvania, the farm in northern New York
State, the factory in Bridgeport, Connecticut, the little,
tar-papered shanty on the wide prairies of Dakota, the
Acadian Valley in the High Sierras of California, had
become Helen MacKnight, M.D., a woman consecrated
to the service of humanity.

Women pioneers in medicine were there. Noble
women who by their unfaltering devotion to their chosen
profession were opening the doors, through which they
had been so grudgingly allowed to enter, to future
generations of women. They clasped my hand, and

when I looked into their eyes I saw there the Grandmothers and Mamas and Aunt Marys of the world.

WOMEN OF THOSE DAYS
JANE STANFORD & PHOEBE HEARST

TODAY, WHEN EVERY VOCATION IS OPEN to women, when our own Congresswoman represents us in Washington, and when Amelia Earhart has flown the Atlantic alone, the status of women at the time of my graduation seems quaint and almost medieval.

"The new woman," said the *Pacific Medical Journal* in 1895, "is a physiological as well as a psychological study. She is evolving herself out of her pleasing, comfortable home-life environments into a cold, distrustful, criticizing world, in which it is doubted she can accomplish as much good in any direction as if she remained in the sphere, medically speaking, to which she is most suited.

"From a physiological standpoint is a woman competent, on account of her delicate nervous organization, to assume charge of the affairs of state? We think not. We are aware that there are women rulers, but do they rule? No. They are surrounded by the wisest statesmen in the land, who direct the government. Obviously there are many vocations in life which women cannot follow; more than this there are many psychological phenomena connected with ovulation, menstruation and parturition which preclude service in various directions. Mr. James Weir, the philosopher and thinker, has recently written an able article in the *Naturalist* on this subject.

"In commenting on this the able editor of the *San Francisco Argonaut* says: 'As the New Woman advances and establishes herself she encounters foes more formidable than masculine distaste and ridicule. She finds herself confronted by the student of the social organism and learns that, in his view, she is but a sign and a warning. That so far from being a pioneer hewing the way for woman into a broader and higher civilization, she is merely a reversion to a type which the race in its progress has generally left behind.'

"To the ebullient New Woman, enamoured of her newness, the theory of Mr. Weir which he expounds in a serious and abstruse article in the *American Naturalist* for September will be as pleasant as an icicle dropped down her back. He thinks that the woman suffragist, the woman who at the tongue point is demanding her rights, chief among which is the right to be not a woman, is a 'degenerate' and he gives plenty of reasons for the unfaltering faith that is in him. The majority of the strident sisterhood, he says, are 'viragebts' or women with masculine traits, and that physical and psychological degeneration of the race must inevitably follow the success of the suffrage movement. He holds in brief, that the New Woman is essentially a he-woman or, as he puts it, all equal rights women have either given evidence of masculo-femininity (viraginity) or have shown conclusively that they are victims of psychosexual aberrancy.

"Chastity, which is the foundation of modesty, sweetness and womanly charm, is the result of the subjection of the female to the male in civilization. Originally, in the savage state, women were often the prizes for which men fought and the victors carried them off. The few remaining women must have served as wives for all the men of the tribe and in this manner polyandry had its inception. Laxity in sexual relations was at first common to all races of primitive men, because of the uncertain tenure by which men held women. Consequently woman had a large estimate of her value and her rights.

"To quote Mr. Weir: 'Polyandry gives women certain privileges which non-andry denies, and she is not slow to seize on these prerogatives and to use them in the furtherance of her own welfare. Polyandry, originating from any cause, will always end in the establishment of a matriarchate in which women are either directly or indirectly at the head of the government.' Mr. Weir recognizes the obvious fact that woman, whether new or not new, is still woman, that she cannot divest herself of sex, and that the bestowal of the suffrage would mean not only the introduction of sex into politics, but ultimately the practical assertion by women of their right to be sexually free, a reversion to the mental habits of our barbarous and polyandrous ancestors. . . . The New Woman would have the ballot, because its possession, she thinks, would do for her what a successful raid on the tribe would accomplish for the women who escaped capture, corner the supply and establish a matriarchate.

"James Weir, the thinker, has but expounded in clear

terms what all manly men and womenly women feel without being able to express their reasons: that the New Woman is an affront to delicacy, a jar upon the sense of congruity, and as offensive in her way as an effeminate man in his.

"The civilization that has borne her as one of its fruits needs looking after."

What were these "ebullient" new women doing at the time that this article was published? The pioneer women in medicine had found that if they desired to enter the profession they were not only confronted by the opposition of the medical schools and faculties, but after graduation there were no hospitals open to them where they might obtain practical experience.

Then, too, even though mothers allowed their daughters to study medicine, they became so worried when the girls were called out at night to attend to their practice that many were compelled to give up the work.

In 1875 Dr. Charlotte Blake Brown, having graduated from the Women's Medical College in Philadelphia, returned to her native San Francisco to practice her profession and raise a family to follow in her footsteps. With her contemporaries, Dr. Bucknell, and Dr. Sarah E. Brown, she started the Pacific Dispensary for Women and Children.

They interviewed seventy of the wealthy and influential women of San Francisco before they found eight women who were willing to act as a board of managers. The purpose of the Pacific Dispensary was "to provide interneships for women graduates in medicine and training for women in nursing and kindred professions." It was opened on Post Street with three beds. The service was soon increased to nine beds, and they moved to other quarters, where greater demands caused another move, and still another, until in 1885 a philanthropic citizen donated a lot far out on California Street.

Through the efforts of Dr. Charlotte Brown, the only one of the original founders left at that time in San Francisco, and the board of managers, enough money was contributed to erect a small Children's Hospital, on the site where now stand the large buildings of a completely equipped modern hospital, grown beyond the most hopeful dreams of its founders. It is a living testimonial to their vision and their devotion to the women of their profession and to all women and children in need of medical care.

In 1890 very few women received hospital care during confinement. Mrs. Alexander, one of the Crocker heirs, inspired by the work done in the Children's Hospital, established and endowed the Alexander Maternity Home in connection with it. It was a small, twenty-bed building. There is now a four-story wing devoted to maternity cases, and a large private maternity service. At present eighty per cent of the maternity cases in San Francisco receive hospital care.

Posterity recalls gratefully the name of another fine woman of those days—Jane Lathrop Stanford.

While in Medical College I went with a group from the Telegraph Hill boarding house to see the new Stanford University. The beautiful buildings, in the style of the old Franciscan missions, were surrounded by fields of California poppies. The buildings were erected and dedicated to the youth of the land by Leland Stanford and his wife as a memorial to their only son, who had recently died.

Stanford University was opened in 1891. There were four hundred and sixty-five students and fifteen instructors. In 1893 Leland Stanford died. The estate became involved in litigation. During the panic of 1893 the income from the vast Stanford holdings ceased. Jane Stanford was advised that it was impossible to finance the University. She refused to listen. She gave up all luxuries. She discharged her servants. She sold the fine horses that had made the Leland Stanford stables famous.

Great men in the educational world, catching the spirit of her devotion, continued to instruct those students who came to the University, not knowing whether or not their salaries would be paid. When it seemed impossible to go on, Jane Stanford said: "We may lose the farms, the railways, the bonds, but still the jewels remain. The university can be kept alive by these till the skies clear." Finally the stress became so great that it seemed necessary to sacrifice them. She packed one half million dollars' worth of the precious jewels that Leland Stanford had given her, in a suit case and went to Queen Victoria's Jubilee, hoping to dispose of them to the people of wealth who would gather in London for the great event.

The panic passed. The jewels were not sacrificed. Jane Stanford gave instructions that, on her death, they be sold, establishing the "Jewel Fund," which is the permanent endowment of the university library.

While Leland Stanford was amassing a fortune in the Union Pacific Railway, George Hearst, a man with only a common school education, obtained in Franklin County, Missouri, was becoming one of the great mining men of the West. He built the first stamp mill in the state in Placer County. Like Stanford, he later represented California in the Senate. He was familiarly known as Uncle George Hearst, and because of his love for horses, as one of the last grand old men of the American turf.

His wife, Phoebe Apperson Hearst, was a woman of great nobility of character and high ideals. I remember her well. She was a handsome woman of fine presence, dressed always in royal purple, queenly in bearing, charming in demeanor.

Although not confronted by the same problems that fell to the lot of Jane Stanford, her contribution to the young men and women of the State opened the doors of the University of California to thousands who might otherwise have been deprived of an education. She defrayed the expenses of an international competition of architects to obtain plans for the present campus and buildings of the university. She encouraged young women by stating to the regents: "It is my intention to contribute annually to the funds of the University of California a sum sufficient to support eight three-hundred-dollar scholarships for worthy young women. The qualifications entitling students to the scholarships shall be noble character and high aims."

And yet woman suffrage was defeated in San Francisco in 1906. It was only saved in the State by the vote of Los Angeles and the interior counties.

While all this controversy was going on, women were not trying to be new women. They were simply endeavoring to enlarge their sphere of usefulness, bringing their vision and intuition to offer it in helpful service.

Women were also bursting their physical bondage. May Sutton Bundy, somewhat handicapped by long skirts and with a sailor hat pinned to her pompadour, was clearing the way for a Helen Wills Moody and a Helen Jacobs.

An item from the society news of the *Argonaut,* August, 1894, states: "Newport has gone in heavily for sports. A few days ago bicycling was enjoyed only by the private clubs. Now it is all the rage. Miss —— sits her 'bike,' the latest slang for bicycle; so does pretty Miss Tucker."

Women were beginning to find that their "limbs" were legs and arms just like their brothers', even though they must be discreetly covered when they ventured into the water.

The following item from the *Delineator,* of August, 1892, gives a quaint picture of the necessary apparatus.

"A certain woman who is quite as charming in the water as out of it told me how she dressed to produce this very desirable result. Choose a suit of dark blue, or better still of black material. In dressing for the water this tasteful woman first dons a thin undervest, and over that an old pair of corsets from which the bones have been removed. Then she puts on a pair of long black yarn stockings, for woolen stockings look much better when wet than cotton ones. Elastic about the knees keeps the stockings in place. Then comes the under part of the black bathing suit, the waist and knee trousers being in one piece. The waist has a sailor collar and the sleeves reach nearly to the elbows. The short skirt would extend to shoe tops if shoes were worn; this is buttoned to the waist and a belt completes the costume."

While we are considering fashions, we might add this item from the society correspondent of the *Argonaut,* dated July, 1894: "The most important event at Windsor was Queen Victoria's new hat. Rumors of its magnificence had preceded her appearance at the castle. The rumors were correct. The august head of the state and church was roofed in a new hat, youthful in shape and fashionable in style and quite covered with ostrich plumes in addition to a large white ribbon bow."

AT CHILDREN'S HOSPITAL ANNIE LAURIE MARY BOTSFORD

WHEN I ENTERED THE CHILDREN'S HOS-pital after receiving my medical degree, there were three women physicians in charge of the service: a resident, an assistant resident, and myself, the only interne. There are now ten internes, and seven resident heads of departments, women who come from medical schools all over the world to take advantage of the fine opportunities offered to women physicians in this institution.

The other women of my class did not care to interne. They were older and anxious to become established. They planned to practice in the city, where assistance was always at hand.

I can never fully express my gratitude to the pioneer women in medicine for the opportunity for practical experience that was made available to me in the Children's Hospital. Had I gone into a country practice without that hospital experience, I would have been in the same dilemma as the interne in another hospital who, being called to a confinement case, the first that he had ever attended, acted as an assistant to nature, who really conducted the accouchement with very little help from him. When it was over, the interne, much pleased with himself, retired to his room and bed. He was soon aroused from his slumbers by a nurse calling: "Doctor, doctor, come quickly, there is another baby!" He had not known that there were twins! Had I made the same mistake in the country and left a house where another baby was imminent, I can picture the complications that might have followed, with some horseback messenger riding furiously after me into the night.

Accidents will happen, even in the best regulated hospital. Our maternity home was above reproach. The lady board, backed by the good women of San Francisco, saw to that. There were free beds for those who could not pay, but there was no place for a fatherless child to be born. One day a young woman, evidently in distress, applied for admission. She was closely questioned about the parentage of the baby who was lustily demanding admission to a world that questioned his right. The unfortunate mother was told, kindly but firmly, that our hospital did not receive "that kind" of case. She was given the address of a home where she might apply. She went down the long stair of the entrance and started across the gravelled court. There was a cry. A nurse came running. I went out. The fatherless baby had arrived. Mother and child convalesced satisfactorily in the Alexander Maternity Home, none the worse for their experience. I have often wondered if that child was as energetic about getting what he wanted in after years.

Experiences crowded thick and fast. There were rounds to be made, charts to be kept, recording temperature, pulse, respiration. The first clinical record charts in San Francisco hospitals were brought by Dr. Emma Sutro Merritt, daughter of the sturdy pioneer of the Comstock, from Paris, where she did postgraduate work after receiving her degree from Toland Medical College.

The printer who copied the chart did not understand what the degree mark, after Temperature, meant. He decided that since it was required for the record of one condition it should be required of all, and for some years the charts read:

Temperature°; Respiration°; Pulse°.

There were surgical dressings to be done. What a nightmare those dressings were. Many of the children were sufferers from tubercular hips and spines and open fistulas led to the diseased bone. These were packed every other day with iodoform gauze. It was my duty as interne in the surgical wards to remove those packs, cleanse the opening and renew the dressing, being sure every time that the probe carried the gauze to the extreme depth of the cavity. There was no anesthetic known at that time except complete anesthesia, and these dressings were done without anything to relieve the pain.

Every other day became a torment to me and to those little sufferers who would plead so hard: "Don't, Doctor, please, Doctor!" It took all the strength I had to crowd that gauze conscientiously to the bottom of the cavity. How I loved those children! They knew it and rewarded me with smiles when it was all over. I, with my one hundred and seventy-five pounds, became the "Little Doctor" to all of them.

When I think of those surgical dressings, I am reminded of the accomplishment of Dr. Mary E. Botsford, who followed me in the surgical service and encountered the same experiences that I had had. She saw patients return from the operating room so saturated with ether that they were ill for a week from the effect of the anesthetic. She told one of the surgeons that she was going to specialize in anesthesia. He replied that she was crazy and could never make a success of it.

Nothing daunted, she entered general practice and gave anesthetics whenever called upon to do so. For the first five years she received no fees for her service in that branch of her practice. That was in the Nineties.

In October, 1931, she was elected president of the American Association of Anesthetists. Distinguished scientists from our own and foreign lands were present. She was presented with a handsome silver trophy.

Dr. Botsford told me recently that when she made application to Dr. McLean to enter the medical department of the University, he said: "If you must study

medicine, you had better go over to the Homeop'
College."

Physicians of the regular school looked with great
scorn on the "homeop's" in those days. Nothing could
have more clearly expressed his attitude toward her
ambition to study medicine.

Although I cringed from those surgical dressings, one
of the most thrilling experiences of my life came when
the visiting surgeon of the orthopedic service allowed me
to perform an amputation at the hip joint on one of his
private patients. It was not an emergency operation and
I had several days in which to "bone" my Gray's
Anatomy and *American Textbook of Surgery,* until
every muscle, every nerve, every artery which would
be cut were impressed on my mind.

When the patient was anesthetized and prepared for
the operation and I stood ready with the knife in my
hand, there was a terrifying instant when it seemed
as if I could not possibly make that first incision in the
smooth, white skin. I wanted to beg the surgeon to
do it for me. But I set my teeth and gripped the knife
in my hand and made it follow the line I knew it should
take. From that moment all personal reaction was lost
in the absorbing interest of the operation. The surgeon
congratulated me on my nerve and steadiness.

Dr. Frances R. Sprague, a graduate of the Women's
Medical College of Philadelphia, was on the visiting staff
of the hospital. All the nurses and even the resident physician were in awe of her. She was tall and erect,
dressed always in a correctly tailored wool suit, with
immaculate "Forsythe" shirt-waists, flat-heeled, made-to-
order, laced shoes, and a severe black turban. Her face

was stern—but how kind, when you came to know it. People said of her that when she walked down the streets of San Francisco she looked as though she owned the place.

As I was the only interne at that time, it fell to my lot to do the dressings on her cases and to make the rounds with her. Needless to say, I was quite unnerved at the prospect. She performed an operation for hernia and directed me in the care of the case. I was so confused by the multiplicity of strange duties and so overwhelmed with work that I became bewildered and thought she told me to dress the case every other day, as I did the others.

When she made her visit on the second day, I accompanied her on her rounds. We came to the hernia case. As soon as she started removing the dressing, she saw that it had not been changed. She looked very stern. "Why has this wound not been dressed?" she questioned.

"I understood you to say that it was to be dressed every other day," I said.

She did not reply. When she had finished she said in a tired voice: "I hope you will find it convenient to do this dressing every day from now on!"

I felt hurt and resentful. I knew she thought I had carelessly forgotten or purposely neglected the case. But there was something about her aloofness that kept me from trying to defend myself. The incident stalked me all day. I was relieved to find there was no rise in the patient's temperature that night, due to the neglected dressing, but I still felt uncomfortable about it. Then, during the night, one of those illuminating flashes that come to us when waking from disturbed sleep outlined the whole scene to me. I saw myself standing with the Doctor at the bed-side of the hernia case on the day of the operation. I heard her distinctly say: "I want this case to be dressed every day." I broke out in a cold sweat. No wonder the Doctor thought I had told a deliberate falsehood! What was I to do about it? The incident was closed. The easiest way, of course, would be to let it go at that.

But I could hear Mama saying: "Nellie, be a good girl!" I could feel Grandmother and Aunt Mary urging me to do the honest thing. I couldn't wait to see the Doctor and tell her about it. When she came I met her in the hall. She greeted me coldly. I plunged into the disagreeable task:

"I am sorry, Doctor. I remember you did tell me to dress the hernia case every day."

I shall never forget the look of surprise and genuine pleasure that illuminated that stern face. From that day on she became a fairy god-mother to me. She took me to Lake Palicitos to recuperate after a bout with an infected arm that threatened to cut short my medical career. She gave me pleasures, things that were unobtainable with my limited budget—Irving and Terry in *The Merchant of Venice,* wonderful meals at the old-time restaurants.

But most gratifying of all, she allowed me to accompany her on some of her most interesting cases. The confinement in Chinatown was one of them. We went to the Sunday afternoon band concerts in Golden Gate Park. Sunday in Golden Gate Park was an event. Society came, driven in fine carriages. The ladies held

their trailing skirts daintily away from their high buttoned shoes. They carried tiny carriage parasols, jointed
so that they could be adjusted to shelter the faces of
the fair ones. With what jealousy complexions were
guarded in those days! We sat in carriages or on
benches and listened to the strains of the "Blue Danube"
and Sousa's stirring marches.

One day in the sand in front of one of the benches
I found a beautiful brooch, set with several fine diamonds. There was great rejoicing when I displayed
it to the doctors and nurses that night. The hospital
was poor and there were so many things needed. It
seemed as if there were always braces that ought to be
furnished, so that Johnny might get up and move about
or Mary could be allowed to go home.

With the reward from the brooch we could meet
some of these pressing problems and then, with what
was left we would celebrate by having a real dinner,
with steak! I advertised the brooch. We all waited,
breathlessly, for the result. I was called to the office.
An exquisitely dressed woman said she had come to
claim the brooch. She asked what reward I wanted.

I explained that I did not want anything for myself,
but, since this was a charity hospital and so many things
were needed for the crippled children, I hoped she felt
she could contribute something towards the work that
was being done. We were so pressed for room at the
time that we were having to send incurable children
back to their families because there was no place to keep
them.

I hoped I might interest her in starting a foundation
for an incurable ward, for which there was a pitiful

need, but I had no opportunity to make the appeal. The beautifully dressed lady informed me that she already had contributed all that she felt she could afford to give to charity. She handed me one dollar!

There was a riot in the dining-room when I exhibited that reward. Seven nurses at one of the tables had just been served seven chicken necks left over from the luncheon which had been held for the lady board of managers that day. My precious dollar went for an oyster loaf, and the nurses on duty and I had a feast in the diet kitchen that night. We used to buy oyster loaves and entrust them to the care of the grip-man, who put them under the big lamp in the front of his car to keep them warm for us, on the way home.

But needs are always met in San Francisco. That warm-hearted newspaper woman, Annie Laurie, writing for the *San Francisco Examiner,* told the people the story of the children who must be turned away because they were incurable.

Her appeal started the fund that was raised, bit by bit, to build the Little Jim ward. Later, through the efforts of the same newspaper, a cottage for contagious diseases was added. This has developed until it has become famous for the treatment of contagious diseases and the training that is given to doctors there.

When I look at this finely-equipped building, I think of the old Out Clinic, where the internes in the Children's Hospital were expected to spend several weeks, providing their own food and living in tumble-down quarters in the poorer district.

One of them told of treating a case of diphtheria. The people lived back of a saloon. They had a fierce dog, and she had to take a policeman with her when she made her calls. There was no antitoxin then. All she could do was to swab the throat of the patient with an antiseptic and hope for the best.

Other women graduates entered the hospital and I was transferred to the service for women and the work in the maternity home. New interests, new enthusiasms, new friends, were mine. One of the internes was my own age. She came from an old San Francisco Jewish family. Her name was Rose Eppinger, but everybody called her "Dick." I grew to love her as I loved Grace and Frances.

She married on leaving the hospital and never practiced medicine afterwards. Her husband assures their friends that one of the great women was lost to the profession when he took his wife away from it, but she protests that she was not lost to the profession, for she taught Dr. Botsford to give her first anesthetic in the Children's Hospital.

Women were making beginnings in the business world. Jessie's cousin came all the way from an art school in Canada to start in San Francisco. She rented a tiny room just big enough to hold her bed and her easel. She did a head of Cleveland, burnt on wood with hot pokers, and put it in the Women's Exchange. Pyrography had never been seen on the coast before, and this portrait aroused great interest and comment.

She received an order to decorate a hall for some function and pressed me into her service when I was off duty. We journeyed to Land's End and Harbor View to gather armfuls of yellow lupine, grown from the seeds that had been broadcast years before by the early settlers at the Presidio. We went to Fisherman's Wharf and wheedled two old fish nets from the fishermen. The fish nets were hung. The yellow lupines stuck in the meshes. The result was a triumph of art! From such beginnings she received the contract to do the Women's Room in the California Building at the Chicago World's Fair. When I go into her very smart, beautifully furnished interior decorating studio, I like to remind her of that head of Cleveland and those lupine-hung fish nets.

After that we pooled our nickels and went across the bay to watch the bicycle races. It is hard to believe that they were just as exciting in the Nineties as the stuttering, deafening motorcycle races of the present—but they were.

Sometimes we joined the Italians who went on Sunday out to the old Italian Cemetery on the hills above Land's End to watch the balloon ascension, or to Harbor View for a picnic, returning at night tired and happy on the horse-cars, reeking of garlic.

A message came from my father. My stepmother was very ill. The local doctor was not able to help her. She wanted me to come. My heart sank. The thought of leaving San Francisco and going back to the valley to face that baffling wall that rose between me and my father was unendurable to me. But I saw my plain, patient stepmother, at whose hands I had received only kindness, lying ill and miserably unhappy. I could not refuse her need of me. I was now twenty-one years old, so I secured my license to practice medicine.

I had made a place in the hospital. The management

offered me the position of assistant resident if I would stay. The internes and nurses made up a package for the "Little Doctor." I was overcome. It contained a fever thermometer, a hypodermic syringe, a hot water bag, a fountain syringe, a Kelly pad—things that they felt I would need in a country practice.

In the afternoon I climbed Telegraph Hill. The sun shone on a golden path that led through the Gate, across the broad Pacific, where sailed the cargoes of the world. On the way down I passed the house with the ship's walk on it. I knew that the old captain had sailed on his last voyage, but I seemed to hear his voice reassuring me: "Keep your sea legs, lass! Keep your sea legs!"

There were no medical students in the boarding house on Telegraph Hill. Toland Hall was deserted. The Medical Department of the University of California, the gift of Dr. Toland, had become a part of the Affiliated Colleges of the University at Parnassus Heights. Ours was the last class to graduate from Toland Hall.

I thought of the words of Dr. Lane, spoken at the dedication of one of the buildings of Cooper Medical College, which was established by the pioneer Dr. Cooper and is now Stanford University Medical School:

"Human memory has its limitations and we scarcely have a right to chide it for lessening its burden by dropping its distant links in the past, and it is probable that, sharing the common fate of all things, the footsteps of coming years will obliterate the individuality of the work of which you are witnesses; yet the work itself will not perish. . . ."

A DOCTOR IN THE
"LAND OF LITTLE RAIN"

✠ COUNTRY PRACTICE ✠
I DEFY MY
FATHER

THAT NIGHT I TOOK THE FERRY. WE glided out of the slip. I looked back on the inspiring tower of the new ferry building that had replaced the old brown sheds. My eyes traveled on to the hills of San Francisco. The lines of Bret Harte came back to me:

> *Serene, indifferent of Fate,*
> *Thou sittest at the Western Gate:*
>
> *Upon thy heights so lately won*
> *Still slant the banners of the sun.*
>
> *Thou drawest all things, small or great,*
> *To thee beside the Western Gate.**

Again the familiar trip: to Reno, then south on the Virginia and Truckee to Mound House, on the Carson

* Chatto and Windus, 1889.

and Colorado to Sodaville, and after a night at the
Sodaville Hotel and Bar on over the desert. My heart
was heavy. I dreaded to go home. There is no one
to whom my heart goes out in such quick sympathy
as to a child who dreads to go home. I know what a
tragic thing it is.

But I soon forgot everything else in my first hand-
to-hand, unaided conflict with death. There were two
physicians in the town. One was an old army doctor,
who refused to consult with me. The other was a man
who treated my degree as a rare joke. He said I might
be a good nurse.

My stepmother needed nursing and tenderness more
than she did prescriptions. She had been over-drugged.
There were hours of terrible uncertainty, when it seemed
she would slip away from me, but gradually she gained
strength. She recovered.

My father was immensely gratified, not by the fact
that his wife had been spared to him, but by my ability
to cure her. He went about the town, telling everyone whom he saw: "My wife is getting well. The doctors gave her up, but Nellie came home and cured her!"

I knew it was useless to ask him to send me back to
San Francisco. My place in the hospital was filled. I
fitted up an office in the front room of the house and
put out my shingle—Helen M. MacKnight, M.D.,
Physician and Surgeon. My father was proud of the
M.D., but resented the Helen. I had been christened
Nellie. That was my name. But I remembered the
words of the Dean, and the sign was not changed. I
put in a small stock of drugs (it would be necessary

to fill my own prescriptions), bought a medicine case, and started in.

My conveyance was a two-wheeled cart with a jump seat. I harnessed and unharnessed the horse myself. I would stand at the back of the cart with the reins in my hand, raise the seat, clamber in and start off. I used to smile sometimes, wondering what those professors with their carriages and coachmen would think if they could see me.

There was little road work done in those days, and the cart would grind through the sand and strike sparks from the boulder-like rocks that were strewn along the way. Then there were the barbed-wire gates in the fences to be reckoned with. One pulls and tugs with might and main to slip the loop of wire over the top and so release the gate. Then when it seems impossible to get it over the last inch, it suddenly lets go, the post springs out of the lower loop and attacks you, winding the strands of barbed wire around you with all the ferocity of inanimate things. Escaping with minor cuts and scratches, you lead your horse through, and then with grim determination you pull and tug at the gate, apparently shrunken several inches in the encounter, to get the post back into the bottom loop and somehow manage to lasso the wire over the top. If your horse stands quietly through this performance, well and good, if not you are plainly out of luck. Fortunately mine was "gate broken."

Patients came to me, mostly chronic cases at first, who had failed to get relief elsewhere and were curious to see what the new woman doctor might do for them. Every

man, woman, and child in such an isolated place has a
personal interest in the health of the community. If
a woman is "expecting," every good wife knows just
when, can tell how long her "morning sickness" lasted,
and will venture an opinion on the sex of the child by
the way the mother is "carrying it." When a woman is
known to be in labor a kind of tenseness settles over the
whole community until word is passed about that it is all
over. Then the length of labor, the sex and weight of
the child, whether "they" wanted a boy or a girl, and
other important factors connected with the case are re-
viewed in detail.

Doctors are supposed to be able to bury their mistakes,
but if they do not wish to have post-mortem discussions
of why and how it happened they had best keep to the
cities. A young doctor, fresh from medical college, can
pass many embarrassing moments in the presence of the
neighborhood midwife. Country people have been
through the stress of illness, without trained medical
assistance so often that they have an astonishing knowledge of human ills gained in the school of experience.

Their kindness is inexhaustible. They will drop everything to go to the bedside of some neighbor, cook the
meals, take care of the children, do the laundry, so that
the sufferer may be kept fresh and clean. Even when
it comes to surgery, they are not the ones to stand help-
lessly by. I remember a case that happened at Benton,
near the Wild Rose Mine. Two Indians, in a drunken
brawl, carved each other with knives, with the result that
one of them was ripped open by a cross-shaped incision
in the abdominal region. An observer assured me that
"the entralls" protruded from the wound and were

covered with the sand and dirt into which the Indian had fallen.

An epileptic, glass-eyed, itinerant doctor of my acquaintance was in Benton at the time and was summoned to the scene. He shrugged his shoulders and said there was nothing to do about it. The Indian would die. But the Indian, Johnny Lynch, was a good Indian when he wasn't drunk, and the citizens of the town did not want him to die if it was in their power to help him.

So they brought Kelty Jim, bar-tender, from the town's main saloon. Now Kelty Jim had been a sailor and the knots he learned to tie and the sails he had mended stood him in good stead when it came to a bit of surgery. A small stream of clean water, from a hot mineral spring, ran by the spot where the Indian lay. Kelty Jim sponged off the sand and dirt with the hot water, replaced the viscera, sewed up the wound with sail stitches and sailor's knots, and Johnny Lynch got well.

You can't put up much of a bluff in a country like that and get away with it.

My father no longer went on surveying trips. It was apparent that he was ready to retire and draw the interest on the investment he had made in me. He stayed at home and watched every move I made with a consuming jealousy. If a man patient came to the office, he watched to see how long he stayed. If it was a longer time than he thought necessary, he would question me about it. He even forced me to ask some of those patients to discontinue their visits. I worked under a terrific handicap. I was beating my hands against the wall—the wall of separation that would not allow me to give myself up to his utter possession.

What trifles may change the course of human destiny! A man came from Silver Peak, Nevada, to consult me about growing deafness. He could no longer hear his watch tick. It was a simple case. The canals of his ears were filled with hardened wax. I put an emollient in over night to soften the wax. The next morning I syringed out his ears, and lo! he could hear his watch tick. It seemed a miracle to him. He went home, spreading the news of the woman doctor.

Soon a message came summoning me to Silver Peak, a mining camp one hundred and fifty miles away. I took the train to Sodaville and there changed to a spur that ran to the one-mill mining town of Candelaria. A man, who had evidently been warming up for the occasion at a near-by saloon, met me. We went over to a team and buckboard that were waiting to take us across the desert. He told me to throw my bag in the back and climb in. When I saw how the horses were tied, each one to a separate post by a stout halter, I realized we were going to have a wild ride, and thought it safest to hold my medicine case in my lap.

The driver took his seat, another man undid the halters, and we were off. That team ran like scared rabbits for the first ten miles. Sometimes we were in the road, sometimes just hitting the high spots through the sagebrush. But I managed to hold my seat and my bag and we arrived at our destination at dawn.

A desert mining camp, in the clear light of early morning, is not an attractive scene. There are no trees to shelter the nakedness of high sham fronts and shed

backs. There is only the whir of machinery to detract from the gaunt ugliness of the stamp mill. There are no signs of life about the doors and windows to draw the eyes from the empty tin cans, that unfailing flora of mining camps. Even the burros drop their ears and look utterly disconsolate.

My patient was the superintendent of the mine. We found him in a bare, board cabin, spotlessly clean. He lay unconscious, a giant of a man, gaunt and unshaven. His head tossed restlessly from side to side on the pillow, while with his big hands he picked aimlessly at the bed covering. On the floor by his bed crouched his Indian wife, like a faithful dog waiting for some sign from its master.

During the drive across the desert I had learned that the patient to whom I had been summoned really belonged to my medical friend who gave me the credit of being a "good nurse." Medical ethics are difficult to live up to on the desert. When people get dissatisfied with one doctor, they send for another, and by the time number two arrives, the emergency does not permit the usual courtesies.

Well, he had said I was a good nurse, and since it was evident that this was a case of typhoid, sadly in need of less medication and more nursing, I forgot ethics and took charge of the case.

I saw that the other doctor had not been at fault. The powders he had left had been emptied on the swollen, parched tongue of the patient at the directed intervals, and a fruitless effort had been made to administer water to wash them down, but they remained to form a thick, glazed deposit, broken like a checkerboard by bleeding cracks. Sordes had settled on the teeth, which the swollen lips failed to cover. The man's beard and hair were matted. Not a pretty picture, but a typical one of the ravages of typhoid in the high altitudes and under the nursing conditions in those inaccessible places.

The Indian wife of this "squaw man" was not to blame. She had done everything she could do. The bed clothes were clean, the cabin was immaculate, but when her man was no longer able to direct her, she sat down to watch him die, according to the "white man's way." In the tribe it would have been managed differently. If any one died in the camp, it became necessary to burn the village and migrate to fresh surroundings. This being a troublesome proceeding, it was much easier to remove the one about to depart for the happy hunting grounds, before he made his exit.

I have driven to a camp to visit a sick Indian, only to find that he was "heap gone." No other information was forthcoming, and it was only by chance that, some distance from the camp, I spied a rude sapling shelter by a tiny stream. Investigating, I found that my patient had been placed there to die. The shelter extended out, like a bridge, across the stream. His equipment for the journey he was about to take consisted of a rabbit's skin blanket, a half sack of pine nuts, and a cup with which, until too weak to move, he could dip water from the stream.

But under my direction this brown-skinned mahala worked untiringly, with a dog-like devotion to her man. No task was too unpleasant, and there were many such, for her to undertake willingly. With the help of the men in camp, we contrived a rude canvas bath-tub, into which the patient could be lowered to reduce the temperature. We took turns sitting by the bed, constantly giving water, a teaspoonful at a time. There was no milk but condensed milk to be had in camp. I learned of a ranch in Deep Springs Valley, miles across the mountains, where fresh milk could be obtained. The services of a man on the regular pay-roll were placed at my disposal, and every afternon he rode horse-back to the ranch, so that he could make the return trip at night, when it was cool. I sterilized the milk, and it was kept in an Arizona cooler, a very efficient ice-box, made of mosquito netting, stretched over a board frame and covered with gunny-sacking, kept constantly wet from a coal-oil can with a hole punched in the side. Sun and evaporation did the rest.

That man was busy as a bird dog. I am sure that he found it a real vacation to go back to work with pick and shovel. Between riding for the milk, hauling the water for baths in barrels for miles over the desert, keeping the coal-oil can filled, splitting wood to keep a fire going in the cook stove in the shed lean-to, to boil water for sterilization of laundry, and disposing of excrement so that it would not become a menace to the camp, he had his hands full. But food and water and nursing won the fight, and in a week's time my patient was far on the road to recovery, and the routine was so well established that I felt it was safe to leave him.

I had spent a week and would have traveled three hundred miles when I reached home. My bill was one hundred dollars! It seemed enormous to me. I was surprised when it was promptly paid in five shining twenty-dollar gold pieces.

All the way home I thought of Grandmother, and hoped that in her abode up there by the beautiful river she knew that I had saved my first typhoid patient. I was elated. I looked forward to getting home, telling my father all about it, and giving him the hundred dollars, my first substantial fee.

My father met me at the station. He was white and trembling with rage. A letter had arrived from Paul during my absence. He had opened and read it. The letter began: "My dear Girl." It was an innocent, friendly letter, but my father read all sorts of jealous imaginings between the lines. He was in an uncontrollable rage. He demanded that I sit down and, in his presence and under his supervision, write to Paul and tell him I never wanted to hear from him or see him again!

Although I prized Paul's friendship, it was not the thought of losing it so much as the injustice of the demand that aroused me. I defied my father. I said I would not endure having my letters opened and read, and my relations to others questioned. I flatly refused to do as he demanded. His rage was a terrible thing to see. I wondered if he would kill me. My stepmother was terror-stricken. She pleaded with him. He got his hat and started for town. Beside himself with passion, he told me that I could leave home, or have the letter ready to send when he returned.

For the first time in my life I realized that I could never reach over the wall that had grown between us. I saw my father for what he was—a cruel, selfish man, who deserted his family and sent for me to come to him only when I was old enough to give him a possessive pleasure. His pride in me was only pride in himself through me.

I never could have left the Papa of Mama's memory. I did leave my father's house. When he returned I was gone. My stepmother afterwards told me that he raged like a mad man all through the night.

❦ *THE WILD ROSE MINE* ❦ *FREEDOM* ❦ *A HORSE* & *BUGGY COURTSHIP*

I RENTED A FRONT ROOM ON THE MAIN street of the town and opened an office. When my father found that my decision was final, he offered to sell me the stock of drugs and my medical books. The shining twenty dollar gold pieces were invested that way.

I bought an old counter from a store and had shelves built behind it. In the room there was an air-tight heating stove, a cot where I slept, and a rough table, which I had made for the examination and treatment of patients. It was not a luxurious place, but it was a peaceful refuge where no jealous, suspicious eyes followed me as I came and went. Grace and her husband lived near-by.

Mary Austin was teaching at the old Academy. She had recently written that exquisitely beautiful book in which she christened the valley, "The Land of Little Rain." She would come in the evening and sit with me and recount fragments of stories that afterwards took shape in "The Basket Woman" and "The Flock."

Strange things happened in that office, difficult to picture now when the telephone is at hand to summon the doctor, and, in an emergency, he arrives in his automobile or perhaps in his aeroplane almost before the receiver is back on the hook. I recall one day when a housewife in a kitchen dress, with hair loosening from the hair pins that held it and falling down her back, came running the length of Main Street to my office with her child in convulsions in her arms. By the time I had procured a wash tub of hot water from my landlady (bath tubs were an unknown luxury) and soused the youngster in it, the office held a good part of the population of the town. They were all as relieved as the mother was when the child was restored to her arms, limp and relaxed, but quite himself again.

For a while I hired a "rig" from the livery stable to answer calls in the country. But an accommodating youngster decided to be born about that time, and through officiating at the ceremony I acquired a fine bay horse as recompense for my services. The hardware store "trusted" me for a new, single top-buggy.

About this time my father deserted my stepmother and went away to the mining camps of the South. He drifted in the region of Randsburg and the Yellow Aster Mine for years. When he was no longer able to provide for himself, I helped to make his last days comfortable, as I knew Mama would have wanted me to do. My stepmother was left penniless. I found that she dreamed of having a little shop where she could sell fancy goods and baked beans and brown bread of her own making. I helped her to realize that dream, and she lived, busily happy, for many years.

I faced the future with new responsibilities, willingly

assuming the notes that my father had signed to raise the money to send me to college, and debts that he had contracted with the promise that he would pay when I graduated and began to practice medicine.

My practice flourished. Even twins happened along to enhance my reputation. I was engaged to confine a woman whom the Army doctor had warned not to have any more children, or she would probably die in the attempt. She had given birth to three girls and the desire, shared by herself and her husband, for a boy had inspired her with the courage to defy the ultimatum.

She studied *Tautology,* a book widely read by expectant mothers at that time, and followed its precepts closely. I have never been sure how much of the credit for the successful outcome of that case should be given to *Tautology* and how much to the instruction in prenatal care that I had received in Toland Hall and the Children's Hospital. At any rate, Aesculapius could not have sent me a greater boon than that patient.

I was called. The woman passed through a normal, uneventful labor, and was delivered of—another girl. I had hoped, as ardently as the parents, for a boy, and sympathized with their disappointment. But on examination, I found that the rotundity that disappears so miraculously when the child is born still persisted. I smiled, remembering the interne who had retired too soon. Without doubt there was another baby, and it might be a boy!

I remember going out to the father, sitting by the kitchen stove, holding his new little girl in his arms. "Don't be too disappointed," I said, "we might have a boy yet!" He looked up at me, entirely puzzled.

"What do you mean?"

"There is another baby, and it might be a boy."

I am sure that the father doubted that I knew what I was talking about. He may have experienced a pang of regret that he had placed his wife in the care of a person with such astonishing lack of the knowledge of the processes of nature. But the twin was born, and it was a boy. I needed no press agents. My patient who had been threatened with such dire misfortune if she ever tried to bring another child into the world had borne twins with no difficulty whatever! Everybody in the valley knew about it.

Although my sign read "Helen M. MacKnight, M.D." in big gilt letters, Dr. McLean had graduated a Dr. Nellie, in spite of his efforts to the contrary, for I was Dr. Nellie to the whole countryside.

Messengers came on horse-back, usually some neighbor who had been summoned and had rushed off with very little idea of what the emergency might be. Barring a "baby case" or an accident, the doctor was left to use her imagination. I carried my own drug store and hospital equipment and nursing aids with me.

I let down the gates in barbed-wire fences to reach women in confinement, babies with pneumonia, and those afflicted with all the diseases and injuries that make up the practice of the country doctor. I loved the work, the opportunity for service. But I felt very much alone. I wanted someone to discuss the difficult cases with, someone to whom I could turn for advice and assistance.

Grace had a baby. I confined her. There was no gas on which women drifted into blissful unconsciousness in those days. Her husband stood on one side of the bed and I on the other, and when the labor pains would come we held her hands and helped her work and pull to bring the child into the world. When her beautiful boy was born, I washed him and dressed him for the first time, as I did all my babies. My babies! I felt that they were mine, and to this day those children who now have children of their own all seem peculiarly mine.

When Frances' baby was born, I tied a sheet to the posts at the foot of the bed and encouraged her to pull on that. Her husband, that tall, powerful man who had been raised in the saddle, was not much help. He broke down and cried like a baby at sight of her suffering. Their boy learned to ride a horse before he could walk.

Someone has said that happiness lies in "the necessity for work, the ability to work, and the work to do." I had all the ingredients that go to make up the formula, but when I brought those children into the world, I realized that a career alone could not make a woman's life complete.

A horse-back messenger summoned me to a little, one-store, mining town, tucked away in the mountains. I took the train to the nearest point and then drove over the desert to my patient. I found a girl of fifteen years, a sheep-man's wife, her blue eyes wide and bright, her face flushed with fever. A midwife, the only succor those women in isolated places knew, had confined her. The young mother was suffering from puerperal fever.

I did what I could for her and after midnight I went to the one hotel and asked for a room. There was only one unoccupied. A doctor, who had come out from

Chicago to work the Wild Rose Mine, had the room,
but he was gone to Silver Peak, to look over their
cyanide plant. Otherwise, he would have seen the case.
He was not practicing, but was always ready to go in
an emergency.

I looked through the Doctor's medicine case with interest and found that the drugs he used were similar to
my own. I wondered what kind of man would be
willing to give up the practice of medicine to work the
Wild Rose Mine, and decided that he must have practiced a good many years to accumulate enough to go
into a mining venture. I left a note telling the Doctor,
who was expected back by noon, what I had done for
the unfortunate child-mother, and asked him to see the
patient and take charge of the case upon his return.

I explained the necessity for an operation and the
fact that I did not have the proper instruments with me,
as I had had no reason to believe it was a case demanding surgery. A lay-over meant two days away from my
own practice, as the train went down the valley one
day and back the next.

On the day of the next down train there was a knock
at my door. I opened it. A young man stood on the
step. His city clothes and derby hat stamped him as a
stranger. When he raised his hat, I thought he was the
handsomest man I had ever seen. The fine head, sensi-
tive mouth, laughing eyes, curling hair, now bronze,
now gold in the rays of the setting sun, made a picture
that time has never erased from my memory.

He came into my office. His presence seemed to fill
the room with youth and vitality. He introduced him-

self. He was the Doctor from the Wild Rose Mine. He wished to see Dr. MacKnight.

When I said I was Dr. MacKnight, he began to laugh. I was so indignant that I felt like shaking him. Then he explained the joke. He had pictured me as one of his pet abominations, a "hen medic." He expected to meet a stern, unprepossessing female, who would look upon his youth and inexperience with scorn. He had heard about me from the mine superintendent whom I had treated for typhoid at Silver Peak, but "No one told me you were just a kid," he said.

It was my turn to laugh, then, and explain to him that I had pictured a middle-aged, professional man, who would probably be inclined to question what I had done and the diagnosis I had made in the case that I had wished to turn over to his care.

He said that when he returned to his hotel in Benton he had found my note and called on the patient. He agreed that she must have an operation. He had taken the train that afternoon and come down to get the necessary instruments, as he had brought none of his own to the mine. I had worked so long, fighting my way against the criticism and scorn of the other physicians of the town, that it seemed a wonderful thing to find a man who believed in me and was willing to work with me to the common end of the greatest good to the patient. It was like renewing one of those fine friendships that had meant so much to me in my college days.

The evening was too short for all the things we found to talk about: the amazing fact that we were the same age, that we had both graduated in medicine before we were twenty-one, he taking his medical degree from Rush Medical College in Chicago, while I was studying at Toland Hall. All these things seemed to draw us together.

He explained that his father, a lawyer, had become interested in the old Mammoth Mine near Pine City, and had encouraged him to go into the mining game. He was excited by the country, the people; it was all a great adventure to him. The next morning he went away with the instruments, but it seemed to me that I would never be alone again. He came back in a few days to report the progress of our patient. The child-mother would recover.

He continued to come, riding his saddle-horse down from the mine, dressed in high boots, a flannel shirt, and a wide Stetson, staying at the Valley View Hotel all night, spending the evening with me and going back in the morning. Ours was a horse and buggy courtship, as we rode to visit my patients. The Doctor still loves to tell how he used to drive with me into the country and be left to sit in the single-top buggy to freeze in the winter or broil in the summer, while I went in and sat with a sick child while the mother snatched a much-needed wink of sleep or washed and dressed a baby.

Recently the old stable in that little mountain town was torn down. An article in the town paper about the horse and buggy days brought a smile to my lips and a bit of mist to my eyes as I read: "In the days of the side-bar buggy, the beribboned whip and the rose embroidered laprobe, the Nevada Livery Stable was a busy place on Sunday afternoons of the Summer time. On such afternoons small boys of Bishop gathered around

the stable and snickered when John, dressed in his Sunday clothes, and with a highly polished boot hanging jauntily over the buggy side, piloted the prancing Jerry through the door. The small boys knew that John was on his way to take Mary for a ride around the eightmile block and they shouted, 'Hi, Johnnie,' and sent him on his way with a red neck. The horse and buggy days are gone and today they are tearing the old stable down. I am sorry to see it go. The horse and buggy days were, after all, the good old days."

Young people had a chance to get acquainted as they drove around the eight-mile block, or had candy pulls, or gathered around the organ to play and sing in the winter, or sat in the hammock in the summer.

I recall moonlit nights when the scent of the blossoming locust trees filled the air, and the Doctor and I sat in a hammock in the little yard with its picket fence on Main Street and played the guitar and sang, "She's my sweetheart, I'm her beau, She's my Annie, I'm her Joe" or "East side, West side, All around the town" and "In the good old summer time."

I told him about my father and Mama and Grandmother and Aunt Mary. Again we found a common bond in the fact that his people came from New York State and Pennsylvania.

He told how his paternal grandfather had been educated as a priest in Ireland, but rebelled against the church and came to Albany, New York, where he set up as a cooper. Perhaps he imbibed too much of the contents of one of the stout barrels. At any rate, he fell into his own mill race and was drowned.

His maternal great-grandfather, a Dutchman, discovered the first coal in Pennsylvania. He found that it would burn and thought that it was a valuable product, so he loaded a flat-boat with it and floated it down the Susquehanna River to Harrisburg. No one would believe the stuff was of any value, and he had to leave it there in sheds.

He afterwards developed coal mines. On his death he directed that the property should never be sold, but that the revenue should be distributed to his heirs and their children's children, through the generations. The children of the fourth generation now look back with gratitude, when they receive their dividends from the lessees of that coal property, to their far-seeing ancestor.

A descendant of Robert Morris, who signed the Declaration of Independence, married one of the daughters and brought her to Bloom, now known as Chicago Heights. It was twenty-seven miles from the Chicago Court House. This young Morris became a farmer. He used to haul his wheat from the farm at Bloom to the river in Chicago, where there was an elevator and a shipping point. At what is now the corner of 179th and State streets there was an inn made of logs, where the farmers stayed all night on their way to market. From there to the river the road was so bad that the wagons would mire in the mud. It was there that the descendants of that Irishman and Dutchman united to found a family. They sent their son to Rush Medical School in Chicago.

Our friendship grew. It seemed as if when I needed him most, the Doctor would come, unsummoned, to my assistance. He talked of his plans for the future—where he would travel, what he would do, when he made a fortune out of the Wild Rose Mine. Gradually he began to include me in those plans. I felt that he loved me, but he did not speak of love and I was glad; I had seen too many friendships broken on the threshold of love. I felt I could never marry a man whose fortunes and those of his family depended on the chance of striking a rich vein or seeing that vein "pinch out."

The Doctor came one evening. He was treading on air. He had brought down a bar of bullion from the Wild Rose Mine and shipped it to the San Francisco Mint. It was the first shipment he had made. He was confident that it would return at least three thousand dollars.

He swept me into his arms with boyish impetuosity. He kissed me again and again. He told me how happy he was to find me and take me away with him, away to far corners of the world, on the money we would make out of the Wild Rose Mine. My heart leaped to his kisses. I wanted to claim him for my own, but I dared not. The shadow of that wall that had come from gold—sifting, gritting—lay between us.

The next week he came to get the returns from his shipment. I saw him walking up the street to my office. I could scarcely believe my eyes. His face was white. The buoyancy was gone from his step. I ran to the door to meet him. I thought he must be ill.

"Sweetheart," I cried, "what has happened?"

He dropped into a chair and looked at me as if I were something he had found and lost.

"The bullion," he said, and his voice sounded old and weary. "I just got the returns. That bar won't net me one hundred dollars! I'm ruined. I've put everything into the Wild Rose, and I'll never get anything out."

I began to laugh and tears of happiness ran down my cheeks.

"I'm so glad! So glad!" I exclaimed.

"Glad? What do you mean?" He looked at me as if he thought I had taken leave of my senses.

"I'm so glad you haven't put everything into the Wild Rose Mine. You haven't put love and youth and health into it year after year. The money invested is well spent, if it has made the years to come safe for us."

"You mean that you don't mind? That you will marry me, even if I am dead-broke, with nothing to offer you but what I can earn in the practice of medicine?"

"What you and I can earn together, dear."

✠ JÉSUS ✠ THE DOCTOR COMES ✠ A BOUQUET OF JASMINE

THE DOCTOR SHUT DOWN THE WILD ROSE Mine, settled up his affairs as best he could, with what money there was left and I.O.U.'s for the rest. He went to Independence, the county seat forty-five miles away, opened an office in the Norman House and started in.

The little saddle animal that had been the Doctor's faithful companion on the trails was now hitched to a cart, and the medicine case that had been put aside for the crucible and scorifiers of the assay office, where he had searched for values in the valueless ore of the Wild Rose Mine, came into its own.

The train that ran up the valley one day and back the next never failed to carry a message to one or the other of the young M.D.'s, whose activities were at first met with scorn, then with apprehension, by those men who were already established.

At Independence there was a big, bluff man who had graduated years before from a medical college in the East. He came West, with one lung gone, doomed to die of tuberculosis. He drifted to Owen's River valley and there, in the shadow of Mount Whitney, while driving over the desert to save the lives of others, saved his own.

He carried a stock of pills and powders in his capacious pockets, and whenever any one stopped him on the street or on the road and solicited his services to relieve them from some disorder, he would search in his vest pocket or coat or trouser pockets, according to the nature of the ailment, and bring forth some remedy that he assured them would relieve their affliction, and it usually did.

No trip was too long for him to undertake willingly, no family too poor to receive his care. He never kept any books and never presented a bill. When he needed some money, he would stop his patients wherever he happened to run across them and say:

"I've got to have some money, and I want you to get it for me damn quick!" The amount was never more than he knew they could pay, and the money was always forthcoming.

Having been free to run things on his own magnificent scale, burying his mistakes and levying tribute according to his needs, he resented having his empire invaded. He met the young pretender in the bar-room of the Norman House.

"So you're a doctor, are you?" he began. "I want you to understand there isn't room for another doctor in this part of the country."

"Well, I'm here!" replied the Doctor.

The older man shrugged and walked away, but there was never animosity between them after that.

The old order changeth. The days when a fever patient was put to bed with all his clothes and a sweater on and starved and doped until he got well or died, practically with his boots on, had exacted a tremendous toll of human life and suffering, and when the new man was called in to treat a patient ill with typhoid at the hotel, the community opened its eyes and took him to their hearts.

Lady Luck, who had proved so fickle in the mining venture, smiled on the young Doctor.

There were the anxious hours when he drove the forty-five miles to talk the case over with me. How we rejoiced when the patient was on the road to recovery.

A patient of mine, whose husband had made a fortune in the soda deposits of one of the dry lakes of Inyo County, consulted me. I advised her to seek a lower altitude to relieve her heart, which had grown weary through long years of struggle in the rarefied mountain atmosphere. She clung to me as she might have to a daughter, and begged me to go with her and see her safely over the summit of the Sierras. And so I went back to San Francisco.

The city was plunged in the excitement of the Spanish War. Bands were playing, soldiers marching, troops sailing. "Remember the Maine" was the slogan heard everywhere. Pictures of Teddy Roosevelt and his Rough Riders greeted the eye on every hand. Roosevelt, the popular hero, with his wide sombrero and his toothful grin, urging his men to do or die! Everyone was singing:

When you hear dem bells go ting-a-ling-a-ling
All join in and sweetly we will sing,
And when the verse am done in the chorus all join in,
There'll be a hot time in the old town tonight.

That song is as indelibly associated with the Spanish War as "Over There" and "The Long, Long Trail" are with the World War.

There were comparatively few men killed in action in the Philippines, but the toll taken by tropical diseases opened the eyes of the medical profession to the necessity for research in the diseases of the tropics. We were no longer an isolated country with only our own native maladies to cope with.

The Occidental Hotel was bursting with officers in gold braid and shining buttons, and khaki-clad soldiers, with their leggings laced up the side, had taken over the town. We stayed at the Palace Hotel, where lovely ladies, with enormous puffed sleeves and trains that trailed behind them like a peacock's tail, graced the brilliant social functions.

My patient became much interested in my career. She felt it was a mistake for me to stay in a little moun-

tain town, and offered to establish me in San Francisco.
To live in San Francisco, just as fascinating, more beautiful than ever! But I had left my heart up in the
mountains.

Many of the characters whom I had known when I
first came to the valley were gone, but there were still
some of peculiar interest. Old Jésus (pronounced *Hay-
sus*) was one of them. There was never a harvest festival or a celebration of any kind that would have been
quite complete without Jésus.

He was a tall, lean Mexican of princely bearing, and
he rode a horse with all the dignity of Montezuma. His
saddle of ornamented Mexican leather, his silver-mounted
bridle, decorated with braided horsehair, his serape
thrown carelessly over his erect shoulders, gave a certain
distinction to any parade.

Jésus was taken ill, and I was called to attend him.
He lived, with his fat Mexican wife and his parrots and
hairless Mexican dog, in a shanty that was little more
than a hovel. But the bed on which he lay was a
beautiful gold-lacquered, four-poster, metal bed, with
bars running between the posts to support a canopy top.
The bed was decorated with carved pineapples. Jésus
told me that it was an heirloom; that he had brought it
all the way from Mexico on mule-back, and every night
set it up to sleep on.

He was suffering from blood poisoning, that much
to be dreaded surgical emergency, known to us now as
streptococcic infection. There were no serums in those
days to combat such infections, and the ravages of the
disease were often attended with frightful results. The

infection started in the hand of his rein arm and traveled fast.

I summoned the Doctor from Independence, and we decided that the only thing that would save Jésus' life was to amputate his arm at the shoulder. I can remember distinctly how Jésus received the news. He had ordered a sheet tied over one of the bars that ran along the top of the posts of the bed. He used it to pull himself up when he became too weak to lift his own weight. He pulled himself up, sitting on the bed as I had so often seen him sit his horse.

"Dios! Jésus, no arm. No ride. Jésus die first!" he exclaimed.

We had to experiment and hope. Every day he submitted to the opening up of new pockets of infection that traveled up the arm and down on to the chest, until the lung was exposed through the incisions. His only complaint was "Ah, Dios!" He fought the infection with all the strength of his firm old body—and won. He recovered, with his arm crooked at the elbow, but no one would know there was anything wrong with it when he was on his horse. He gave me the beautiful bed that I had admired so much. It was his most prized possession and the most heart-felt gift I have ever received from a patient.

The rush to the Klondike was like a call to battle to an old war horse; men left their wives and families and went to join the throng who struggled over the Chilcoot Pass and shot the White Horse Rapids.

The Doctor's practice had grown beyond his fondest expectations. The mining debts were paid, and now we were confronted with the problem of deciding where to establish our home together. The mining activity that supported the lower end of the valley was becoming less important than the fields of grain and alfalfa and the heavily laden orchards that stretched from foothill to foothill with the promise of homes and plenty to those who put down their roots in the soil. So the Doctor came to Bishop and opened an office on Main Street in the back of the only drug store the town afforded.

We made our first investment in a home on West Line Street, where the poplar trees marched like soldiers out on the country road that opened on a vista of Mount Tom, the hoary-headed benignant peak that watched over the destinies of the town of Bishop. My office was to be in the front room of our home.

We were married on a beautiful morning in June. My wedding dress was a crisp, white organdy, with a ruffled, gored skirt that touched the floor all around. The waist had a high collar and long sleeves. The wedding bouquet was a bunch of fragrant jasmine, sent from her box-hedged garden by the wife of the man who kept the Temple of Folly saloon.

My stepmother brought long sprays of pink roses to decorate the sitting room behind my office. A small group of friends came to witness the ceremony, and the gold band that plighted our troth was slipped over my finger. Not a very sumptuous affair, had I paused to remember the pageant of the Fair-Oelrichs wedding—pageantry that might have been mine if the lode had chanced to run in a different direction.

But those days were past. I faced the future praying

that I might meet life with the same strength and forti-
tude that were Mama's and Grandmother's and Aunt
Mary's.

The romance of the Old West colored our wedding
day. Friends had found a Concord stagecoach stored
away in one of the livery stables. With a flourish, an
old-time stage driver reined his high-headed team of
six horses to our door, and the wedding party was driven
over the same route that that old coach used to travel,
to Frances' home on the big ranch.

My going-away dress was a striped light-and-dark
blue lawn with ruffles, and starched petticoats with more
ruffles.

How the meadow larks sang, to our delight! All
along the way a frail desert flower clung to the harsh,
dry sand and greeted the morning with perfumed incense. The poplar trees by the roadside rustled their
leaves with such fullness of life that I would not have
been surprised to see them curtsy and come strolling
down the road to meet us. Tiny rabbits scurried across
the road, their white tails flashing into the sheltering friendliness of gray-green sagebrush. Cock quail
proudly led their families to breakfast under some seed-
giving shrub. Collies, guarding the bands of sheep,
wagged their tails in friendly greeting. Lizards scram-
bled over rocks and nearly lost their tails at sight of
the merry party in the big Concord stage.

And how Frances' house seemed to open its arms and
gather us in with true Western hospitality. Her husband, tall and darkly handsome as a Spanish Don,
greeted us proudly with his sturdy boy, arrayed in minia-
ture chaps at his side. Jessie and Grace were there

with their husbands and other friends of the old Academy days.

What a banquet we had! Barbecued meat, juicy and tender as only meat that has fattened on the mountain meadows can be, a wedding cake sent out from Goldberg Bowen's in the "City" and accompanied by wines and other rare delicacies, strange to the tables of the mountains.

When we returned to our new home that night, there was a charivari and all the people of the town came to greet us with much noise and joyful congratulation. A charivari is looked upon as a hoodlum, disgraceful thing nowadays, but, like everything else, it is the spirit of the thing and not the thing itself which determines whether it is good or bad.

Even an old prospector friend was inspired by the occasion to pen a poem, which he entrusted to us the next day:

> *Our Dr.'s heart seems lighter,*
> *Her foot falls soft and light,*
> *And to me she looks much brighter*
> *Since she's shed the name MacKnight.*
>
> *We watched her as a student,*
> *For we had known her as a girl,*
> *Her deportment was so prudent*
> *It outshone the purest pearl.*
>
> *Now since a Doctor she hath wed*
> *There'll be a Doctor flock.*
> *Should you need a Doc while sick abed*
> *Call the double dose of Doc.*

One of the loveliest happenings of the whole day was when, after the last boisterous guests had departed and we had gone to our room, there came from beneath our window lovely Spanish music, played on a violin and guitar. Jésus had brought his Mexican friends to serenade us.

NOT TO BE
EMBITTERED

⚔ *THE TWENTIETH CENTURY* ⚔
TONOPAH ⚔ *THE WAR*

AND SO THEY WERE MARRIED AND LIVED happily ever after. Perish the thought! What a very boring existence that would be. If there were no valleys, there would be no mountains. Peaks of joy and valleys of sorrow lay ahead, but we faced them together. Young doctors can look very dignified and serious, but they can be just as sentimental as other young married people. The Doctor put a telephone line from our house to his office in the drug store, about a block away, so that we could talk to each other. It was the first telephone in the town.

There is something about a country practice that weaves one into the pattern of the life of the community. We shared the joy of birth and the sadness of death with the people of the valley. We saw houses built on the old ranches for sons and daughters, and new families putting down their roots in the land that their parents had reclaimed from the desert.

A baby was born to us in the bed that old Jésus had brought all the way from Mexico to the valley. A dark haired baby girl. We had a double buggy now and a team of the fastest horses in the country, and we used to bundle up the baby and take her along to sleep soundly in some corner while we sat watching through the night with some family where birth or death was imminent.

Three weeks before the baby came, I attended a woman in confinement, three weeks afterwards, another. So much for the physiological and psychological limitations of women in the practice of medicine.

Then came the first shadow that might have grown to a wall between us. Gold was discovered across the White Mountain range, in Tonopah, Nevada.

Jim Butler, a man who had known the great placer mines, who had watched the fortunes of the Comstock rise and fall, and had remained through it all a poor man, was always a prospector. He owned a small ranch in Nevada and when things were slack, he and his wife, Belle Butler, would hitch their burros to a buckboard and strike out. One night they made a dry camp and in the morning, while rounding up the burros, Jim noticed that one of them had loosed some rock that looked as though it might carry values. It was different from anything he had ever seen, and he scarcely considered it worth sampling. But his wife insisted that they take some of it along. She named the place *Tonopah,* an Indian name, meaning: no wood, no water.

Those samples were taken from what afterwards was known as the Buckboard Mine, on the Mizpah Lode. They assayed 350 ounces in silver and $152 in gold to the ton. It was not long before, in the words of Jim

Butler: "The moneyed kings came riding, in the old-fashioned coaches, through sand and dust to see her wonderful wealth."

But when the moneyed kings arrived they found a man who was working in the interest of the miners. He was not hoodwinked by those powerful banks that had controlled the fortunes of the Comstock, and came, endeavoring to tie up the new camp with a small bond. An expert who was sent out by the mining capitalists told Jim he might consider the property if he were sure the ledge went down.

Jim's reply was characteristic: "Well, by God, it doesn't go up!"

And it didn't. Pay ore was shipped from the grass roots and in Goldfield, a later find, sagebrush was pulled up and the soil shipped to the mint.

The valley was agog with excitement. Tradespeople loaded their goods on freight wagons and started across the mountains. Farmers followed with hay and grain and produce, which they sold at fabulous prices. The Doctor went, thrilled by the stories of the new bonanza. He returned, painting in glowing words the opportunities in the new, wide-open mining camp. They needed doctors, and being there on the ground would give a man the opportunity to get in on a lease with every chance of making a fortune. I listened, fearfully, thinking of our baby girl, and remembered another little girl who listened wonderingly while her father talked of "Gold" and "Out West," and the wonderful opportunities that were there.

We discussed the matter. It would mean separation. Tonopah was just over the mountains, but separation is not a matter of distance but of the things that come in between. And so, generously, whole-heartedly, the baby's father gave up the chance of making a fortune to stay with his little family in the valley.

But some of that gold from Tonopah came to the Owen's River valley, and we all shared in the wealth brought into the community by the stimulus to trade and agriculture. The valley grew and new homes appeared. The power that was latent in our streams was harnessed to provide light and power for the mines across the mountains, and for the towns and ranches of the valley. We had never had gas, so that the old coal-oil lamps and acetylene buggy lamps were our only light until electricity was developed from the streams. Great power houses were built on the lake and stream where I had camped and caught my first mountain trout with my father.

Twenty-animal teams drew long freight wagons, loaded with huge pipes and giant transformers, through the town, up the mountain sides, over new roads that were great gashes along the canyons above the streams. Hundreds of men were employed. Terrible accidents happened.

There were hair-raising experiences when the Doctor was called on velvet-dark nights, when we drove over strange roads, with the mountains towering above us on one side and on the other dropping into inky blackness that hid the stream at the bottom of the canyon. I would walk on the outside edge of the road, carrying a lantern while the Doctor drove the frightened team, hugging close to the mountain side, where rock slides and boulders threatened the perilous ledge.

Greek workmen were brought in to lay the pipe lines and, seeing the succulent, poisonous wild parsley growing, ate it and died of the poisoning.

People coming into the valley brought epidemics. We had been peculiarly free from contagious diseases, but now measles, scarlet fever, whooping cough appeared. The Indians were especially susceptible, as they had established no immunity and with the unenlightened care they gave their children, measles often developed into pneumonia, and scarlet fever and whooping cough left distressing complications.

The fact that there was now a Government school for the Indians made very little difference in their mode of life. Although they could go and live on government reservations, they chose to stay in the valley and work for the white people whom they had known from childhood.

Although the older white doctors resented the encroachment of the younger physicians, the Indian doctors welcomed us as gifts of the gods. Medicine men were chosen by the tribe by some unusual occurrence at their birth, or by some outstanding circumstance that set them apart from the others. They had no voice in the matter. When they lost three patients, they were quietly assisted on their way to the happy hunting ground, where their patients had preceded them. The Government tried to interfere, but was powerless to control this tribal custom.

Even though the Indians willingly employed white doctors, they still had a superstitious faith in the herbs and medicine dances and the barbaric custom of burning with a charred stick until the body was a mass of sores.

They covered their wounds with pitch, and still clung to their sweat houses.

The Indians were urged by the Government to send their most promising boys and girls to the Carson Indian School or to the Carlisle Indian School. The indoor life, so different from the campoodie, often caused them to develop the great white plague and be sent home to die. There was one young Indian girl, the flower of the tribe, who was sent home from Carson, suffering from the last stages of acute tuberculosis. We were called to the campoodie. Flora's father, Peeper, was one of the fine Indians of the Paiute tribe. I shall never forget his tragic face when he met us and took us to the wickiup where Flora, emaciated and parched with fever, lay huddled in the rabbit-skin blanket.

The next visit which we made found Flora's chest and abdomen covered with burns—the old tribal idea of drawing out the sickness. We knew that there had been medicine dances and incantations to drive away the devil sickness. We came again to the camp at sunset. We heard the wailing of the women. We knew that Flora had gone on to the happy hunting grounds.

The sky was ablaze with color, but the campoodie was already in the shadow of the mountains. Peeper sat alone, some distance from the camp, bowed over in silent grief. We went to him. The Doctor asked:

"What's the matter, Peeper?"

"I heap sick," Peeper replied.

"Where you sick?" the Doctor asked, sympathetically.

"Sick in here, all same Plora!" Peeper made a gesture to his breast.

We did what we could for him. Left remedies. I

don't know whether he took them or not. When we returned to the campoodie we found him, always sitting in the same place, and heard him make the same replies to our inquiries:

"Heap sick, in here, all same Plora!"

In three days Peeper was dead. It is unscientific to say that a patient died of grief or a broken heart, but I have no other diagnosis to offer in Peeper's case.

The town of Bishop began to take itself seriously. The census showed over the required number of people in order to incorporate. And so our son was born in a young city, the first incorporated town in eastern California, with a telephone system, a water supply and sewer system, electric lights, bath tubs and a Board of Trustees. His father had an X-ray machine in his office, and he had built an ice plant in town which froze the mountain water into great blocks and provided ice up and down the valley along the narrow gauge railroad, and to the mining camps by fast stage.

The years between were full years for us. Years made precious by our little family, years brightened by loyal friendships.

☙ *AN AQUEDUCT* ☙
A SYMBOL

THE PEOPLE OF THE VALLEY HAD ALWAYS cherished a dream that some day the Government Reclamation Service would impound the surplus water in the mountains, so that thousands of acres of the fertile desert might be brought under cultivation. The Government engineers arrived. But Los Angeles coveted not only the surplus water, but all of the water from our clear mountain streams.

The people of the valley raised their voices in protest when they saw the reclamation project, that had promised so much, fold up its tents and depart; saw the lands of the valley withdrawn from further settlement; watched, powerless to stay their tragedy, as one by one the irrigating canals, that were their only protection against the encroachment of the desert, were acquired by the Southern city. A broad gauge railroad was built to unite the narrow gauge Carson and Colorado with the main line at Mojave, and furnish transportation for materials to build the longest aqueduct in the world. The stage that had carried passengers from Keeler, through the deep sand around Owen's Lake, past Olancha, to which point the famous Twenty-Mule-Team Borax was hauled from Death Valley, on by Coyote Holes and Indian Wells, Red Rock Canyon and the Eighteen Mile House to Mojave, drove on to join the caravan of history.

We gave up our team and double buggy for an automobile. We struggled through the sand and over the hills, always wondering at the bottom if we would ever get to the top. We cut sage-brush to lay in the sandy roads to increase traction. We had a puncture every few miles, and bent our backs over a hand pump to inflate the new tire. I have had many a Panama hat ruined when I was thrown into the top of the car as we leaped the irrigating ditches. Many a time our engine flooded and died when we plunged into bridge-less streams and the Doctor waded in, knee deep, and brought rocks and brush or walked miles to procure a team of horses to pull us out.

Then came that momentous day when white people and Indians, men, women and children, made a pil-grimage to Lone Pine, that "Little Town of the Grape-Vines" at the foot of Mount Whitney.

Silas Christofferson, a fearless aviator, was induced to come to Owen's River valley and attempt to fly over the highest mountain in the United States. It is evident that his hosts felt that the chances of his being able to accomplish the feat were about even, for the agreement was: "Two thousand dollars if you do it, and only expenses if you fail."

When we saw our first airplane we were all like the man who, on seeing his first locomotive, exclaimed: "They'll never start her!" and when that feat was ac-complished was sure: "They'll never stop her!" We watched in awe while the man-made eagle climbed the skies to conquer the snow-capped king of all the peaks. Many strange and thrilling things had come to pass, but this was the most unbelievable of all.

That dread spectre of war was drawing nearer and nearer. News came of the sinking of the *Lusitania*. Men grew white and women looked at their stalwart sons with a new tenderness. Then came that momentous June fifth: Registration day for the new draft army of the United States.

Boys of Inyo County who had never spent a night away from home, boys who had never been on a railroad train, donned the uniform of Uncle Sam and went gloriously forth to the great adventure, while those at home did double duty on ranch and range and kept the home fires burning.

The Doctor, his hair gray at the temples now, answered the call. I taught our children, as Grandmother had taught me, that there was no country like our country, no flag like our flag. But the family was soon united, for the Doctor became part of the Medical Corps whose greatest service started when the Armistice was signed. The children and I journeyed to New York to be with their father.

We lived there while, as commander of Hospital Train No. 1, he cared for sick and wounded soldiers who came from the great receiving hospitals—Fox Hills, Grand Central Palace, Camp Mills, Green Hut, in New York, to entrain at the Grand Central and the Pennsylvania stations for their homes on the prairies and the deserts and in the mountains of the country they had helped to make safe for democracy.

But what of the mountain valley to which the boys came home? The great aqueduct basked complacently in the land of little rain. Green fields were becoming brown. The desert was claiming its own. Los Angeles bought the ranches and Los Angeles bought the towns. She paid a fair price. But there is an intangible something that money cannot buy.

Families scattered. Neighbors bade farewell to neighbors who had grown dearer than brothers through the years, and the Mamas and Grandmothers and Aunt Marys faced the problems of creating a home in new scenes. The houses that sheltered the hopes and fears of the families of the valley stare through vacant windows across the fields that are rapidly returning to the sage-brush of the desert. The orchards that the pioneers planted for their children's children have been uprooted and left to bleach on the sand. There was a legend written long ago of the little village of Grand Pré. . . .

And so we came to live in the Berkeley Hills, across the bay from that beautiful city that has always been "the City" to me. I often take one of the ferry boats that still glide into the slips at the foot of Market Street. I climbed Telegraph Hill recently. Automobiles were driving up the wide boulevard to the fine balustrade that overlooks the bay. In the distance the campanile of the State University stood out in slender beauty against the Berkeley Hills. Farther north the Richmond oil tanks squatted in smug assurance. The broad expanse of the Embarcadero was dynamic with traffic. The great smokestacks of steamers from every land marked the vessels that lay at anchor along the wharves.

An airplane flew over my head, carrying mail that will be delivered in New York in forty-eight hours, mail that took thirteen days to reach the same destination in the days of the Pony Express. The U. S. *Macon* swam through the air, like a huge silver fish, on its way to the hangar at Sunnyvale. The sailing vessels are no more. The doom of the ferry boats is written in the plans for the Transbay Bridge. The Golden Gate will soon be spanned by an arch of steel. The Coit Memorial Tower stands where a signal pole, in the days that are no more, flashed the news of incoming vessels from the top of

Telegraph Hill. But the eucalyptus trees, transplanted here from far-off Australia, still serve as tent poles for the curtains of fog that drift in from the ocean.

The kaleidoscope of life turns, showing ever-changing, multi-colored patterns. . . .

But love and faith and hope endure. The gold wedding ring on my finger is a symbol of the love and faith and hope that has permeated the whole design of life with my husband, who has been content:

"To be honest; to be kind.—To earn a little; to spend a little less. To make upon the whole a family happier for his presence. To renounce when that shall be necessary and not be embittered. . . ."

GENNY SMITH BOOKS

*offers these other publications on
California's eastern Sierra region.
Genny Smith, editor.*

MAMMOTH LAKES SIERRA

C. D. Rinehart, E. Vestal, B. Willard, and G. Smith. Fourth ed
1976, 192 pages, paper.

DEEPEST VALLEY:
GUIDE TO OWENS VALLEY

Revised edition planned for 1984.

OWENS VALLEY
GROUNDWATER CONFLICT

P. H. Lane and A. Rossmann. 1978, 28 pages, paper.

EARTHQUAKES AND YOUNG VOLCANOES
ALONG THE EASTERN SIERRA NEVADA

C. D. Rinehart and W. C. Smith. 1982, 64 pages, paper.

OLD MAMMOTH

A. Reed. 1982, 194 pages, cloth and paper.

For prices and mail order information:
William Kaufmann, Inc.
95 First Street, Los Altos, California 94022